W9-BWB-626

MMPI
INTERPRETATION MANUAL FOR COUNSELORS AND CLINICIANS
Third Edition

Jane C. Duckworth, Ph.D.
Professor of Psychology—Counseling
Department of Counseling Psychology
and Guidance Services
Ball State University

Wayne P. Anderson, Ph.D.
Chair, Joint Training Program
   Counseling Psychology
Professor of Psychology—Counseling Psychologist
Counseling Services
University of Missouri—Columbia

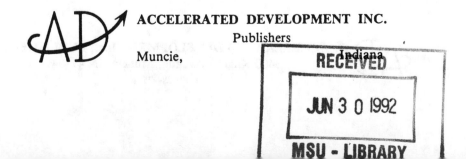

ACCELERATED DEVELOPMENT INC.
Publishers
Muncie, Indiana

MMPI
Interpretation Manual
For
Counselors And Clinicians
Third Edition

Library of Congress Catalog Card Number: 86-70660

International Standard Book Number: 0-915202-57-3

© Copyright 1986 by Accelerated Development Inc.
First Edition Copyright 1975
Second Edition Copyright 1979
Third Edition Copyright 1986

Technical Development: Tanya Dalton
Judy McWilliams
Sheila Sheward

Graphic Artist: Cheryl King

Printed in the United States of America

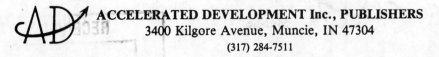

ACCELERATED DEVELOPMENT Inc., PUBLISHERS
3400 Kilgore Avenue, Muncie, IN 47304
(317) 284-7511

PREFACE

Readers of this third edition, who are familiar with the first two editions of this book, will immediately be aware of one of the changes that has occurred for this edition, Dr. Wayne Anderson has become a co-author of this edition. Dr. Anderson brings a wealth of MMPI research experience to this edition, as witness the references bearing his name in the bibliography. In addition, he has been a clinician and teacher for over thirty years, making him eminently suited to write about the interface between the research and clinical aspects of the MMPI. His most visible contributions to this edition of the chapters on interpreting the MMPI (Chapter II) and the use of the MMPI with different races and cultures (Chapter III). The not-so-noticeable contributions about interpretive strategies for certain scales and the broadening of the focus of this edition through his new and at times unique perspective of the test.

My contributions to this edition have been updating the research noted for each of the scale sections, adding a section on the MacAndrew Addiction Scale, and revising the introductions to each of the scales to more accurately reflect our latest thinking about the meaning of each scale. In spite of occasional differences of opinion, we are both committed to the "normalizing" of the MMPI for those populations where it is called for (See Chapter II). We believe this book makes a unique contribution in identifying positive aspects of moderate elevations of the Clinical Scales and the contributions that the Research Scales can make to that end. This makes the MMPI a much broader personality assessment instrument and uses its richness and complexity to the fullest.

In conclusion, I believe some of the points made in the preface to the original edition of this book published in 1975 deserve to be restated. Comments have been added to clarify some of these original statements.

The first purpose of this book is to present MMPI information for practitioners whose clients are basically normal. By normal I mean those clients who typically do not require hospitalization and in most instances can be helped without extensive alteration of the personality. By normal, I do not mean that the clients do not have problems because they are seeking some kind of help.

My second purpose for this book is to collect from various sources the information concerning the MMPI which would be useful for work with these normal, non-hospitalized populations. In this edition, we have included much more information about the hospitalized populations, since many of these people are being discharged quickly and appear for continued care in mental health centers. My experience has been that this information is scattered throughout many books and journal articles, and as such is not readily accessible in any one place. This is still a continuing problem. We believe one of the major contributions of this book is that we, the authors, have evaluated the articles and books and have digested the material from them, so that you, the reader, are saved time and energy to devote to your clinical practices. Being clinicians, we always scrutinize books and articles on the MMPI from the point of view of their usefulness to the practitioner. From hundreds of hours of reading comes the information that is listed for each of the scales.

The third purpose for this book is to present information about and interpretations for the Research scales (**A, R, Es, Lb, Ca, Dy, Do, Re, Pr, St,** and **Cn**). Added to this edition is information about the Mac-Andrew Addiction Scale, an extremely useful one for diagnosing alcohol and drug addiction.

The fourth purpose for this book is to present the material in such a way as to be accessible easily and quickly. To this end I have used a combination of an outline format and a written paragraph form.

You, the reader, deserve a thank you for taking the time to fill out the Feedback and Suggestions sheets at the back of this book. Many of the suggestions which you have made to the first and second editions have been implemented in this edition of the book. As an example, many of you have mentioned David Lachar's excellent interpretive manual as one which you have found to be useful. References to it are included in this edition. We highly recommended you buy this book to get the full benefit of Dr. Lachar's expertise. Additional books and articles which will be useful to you to read in greater detail are listed in the Acknowledgements section. With these aides and this third edition of the *MMPI Interpretation Manual,* we believe you will be fully prepared for the often complex and challenging job of interpreting the most widely used personality test in the world, the MMPI.

Jane Duckworth

Jane Duckworth

ACKNOWLEDGEMENTS

The selecting, rewording, and editing of the material in this book have been based primarily upon our use of the MMPI and experience as practitioners and teachers. However, we have drawn heavily from several sources. Therefore, we acknowledge our special indebtedness to the following authors and their works and suggest that these books and articles would make excellent additions to your professional libraries.

1. Dahlstrom, W.G., Welsh, G., & Dahlstrom, L. (1972). *An MMPI handbook: Vol. I. Clinical Interpretation.* Minneapolis, MN: University of Minnesota Press.

   This is the "granddaddy" of MMPI books written by the people who know about the origin and development of the MMPI than any others. This book is recommended as a basic book on MMPI.

2. Gilberstadt, H., & Duker, J. (1965). *A handbook for clinical and actuarial MMPI interpretation.* Philadelphia, PA: W.B. Saunders.

   This book is one of the major "cookbooks" on the MMPI. Nineteen profiles most commonly found for males in VA hospitals are presented along with pertinent information concerning diagnosis, treatment, and so forth.

3. Graham, J. (1972). *The MMPI: A practical guide.* New York: Oxford Press.

   A very useful book that gives an overall view of MMPI interpretation. Of special interest is the information on two-point codes, which Dr. Graham has researched extensively, and the chapter on interpreting the MMPI.

4. Greene, R. (1980). *The MMPI, an interpretive manual.* New York: Grune & Stratton.

   Another very useful book giving an overall view of MMPI interpretation. Of special interest in Dr. Greene's book is an innovative way of assessing the validity of a profile.

5. Gynther, M., Altman, H., & Sletten, I. (1973). Replicated correlates of MMPI two-point code types: The Missouri Actuarial System. *Journal of Clinical Psychology, 29,* 263-289.

Schwartz and Green (1983) have found that among the actuarial systems, the Gynther et al. approached is the most useful in diagnosing college students. They summarize their article by recommending the system discussed in this article for making diagnostic decisions within a college center.

6. Kunce, J., & Anderson, W. (1976). Normalizing the MMPI. *Journal of Clinical Psychology, 32,* 776-780.

One of the few articles that discusses the "normal" aspects of moderate MMPI elevations.

7. Lachar, D. (1974). *The MMPI: Clinical assessment and automated interpretation.* Los Angeles, CA: Western Psychological Services.

This book presents an interpretive system consisting of statements based upon Validity and Clinical scale elevations and profile configurations. These statements can then be compiled into an interpretive report.

8. Marks, P., Seeman, W., & Haller, D. (1974). *The actuarial use of the MMPI with adolescents and adults.* Baltimore, MD: Williams and Wilkins.

Another "cookbook" presenting 16 profiles for adults and 29 for adolescents. This book is one of the few to discuss adolescent MMPIs and their interpretation.

9. Trimboli, R., & Kilgore, R. (1983). A psychodynamic approach to MMPI interpretation. *Journal of Personality Assessment, 47,* 614-626.

This article presents an excellent overview of the MMPI Clinical scales and their interactions with each other. Despite the title, the psychodynamic point of view is not the only approach taken in interpretation.

We also owe a large debt of gratitude to Alex Caldwell for material gathered from his talks. We have tried to acknowledge his contributions wherever they occur, but there may be instances when an idea we feel is ours has been given to us by him.

Jane Duckworth   Muncie, Indiana
Wayne Anderson   March, 1986

CONTENTS

LIST OF FIGURES

xi

CHAPTER **I**

INTRODUCTION

This MMPI book has been written primarily for counselors and clinicians who work with three types of populations: university counseling center clients, private practice clients, and mental health clinic clients. These populations are not usually psychotic or neurotic but are likely to be people who are functioning adequately in their world but having problems in one or two areas. These problems may be longstanding ones, but more usually they are the result of situational pressures and stresses. These pressures may range from mild (such as selecting an academic major) to severe (such as divorce or death in the family).

1

The MMPI was developed in the 1930s and 1940s as a complex psychological instrument designed to diagnose mental patients into different categories of neuroses and psychoses. Since that time its use has extended to all kinds of settings, including employment agencies, university counseling centers, mental health clinics, schools, and industry. Its use also has been expanded to include research and screening. Most importantly, its diagnostic origins have been expanded to include a person's behavior, attitudes, thought patterns, and strengths; data which are extremely useful to the practicing counselor and therapist.

The MMPI as originally constructed had eight Clinical scales (scales **1** through **4** and **6** through **9**). Two additional scales, **5** and **0**, have since been added to the Clinical scales. Originally the MMPI Clinical scales were intended to place persons into various diagnostic categories. Designers of the test expected that people taking the test would have an elevation on one scale which would then indicate the diagnosis for that person such as schizophrenic, hypochondriac, and so forth. It was soon discovered that this was a very limited approach, and consequently, three major developments occurred.

First, MMPI interpreters began describing the behavior associated with the various elevations instead of just placing people into diagnostic categories. This development provided information useful to the counselor and clinician in the treatment of the person.

The second development was to use the varying scale elevations to differentiate intensity of behavior and thinking. For example, scale **2**, which was originally only interpreted as depression, is now used to differentiate between people who are feeling "blue" (lower elevations) from those who are severely depressed (higher elevations).

The third major interpretative development of the MMPI was the use of the whole profile for analysis, rather than only one, two, or three high points. This approach has added subtlety and richness to the interpretations.

An initial improvement of the MMPI, occurring soon after it was developed, was the addition of four Validity scales to the Clinical scales to measure the test-taking attitude of the person. This addition is one of the major strengths of the MMPI. These Validity scales note the number of Items omitted (**?** scale), the amount of obvious social virtues claimed by the person (**L** scale), the amount of "different" or bad experiences the client is reporting (**F** scale), and the amount of good feelings the person is reporting (**K** scale). No other psychological instrument, to our knowledge, is so thorough in attempting to determine the client's mental set at the time of test administration. These Validity scales are typically shown first on the MMPI profile so that the test-taking attitude of the person can be taken into account in interpreting the Clinical scales which appear in the second section of the profile.

In addition to these two sets of scales, over 550 experimental scales have been developed to measure such diverse areas as alcoholism, ego strength, dominance, anxiety, and status needs. Some of the research scales which we have found especially useful form the third section of the MMPI profile and we have included a section on them in this book.

One of the difficulties some people have in using the Research scales is getting them scored so they can be interpreted. However, there are many computer scoring services and home computer scoring systems that score these scales. If the MMPI is manually scored, the items for the Research scales mentioned in this book are listed in Appendices A and B of this book and scoring keys can be made from them. Keys are also available from Psychological Assessment Resources, Inc., P.O. Box 98, Odessa, FL 33556. Profile sheets also are available from them for plotting these scales.

Thus the MMPI, as used in this book, has three sets of scales: the Validity scales, the Clinical scales, and the Research scales. We tend to use these three sets of scales in the following way. We look at the Validity scales *for the mood and/or test-taking attitude of the person.* Then we look at the Clinical scale elevations *for problem areas* (except for scale **5** where an elevation may not be a problem) and finally we note the Research scales *for additional problem areas as well as some areas of strength.* The use of these scales is explained more completely in the introduction to each set of scales.

FORMAT AND USE OF THIS MANUAL

The following format is used in this book in presenting the chapters on the Validity, Clinical and Research scales. An introduction and

3

general information about the scale is presented, then high score interpretations are given, usually divided into moderate elevations (60 through 70 T-score points) and marked elevations (70 T-score points or above). These interpretations are followed by the low score interpretations (usually 45 T-score points or below). Combinations of scales are then noted and the interpretations for them are given. All Clinical and Validity scales in the combinations are at a T-score of 70 or above, unless otherwise noted and are listed in order from the highest to the lowest peaks. Research scale combinations use scales at a T-score of 60 or above. If a scale in a combination is lower than a T of 50, the symbol "—" above the scale number is used, for example 5 in 4-5̄.

At times a scale score may fit in more than one interpretive category. For example, a Clinical scale score of 70 could be interpreted as a moderate elevation (T = 60 through 70) or a marked elevation (T = 70 or above). When this happens, use whichever interpretation seems to fit the situation best.

Information should be gathered from the chapters concerning the Validity, Clinical, and Research scales according to the high and low points present in the profile to be interpreted. The T-score range between 45 and 60 is not usually interpreted for the Validity and Clinical scales but is in some cases for the Research scales. A profile may be interpreted using only the high and low score sections or it may be interpreted using combinations (with or without the information in the high and low score sections) if the profile scales are high enough to be in a combination (above 70 T-score points for the Clinical and Validity scale combinations or above 60 T-score points for the Research scale combinations).

For the reader who is new to interpreting the MMPI, the best way to become acquainted with the various scales is to read the introductory remarks for each of the scales. As one continues to work with the MMPI, the more detailed information listed under the high and low points of the scales becomes useful. Finally, as one becomes yet more skilled in the usage of the test, the combinations with their more intricate interpretations become useful. A word of caution is necessary about the Clinical scale combinations. Only the highest two or three scales above 70 T-score points are considered as a combination. The other Clinical scales above 70 should be interpreted by referring to the respective high point sections of the scales involved.

New to this edition are two chapters which should be useful in learning interpretive skills. Chapter II, Interpreting the MMPI, and Chapter

4

III, Race and Culture, give the reader an overview of important points to consider regarding the difficult task of making the best MMPI interpretation possible. Also included from the second edition of this book is a chapter (Chapter VII) which contains information as to how the two of us interpret the MMPI. The reader may find Chapters II, III, and VII useful in understanding how we apply some of the points we make throughout the book.

We recommend that the whole book be read through first in order to get the total picture of the MMPI we are presenting. After the overview, separate sections can be used as needed.

—NOTES—

CHAPTER **II**

INTERPRETING THE MMPI

Like any other high level skill, learning to interpret the MMPI takes time. This is a test where much of what one can say is dependent on the interaction of many factors. To the reader learning all of these factors may seem to be a massive task. This interaction, however, is what makes the test such a rich source of information about clients. Its complexity adds to rather than detracts from its value as an appraisal instrument.

7

In this section we will discuss three areas basic to interpreting a profile: (1) how to use sub-grouping of scale items especially for scales between 70 and 85 T-score points; (2) how one clinical scale modifies the interpretation of another; (3) how the research scales can be used to add to the predictive power of the test. In addition we will discuss how to interpret what some people consider very difficult tests, those that are only moderately elevated (60 to 75 T-score points). A richness of material is here which we believe has been relatively untouched except by the previous editions of this book in the discussion of moderate elevations and by a few research articles (e.g., Kunce & Anderson, 1976).

ITEM SUB-GROUPS

Many of the Clinical scales on the MMPI are made up of subgroupings of items that are similar in content. When working with a client, knowing which of these subgroups are being endorsed sometimes is useful in obtaining a more accurate picture of what the person is feeling and thinking.

Many people have suggested subgroups for scales of the MMPI. The most known subgroups are those that have been developed by Harris and Lingoes (1955). They have subjectively divided scales, **2, 3, 4, 6, 8,** and **9** into groups of items that have similar content. For example, scale **4** (anger) has been divided into four subscales, familial discord, authority conflict, social inperturbability, and alienation. The other MMPI scales, **1, 5, 7,** and **0** were found to have uniform content and therefore subgroups were not developed. We believe that knowing to which scale subgroups a client/patient is responding is useful in order to get the most accurate picture of how that client/patient is feeling, thinking, and behaving.

We find subscales to be especially useful when the client/patient has a T-score between 70 and 85 on the appropriate scale. In this range the person could be choosing items from only one or two of the subgroupings rather than all of them. For example, one person with a **4** scale of 75 could have that elevation because of endorsing items reflecting family problems (family discord) whereas another test taker could have an elevation on the **4** scale because he/she is denying social anxiety and dependency needs (social imperturbability). When a scale score is above

85 T-score points, however, the person most likely is answering at least some items from all the subgroupings in order to get that scale elevation and therefore the subgroups are not as useful.

CLINICAL SCALE INTERACTIONS

Clinical scale interactions become important to answer two questions: (1) how is the highest point scale interpretation *modified* by other scale elevations? and (2) how does a scale *modify* other scales when it is a lower point in a two or three point code?

The interpretation of any one scale will be modified by the other scales that are elevated along with it. In each scale chapter in this book we discuss high point codes. These are usually two point codes but some three point codes are included when the third scale seems to be an important modifier of the two higher scales. The second and third highest scales may modify the highest scale in ways that change rather markedly what is said about an individual. Sometimes the scale which has the lower elevation accentuates or makes more pathological a tendency indicated by the high point scale. At other times a lower elevation may repress or diffuse a tendency, and at still other times it may significantly change the interpretation of a scale. With scale **4** as an example let us examine these three possibilities. An individual who has a high **4** with no other significant elevations is usually seen as impulsive, rebellious, egocentric, and having poor relationships with parents and authority figures in general. These individuals also have low frustration tolerance. This combined with their poor self-control often results in aggressive outbursts.

An elevation on scale **9** (psychic energy) will accentuate the characteristics we expect of a **4** scale elevation making the pathological characteristics not only more likely to appear but energizing them. Therefore, an individual with a **4-9** pattern will be even more impulsive and irresponsible than one with just a high **4** scale. The **9** scale adds a dimension of restlessness and a need for stimulation which "pushes" these individuals into trouble. On the other hand, an elevation on scale **3** (denial) will moderate the effects of the **4** scale and the usual behavior connected with a scale **4** elevation will be seen only on relatively rare occasions usually as sudden anger or rage, to a degree which is inappropriate to the situation. Most people will see this acting out as out of character for the individual since under ordinary conditions the person will be quiet and somewhat withdrawn.

The addition of a high **8** scale along with the high **4** scale changes the interpretation of the **4** scale elevation also since the **8** scale elevation adds a more pathological dimension of confusion and bad judgement. Individuals with **4-8** elevations will have a long history of problems as a result of their not understanding social norms and chronically misinterpreting the expectations of others. While an individual with a high **4** scale is frequently likeable on initial contact, individuals who have the **4-8** combination are not.

We have been discussing how a particular high point is modified by the addition of another scale elevation. We also can look at what a particular scale does to other scales when it is the second highest scale and modifies the highest one. From the above discussion we should suspect that a high scale **9** tends to energize other scales and that a high scale **3** tends to modify or lessen the pathology of other scale elevations.

An elevated scale **8** also modifies other scale interpretations. A high scale **8** by itself usually reflects an individual who has difficulty relating to others, is confused, and may be actually delusional or hallucinating. When scale **8** is the second highest score in a two point code, different aspects of this scale will be apparent and the interpretation of the high point will need to be modified accordingly. For example, when scale **1** is the highest point, it indicates considerable bodily concern and symptoms which are not logically connected to any standard illness. When scale **8** is added as a secondary elevation, these bodily concerns take on a bizarre quality, one where the somatic concerns may be of a delusional nature. As was already mentioned when the **8** scale elevation was secondary to a high scale **4**, the delusional quality of the **8** scale was not as apparent, instead the bad judgment and chronic inability to relate to others became more noticeable. Finally when the **8** scale is secondary to scale **7** (anxiety) we are not as likely to see either delusions or bad judgment, instead we see a pattern of chronic worry and tension, an awareness and a concern on the part of the patient that his/her thoughts are inappropriate. Thus, to look at the interaction of the two or three highest scales is important so as to become most accurate in interpreting a profile.

Of additional interest is whether a secondary clinical scale elevation activates or modulates the behavior, thoughts, and feelings indicated by

10

the highest scale. The following is a listing of the clinical scales and our assessment of their activator/modulator potential when they are elevated secondary to another Clinical scale.

Scale **1** (physical complaints) modulator
Scale **2** (depression) modulator
Scale **3** (denial) modulator
Scale **4** (anger) activator
Scale **5** (masculine-feminine interests)
      for men-modulator, for women-activator
Scale **6** (suspiciousness) activator
Scale **7** (anxiety) activator
Scale **8** (confusion) activator
Scale **9** (energy) activator
Scale **0** (extroversion-introversion) modulator.

RESEARCH SCALES

We have found the research scales in Chapter VI of this book to be of real value in interpreting profiles. We regularly use the research scales for a number of purposes, (1) to modify the interpretation of the clinical scales, (2) to help with our predictions about therapy outcomes, and (3) to add new information not available from the clinical scales.

One of the most useful scales for modifying the interpretation of the clinical scales is the **Es** scale (Ego Strength). We find that the ego strength scale is one key to whether or not to use attenuated pathology interpretations, suggested by Graham and McCord (1982), for scales that are moderately elevated (65-70 T-score points) or to go with interpretations which suggest more positive characteristics (Kunce & Anderson, 1976, 1984). (See the next section, Moderate Scale Elevations, for a more complete discussion of other cues to using the pathological or positive interpretations.) When the Clinical scale is between 65 and 75 and the **Es** is below 50, we use the more negative interpretation for the Clinical scale. For example, with a scale **4** elevation of 70 and an ego strength of 40 we would give a more pathological interpretation. We would speak of an impulsive, rather unreliable individual who has frequent minor problems with authority figures. On the other hand if the scale **4** were 70 and the **Es** score were 60, we would speak of an individual who was enterprising, social, and probably dedicated to making some changes in the social system but from a non-hostile stance.

Second, even in those individuals where their profiles are such that one would tend to use the more pathological interpretations (Clinical scales are above 70 T-score) the Es can be used to modify the interpretation. Anderson and Kunce (1984) have found that clients in a university counseling center who have an elevated 8 scale show different degrees of pathology, not so much on the basis of the height of the 8 scale score but on the difference between the 8 scale and the Es scale score. That is, a moderately elevated 8 scale with a very low Es was more predictive of bizarre ideation than a high elevation on the 8 scale with an elevated Es.

How responsive an individual will be to treatment is often predicted from the Clinical scales. The usual expectation is that an individual with a 1-3 pattern will be rather unresponsive to psychological interventions, while an individual with a 2-7 profile will be actively involved in and responsive to psychotherapy. The research scales add another dimension to therapy predictions since they can predict additional ways in which the individual will help with his/her own therapy or ways in which resistance will be shown. The relationship between the A scale and the R scale is an example. The A and R scales were both derived from a factor analysis of the MMPI. The A scale relates to the client's feelings of being psychologically disturbed and taps a general maladjustment dimension. It intercorrelates highly with most measures of pathology on the MMPI. The R scale on the other hand does not correlate highly with many other scales and seems to tap a dimension of control of feelings which can be of a repressive nature. In any case, when the A scale is elevated above 55 T-score points and R is below 50 T-score points, therapy tends to proceed quite well. The person is both feeling disturbed (A scale) and not repressing the awareness of these feelings (R scale). On the other hand when both the A and the R scales are above 55 T-score points, elevation of the R scale seems to prevent the client from discussing pertinent material even though the person recognizes being psychologically disturbed (A scale).

Finally the research scales may add information about a client/patient that is not given by the Clinical or Validity scales. The Dy and Do scales (Dependency and Dominance) can be most useful in indicating how a person will react interpersonally. If the Do scale is above 50 T-score points and the Dy scale is below 50, the individual likes taking

12

charge of his/her life and is not psychologically over-dependent on others. If, however, both the **Do** and **Dy** scales are above 50 and the **Dy** scale is higher than the **Do** scale, the person is likely to be passive-aggressive. This type of individual tends to be a game player in TA terms and while saying one thing, "help me run my life (**Dy**)," really has a stake in making sure the individual who is trying to help does not succeed, "see, you can't do it well either (**Do**)." Passive-aggressiveness is not indicated by any of the Validity or Clinical scales. The only place it can be seen clearly on the MMPI is on the **Dy** and **Do** scales.

Other research scales that add information not indicated by Validity or Clinical scales are the **Lb, Re, Pr, Cn,** and **Mac** scales. Each of the scales' contribution to an MMPI interpretation is discussed in the introductory remarks for that scale. Being aware of these scales' contributions can enhance the accuracy and applicability of your MMPI interpretations.

MODERATE SCALE ELEVATIONS

While originally developed for diagnosing psychiatric patients, the use of the MMPI has been broadened to include testing a much wider range of individuals for a variety of nonpsychiatric purposes. In most populations if all of an individuals T-scores on the MMPI profiles fall between 45 and 60, we usually can not make a very individualized report on that person's personality characteristics. However, given a profile which has moderate elevations (T-scores between 60 and 75) we have found that often as much can be said about the personalities of these individuals as can be said about individuals whose profiles have higher elevations.

In a nonpsychiatric setting, however, when one has a profile with moderate elevations a problems exists in deciding what kind of interpretive approach should be used. A very frequent approach is to interpret the moderately elevated scale scores as if they indicated lesser degrees of the pathology which is connected with higher elevations. Graham and McCord (1982) represented this position when they stated,

Probably the most commonly used approach is to generate for our normal subjects what Dahlstrom and Welsh (1960) have called "psychologically

13

attenuated" descriptions of more clear cut psychiatric patients. We determine what a more elevated score on a particular scale would mean for a clinical subject, and we modify the inferences subjectively for our more moderately elevated score for our normal subject. For example, if we would characterize a psychiatric patient with a T-score of 90 on scale 2 as depressed, a normal person with a T-score of 65 or 70 probably would be described as unhappy or dissatisfied. (p. 4)

Struck with the discrepancies between the potentially pathological implications of moderately elevated scores and the good personality adjustment of individuals in some populations who have these elevations, Kunce and Anderson (1976, 1984) have asked the question, "Why would well-functioning, academically able individuals score in a pathological direction on some of the scales?" Their investigation of the literature led them to support the position that in some populations moderate scale elevations on the MMPI are related to positive personality traits. Their position on this point therefore is in opposition that held by Graham and McCord (1982).

Kunce and Anderson argued that while a certain scale configuration often may be associated with certain kinds of pathology in a psychiatric setting, a similar profile may or may not be connected with the same pathology in a nonpsychiatric setting. Thus, it does not follow that a nonhospitalized person who has a moderately elevated peak score on the scale 8 will show schizophrenic symptomatology, even though persons hospitalized for schizophrenia do have elevated scale 8 scores.

Kunce and Anderson postulated an underlying personality dimension for each scale which could have either negative or positive characteristics when it is moderately elevated. In a psychiatric population the characteristics the client/patient will show are almost always the negative aspects of the dimension but in some populations these same moderate elevations are related to positive traits. For example, the dimension underlying scale 7 is organization. Under conditions which we will be discussing in this section, individuals with moderate elevations on this scale will show a good ability to organize. They will be punctual, decisive and methodical, and probably function well in managerial or mechanical occupations. A problem arises when individuals with these moderate elevations are put under stress. The scale 7 scores of individuals with these positive traits will probably become more elevated, and their behavior will become maladaptive. They may develop an over-reliance on obsession with minutia and engage in ritualistic behaviors or constant checking (e.g., to see if they have locked the door). What had

14

been a personality asset paradoxically degenerates into ineffectual adjustment. However, an important recognition is that maladaptive personality characteristics inferred from the MMPI in these cases with nonpsychiatric clients may represent transitory reactions rather than enduring traits.

In the appropriate chapters on the Clinical scales we will discuss the possible positive interpretations for each scale but to help the clinician follow our reasoning on this point we will point out the underlying dimensions for each scale and a sample positive term which would apply for moderate elevations for each of the Clinical scales: scale **1**, conservation (conscientious); scale **2**, evaluation (deliberate); scale **3**, expressive (optimistic); scale **4**, assertion (venturesome); scale **5**, role-flexibility (dilettante); scale **6**, inquiring (investigative); scale **7**, organization (methodical); scale **8**, imagination (creative); scale **9**, zest (eager); scale **0**, autonomy (independent).

This raises the question of when does a clinician use an attenuated pathology approach and when does he/she use a more positive interpretation for moderate scale elevations. Three groups of factors exist and in various combinations help build the case for using either the attenuated pathology approach or the positive strengths approach to interpreting profiles which have scale elevations in the moderate range. These factors are (1) the reason the test was administered,(2) the personal characteristics of the test taker, and (3) test scale variables, especially research scales.

REASONS FOR TAKING THE TEST

Under the following conditions, the clinician should ask in each instance if a more positive approach might be called for in interpretation of the MMPI. When the test is being used for the following conditions a more positive approach may be appropriate:

1. for personnel screening for positions where the psychological adjustment of the applicant is not critical,

2. to help agencies and courts in making judgments in cases such as child custody,

3. for students in graduate classes where taking the test is part of the learning situation,

4. with a normal population as part of a research study, and

5. for clients in college counseling centers and in private practice.

The use of the MMPI with three of these groups merits further explanation.

Students in Classes

Our experience has been that well functioning graduate students often have moderately elevated scale scores. When they take the test for a graduate course in testing and find that they have moderate elevations, especially those with 70 to 75 T-scores on scales **4** and **9,** they become overly concerned about their adjustment. Instructors need to recognize that for most of these students the more positive description of the underlying dimension gives an interpretation which is closer to the actual behavior (and strengths) of these students.

Research Study Use

Two examples of the MMPI used for research will be discussed: one where we feel the authors made a mistake by using an attenuated pathology explanation and a second where the author recognized that a more positive set of descriptors were needed. The first is a study by Rosen and Rosen (1957), where from a group of business agents, the most successful were selected for study. They found that these agents had mean T-scores greater than 60 on scales **1, 3, 4, 6,** and **9.** The authors interpreted these scores as reflecting the high stress that these men felt from their jobs. Given that these subjects had been selected as outstanding performers and that their **Es** scores averaged greater than 60, the authors explanation might have been reformulated and the subjects described as optimistic, energetic go-getters.

A second example, one where the author did not conclude that moderate elevations meant attenuated pathology, is found in MacKinnon's (1962) work with creative architects. MacKinnon emphasized that when the creative architects' MMPI scale scores were moderately elevated these scores did not have the same meaning for their personality functioning that it would for other persons. These creative architects

16

were getting along well in their personal lives and professional careers. He felt that the manner in which these creative subjects described themselves in the MMPI as well as in their life history interviews was less suggestive of psychopathology than it was of good intellect, complexity and richness of personality, lack of defensiveness, and candor in self description, in other words, an openness to experience and especially an openness to the experience of one's inner life.

Client's in Private Practice

When the MMPI is used with some client populations the therapist may be misled if only the negative descriptors for moderate scale elevations are used. As the public becomes more psychologically sophisticated and people are increasingly willing to seek help with their personal problems, more persons who are basically well adjusted and who have a minimum of personality problems will consult psychologists for help. The clinician must be careful not to over-read scale elevations with this group. These clients bring many positive personality characteristics to therapy in spite of their moderately elevated scale scores on the MMPI.

Along these same lines Daniels and Hunter (1949) found that occupational groups differed on their mean MMPI profiles. For some groups moderate elevations appeared to be normal and not an indication of attenuated pathology. For those readers who would like further evidence on this issue we would suggest an article by Kunce and Callis (1969) "Vocational Interest and Personality."

While we are stressing that the clinician should be alert to the possibility of using positive interpretation in non-psychiatric populations, even among hospitalized psychiatric patients moderate elevations may have positive characteristics connected to them. After considerable experience with different client populations, Hovey and Lewis (1967) prepared a library of statements for each scale of the MMPI but with a difference. They included positive traits which they found to be associated with elevated scores as well as negative traits. They felt that one apparent advantage of their library of terms over some other systems was that it contained a substantial portion of non-negative and positive statements. They believed this was one way to avoid descriptions of patients only in terms of liability statements.

Hovey and Lewis go on to state that their experience indicates that T-scores around 60, rather than 50 are optimal for most of the Clinical scales. They also observed that when some T-scores are under 50, they are likely to reflect negative characteristics, just as they do when they approach a 75 T-score. However, they recommended that when the clinician in a psychiatric setting is selecting positive statements for a profile, that he/she be aware that a T-score of 75 is the upper limit for using positive traits. Also, they suggested, based upon their evidence, that positive statements should be used with caution if the score for scale **F** is above 70, if scale **8** is above 80, or if any two scales are above 80. In our discussion of individual scales we will include the positive statements suggested in the work of Hovey and Lewis (1967) as well as those given by Kunce and Anderson (1976, 1984).

SUBJECTS PERSONAL CHARACTERISTICS

Some personal characteristics of the individual who has taken the MMPI also would lead us to consider a more positive interpretation of moderately elevated scores. Some of these characteristics are

1. present functioning,

2. past social history,

3. intelligence and educational level, and

4. openness to admitting personal inadequacies.

Present Functioning and Past Social History

If the individual is "making it," that is, is successful in some occupation and reports that in general his/her life is going well, positive interpretive statements probably apply. This also is true if the test taker reports that his/her past life has been well-adjusted.

Intelligence and Educational Level

Both of these factors seem to be connected with higher scores on some scales of the MMPI. Researchers usually find that more intelligent college students routinely have moderately elevated scores on some scales with no more symptoms of pathology than shown by college students in general. A representative study is the one done by Kennedy (1962) on the MMPI profiles of a group of mathematically gifted adolescents who had an average I.Q. of 135. The mean scores for males on scales **2, 3, 5, 7,** and **8** were 58, 66, 64, 58, and 59 respectively. The moderately elevated scores for females were scales 3-60 and scale **K**-57. The reader should keep in mind that this means that many of the gifted students had scores higher than these means. The average age of this group was 17 and they did not show any clinically evident signs of psychopathology.

A number of other studies also support the position that college students tend to have higher than average scale scores on the MMPI and also frequently have more positive personality characteristics (Norman & Redlo, 1952; Goodstein, 1954; Rosen, 1956).

Openness to Personal Inadequacies

Gilliland and Colgin (1951) working with MMPIs of 14 groups of students from three campuses found that normal college students typically were moderately elevated on a number of scales. At one university 39 percent of the students had one score over 70, 14 percent had two scores over 70, and 7 percent had three scores over 70. Rather than accept the conclusion that a high level of abnormality existed in these groups, the authors posit that college students are less inhibited and freer to give answers which indicate deviations from normal since they have less at stake than hospitalized patients. Whatever the cause, they feel that extreme caution and tentativeness should be attached to any pathological diagnosis given to this population based upon personality test score alone.

RESEARCH SCALE VARIABLES

A third consideration in the interpretation of moderately elevated scores is the presence or absence of other elevations on the test itself, particularly those of the research scales. The research evidence on the ego-strength scale is an example. With populations such as college students and creative individuals, ego-strength scale scores tend to be elevated above 60 T-score points. As has been mentioned before, our interpretation policy has been that one should take a positive interpretative stance when confronted with moderately elevated scores on the psychiatric scales if they are accompanied by elevated ego-strength scores (Barron, 1969; Kleinmuntz, 1960; Kunce & Anderson, 1976).

We also feel that a normal **F** (50 T-score points or below) and an elevated **K** (above 55 T-score points) in a nonpsychiatric population warrant considering a positive interpretation of moderately elevated scale scores. As the reader will see in our section on Validity scales, we believe the evidence supports the conclusion that in a non-psychiatric population, high **K** represents something very close to good ego strength and self respect. Another combination we would use as suggestive of positive interpretations would be low **Dy**, high **Do**, and **St**.

In summary, we suggest two ways of approaching the interpretation of a nonpsychiatric population MMPI profile which has scales with moderate elevations (T-scores of 60 to 75): (1) attenuated pathology or (2) positive strengths. The reasons for taking the test, the personal characteristics of the individual, and other scale levels, especially the research scales should all be considered in making the decision as to which interpretation to use. As a final suggested guideline, if false negatives (labeling people pathological when they are not) are more undesirable in interpretations, then use the positive strength interpretations. If false positives (labelling people psychologically healthy when they are not) are undesirable in an interpretation, then use the attenuated pathology interpretations.

EFFECTS OF RACE AND CULTURE ON MMPI PROFILES

In this chapter's first section on race we will be concerned only with MMPI interpretations for Blacks. We are limiting ourselves to this one race because research concerning other races is still quite sparse and even more contradictory than that concerning Blacks. We will cover interpreting the MMPI for people from other cultures and with different languages in the second section of this chapter.

RACE

Controversy exists about a number of issues that we feel need to be explored by all clinicians who are in a position to interpret tests which have been administered to Blacks. Questions being debated by authors in the field include the following:

1. Are there differences between Blacks and whites on the MMPI?

2. If these differences exist, are they due to test bias or do they reflect some real differences in behavior between Blacks and whites?

3. Are new norms needed for Blacks?

4. What factors influence the different elevations in some Black profiles?

5. How does a clinician know when to use different norms for Black clients?

The simplest approach to interpreting MMPI profiles of Black Americans would be to treat them as if they were no different than those of a group of white Americans. As will become apparent to the reader, support is in the literature for this position (e.g., Pritchard & Rosenblatt, 1980). However, in some settings and with some clients we feel this will lead to misdiagnosis and the attribution of psychiatric problems where no such problems exist. Before presenting our suggestions for an approach which will help the clinician to individualize test interpretations for Blacks, we need to explore some possible answers from the literature to the questions which were just outlined above. Knowing the issues involved in the current controversy about the effects of race upon personality should help in more adequately interpreting profiles of Black individuals.

The first question that must be answered is, "Are there race differences on the MMPI?" This is not an easy question to answer since the research findings seem, on the surface at least, to be very contradictory.

A case has been made that there are no significant differences in mean scale scores between the MMPI profiles of Blacks and whites taken from the same clinical population. This case has been made by Pritchard and Rosenblatt (1980) who gathered and analyzed what they felt were all of the acceptable studies on Black-white differences. They found that there were no MMPI scales for which significant racial differences occurred more frequently than nonsignificant differences. If some studies found significant racial differences for certain scales, a larger group of studies would report that there were no differences.

Pritchard and Rosenblatt concluded that little, if any, evidence exists that Blacks score substantially higher or lower than whites on the MMPI scales. They also feel that even if a researcher finds differences between the elevations of Blacks and whites in a particular population this might reflect actual differences in pathology since researchers that argue otherwise have not shown that different elevations have occurred for Blacks and whites with the same level of pathology.

On the other side of this question of race differences, some prominent and frequently quoted researchers (Gynther, 1972; Gynther & Green, 1980) have said that not only do racial differences exist but that these differences are at a level of significance where separate norms should be used for Blacks. Gynther and Green (1980), also have done an extensive review of MMPI studies of racial differences. In addition, they subdivided the studies on race differences into three categories, those dealing with normals, those involving deviant groups (psychiatric patients or prisoners) and those involving drug addicts.

In their review of the 11 studies which had been done on normals, Gynther and Green found that Blacks and whites scored similarly on all scales except F, 8, and 9. On these three scales Blacks scored significantly higher than whites by 5 to 10 T-score points. These authors point out that these are not just any scales, but rather are those that are frequently used to make assertions about serious pathology. Therefore, if normal Blacks are scoring higher on these scales, they frequently will be misclassified as having serious pathology if standard norms are used.

Their second subgroup consisted of Blacks and whites in deviant populations. They found that Blacks still scored higher on certain scales, even though in general, these differences in the scores were not as great as they had been for Blacks in normal populations.

23

The third group of studies investigated by Gynther and Green consisted of five studies which used drug addicts as subjects. Here they found a very different pattern for Blacks and whites than was found in the two previous groups of studies. In these studies whites typically got higher or more deviant scores than Blacks, especially on scales 2 and 7 but also on scales F, 3, and 0. Also evidence was present in these studies to enable them to conclude that whites who become drug addicts are more disturbed than Blacks and therefore their elevations on the MMPI probably are accurate reflections of that fact.

Gynther and Green thus concluded that significant differences do exist between Blacks and whites on Scales F, 8, and 9 of the MMPI with Blacks scoring higher in general than white subjects in normal and psychiatric populations, and lower than white subjects in drug abuser populations. Gynther and Green believe that when using the present MMPI norms clinicians frequently misdiagnose Blacks in nonpsychiatric populations as more pathological than they really are since they routinely score higher on these three scales. This then leaves us with a more difficult second question to answer, "Are these differences due to test bias or do they reflect some real differences in behavior between Blacks and whites?"

Just what these scale differences mean is not immediately clear from the literature and a number of positions can be supported: (1) the higher scores mean more pathology, (2) the higher scores do not mean more pathology and allowances must be made for them, or (3) even when Blacks and whites get the same score on a scale it may not reflect the same behavior. We will cite a study in support of each of these positions before going on to explore a solution to the dilemma.

Butcher, Braswell, and Raney (1983) in their recent study ask the question whether or not the finding that Blacks have more MMPI scale elevations than whites means that the MMPI scales "overpathologize" for Blacks. Their findings suggest that the MMPI scale differences between the races most likely are a reflection of actual differences in symptoms between the groups. As an example, in their study, Blacks more frequently had paranoid symptoms than the other groups and this was reflected in higher scores on scales 6 and 8.

On the other hand, Elion and Megargee (1975) worked with offenders and concluded that scale 4 is valid for Blacks only if clinicians "mentally subtract" five points from the 4 scale T-score to correct for racial bias.

Even when Blacks and whites get the same score on a scale, it may not reflect the same behavior. This is shown in a study by Smith and Graham (1981) who found that high scores on the F scale for white patients were associated with psychopathology, including emotional withdrawal, hallucinations, and thought disorder, however, for Black patients this was not true. Their conclusion was that elevated scores on the F scale do not have the same pathological implications for Black patients as they do for white patients.

Does this then mean that separate norms for Blacks are needed? The strongest case against using different norms has been made by Pritchard and Rosenblatt (1980). As was mentioned before they stated that there is currently no evidence that the MMPI makes more predictive or interpretive errors for Blacks than for whites.

We believe, however, that while separate norms may seem not to be necessary for Blacks from some populations, for other populations of Blacks separate norms would be appropriate. This brings us to our fourth question, "What factors influence the differences between the MMPI profiles of Blacks and whites?"

McDonald and Gynther in 1963 were the first to propose that the MMPI differences between Blacks and whites were a consequence of different patterns of interests, values, and expectations. They stressed that these differences did not mean that the higher scores of Blacks meant that Blacks were more pathological. They hypothesized that the greater the separation between the races, the greater the differences to be found on MMPI scale scores. This anticipates a point that we will be substantiating later in this section that Blacks with limited contact with the white culture may score higher on certain scales but that these higher scores should not be interpreted as psychologically deviant.

An alternate hypothesis for the differences between Blacks and whites on the MMPI is given by Butcher, Braswell, and Raney (1983) who believed that who gets referred for treatment may differ from one culture to another. Behavior which is accepted or at least ignored in one culture may lead to hospitalization in another. In addition certain problem behaviors may have a higher base rate in one group than in another group because different prevailing social conditions predispose its members to different psychological problems.

While the two studies cited suggest that factors exist that might make for differences in Black-white MMPIs several studies have attempted to control variables besides race which might influence elevations. Bertelson, Marks, and May (1982) matched Black and white psychiatric patients on a number of crucial variables, race, sex, residence, marital status, hospital status, type of employment, socioeconomic status, age, and number of years of schooling. With all of these variables matched, they no longer found any scale elevations which could be attributed to race.

Another approach to understanding race differences on the MMPI was taken by Holcomb, Adams, and Ponder (1984). They were interested in the effects of removing intelligence as a factor in the scale scores of a group of Black accused murderers. This group of Blacks had significantly higher scores than white accused murderers on the F and 9 scales, but did not differ on the 8 scale. These differences disappeared when the effects of nonverbal intelligence were removed statistically.

Research which has been done by the second author (Anderson) indicates that difference in intelligence test scores between Blacks and whites is directly related to the degree of acculturation of the Black subjects into white society. An indication of the degree of acculturation in this study seemed to be where the Blacks were reared and whether they attended a segregated school. Those Blacks reared in the south and sent to segregated schools had intelligence test scores below those of Blacks reared in Northern city ghettos who attended non-segregated schools. In turn these Blacks had lower scores than Blacks who attended non-segregated schools and were reared in non-ghetto areas. All of this adds support to the McDonald and Gynther (1963) hypothesis that the greater the separation between the races the greater the likelihood that they will have higher scale scores on certain scales of the MMPI, most likely F, 8, and 9 (Gynther & Green, 1980; Elion & Megargee, 1975). Therefore, while Black-white differences seem to be dependent upon a variety of factors, what may be a major one that helps explain some of these differences seems to be the degree to which a particular Black individual has been acculturated into the white society.

How does different cultural exposure affect the personality of Blacks? In speaking of Blacks who come from areas containing a major degree of prejudice, Grier and Cobbs (1969) stated, "For his own survival, then, he must develop a cultural paranoia in which every white man is a potential enemy unless proved otherwise and every social system is set against him unless he personally finds out differently" (p. 149). Doob (1960) has hypothesized that a group in transition from one culture

26

to another would be under unusual strains and therefore should be more discontent, aggressive, and interpersonally sensitive than groups which are not in transition. Therefore MMPIs from people who are experiencing prejudice or who are in transition should be elevated to reflect the strains being experienced.

White (1974) recognizing that Blacks differ in degree of acculturation developed the Race-Sensitive (**Rs** scale) for the MMPI. This **Rs** scale score provides an indication of the degree to which a particular Black deviates from the modal MMPI performance of whites. If a black scores high on this scale, then allowances need to be made on the **F, 4, 8,** and **9** scales for his/her differences in acculturation into the white society. The scale appears in appendices A and B. The formula for adjusting the **F, 4, 8,** and **9** scales for the degree of acculturation is as follows: **F** scale score minus .2 times **Rs** raw score, **4** scale score minus .3 times **Rs** raw score, **8** minus .6 **Rs** raw score, and **9** scale minus .3 **Rs** raw score.

Guidelines in Interpreting Black Profiles

On the basis of the research which we have reported in this section on race we would suggest the following guidelines be used in interpreting a profile from a Black individual.

1. When working with a nonpsychiatric population of Blacks, for example clients in private practice or college students, and it seems clear-cut that the client is acculturated into white society, we recommend that the MMPI be interpreted in the same way that you would interpret the test for a white client.

2. If the client is a Black from a nonpsychiatric population and it is clear he/she is not acculturated into the white culture, we recommend that you make allowances for elevated scores on **F, 4, 8,** and **9.** As a rule of thumb we would recommend that you take 10 raw scores points from the **8** scale score and 5 raw scale score points from the other three scales.

3. If the client is a Black from a nonpsychiatric population, and you are not sure if the Black client is acculturated into the white culture, we recommend you use White's Race-Sensitive Scale (**Rs**) to help make that determination. If the client makes a high enough score on the **Rs** scale, you then can make the allowances for the **F, 4, 8,** and **9** which he recommends.

27

4. If the client is a Black and already judged by others to be deviant, either by being incarcerated or placed under psychiatric treatment, treat the MMPI scores as being truly reflective of the individual's condition. If the Black has higher scores than a white in a similar setting, most likely the MMPI scores are indicating more pathology.

5. If you are working in a drug treatment program, expect that, in general, the MMPI profiles of Blacks will be lower than those for whites. Again, the higher scores of the whites represent more pathology.

CULTURE

In this section, MMPI interpretations for people from a different culture and/or people who are primarily fluent in another language will be discussed. In the United States we have a large population of individuals whose first language is not English. Recently a large influx of Mexicans, Cubans, and Vietnamese people have come into the U.S. and some of these people are being tested in mental health facilities and other social service agencies. In colleges and universities there are a large number of foreign students from other countries, especially from such countries as Iran, India, and Nigeria. The need to interpret MMPIs for these different cultures raises two questions: (1) Does thinking in a foreign language affect the measurement of personality, especially on the MMPI? (2) If it does, how does it modify the interpretation of MMPI profiles for populations like those listed above?

Much information has been obtained regarding national (cultural) differences on the MMPI by Butcher and Pancheri and reported in their 1976 book on cross-national MMPI research. They studied differences between normal American subjects and normal individuals from Israel, Pakistan, Mexico, Costa Rica, Italy, Switzerland, and Japan using different translations of the MMPI. They initially felt that it was doubtful that the structure and content of personality would be the same in all countries. However, after study they found an impressively similar factor structure for the MMPI not only for Western European groups but for other national groups as well. As one would expect when comparing samples of subjects of such diverse origin, some differences existed in factor loadings for some scales, but for most purposes it can be assumed that whatever personality structure underlies the MMPI for Americans seems to apply to other cultures as well.

The authors concluded that, "It is evident from the factor-analytic study that the factor structure of the MMPI is maintained across different cultural samples not only when dealing with normal populations, but also when pathological subjects from different countries take the MMPI in their native languages" (p. 134).

The authors also present the results of item analyses, and a study of extreme item-endorsement to demonstrate that the MMPI item pool has a high degree of generality for normal populations speaking in other languages. That is, normal subjects from different countries taking the test in different language translations respond to MMPI item content in an essentially similar manner. This does not mean, however, that their MMPI profiles look exactly like those of the American population. A study of the mean profiles of normal individuals from the different national groups studied by Butcher and Pancheri shows that the mean profile of the Swiss and Italians are most like American samples, Mexican and Costa Rican samples are somewhat different, and the Pakistani and Japanese mean profiles are so different that if these MMPIs were used to screen for pathology, there would be many of them falsely labeled pathological.

While Butcher and Pancheri were impressed with the ability of the MMPI to discriminate between different diagnostic samples across cultures, they did feel, however, that sufficient differences do exist between Western and non-Western subjects in endorsement patterns for scales that measure psychopathology to caution against blind acceptance of MMPI scale scores and to suggest the need for additional research to verify the generality of these scales.

Summation of Cultural Effects

In summation, the above studies seem to indicate the following:

1. For an individual from a different culture who is part of a normal population, the reasonable expectation is that the clinical scale scores are elevated in direct proportion to how dissimilar that culture is to the American culture. More elevated profiles and therefore more false positives (calling people pathological when they are not) can be expected when

29

making judgments about such national groups as Iranians and Japanese because these cultures are quite dissimilar from the American culture. Fewer false positives will be found when judging pathology in such national groups as the Germans or French because these cultures are quite similar to the American culture.

2. Some scale elevations for people from a normal population will not indicate the same symptoms cross culturally. For example Butcher and Pancheri found symptom exaggeration on the MMPI for Italians. They felt this might be a manifestation of the general characteristic of Italians to dramatize problems. A good way to become acquainted with some of these cultural symptom differences would be the book by Butcher and Pancheri.

3. When working with a psychiatric or other deviant population, the MMPI should be a moderately good indicator of degree and kind of psychopathology. While caution is essential, apparently rather good overlap exists in symptoms of psychiatric problems from one group to another.

CHAPTER IV

VALIDITY SCALES

Of primary consideration in the interpretation of any inventory is the attitude of the person taking the test. Most inventories either have no way to check this attitude or have a simplistic approach to the problem. The MMPI is unique in this area. Four separate scales have been developed to measure the test-taking attitude of the subject, the **?, L, F,** and **K** scales. Of these scales, two (**L** and **K**) were designed to measure the person's trying to look better on the test than he/she really is, and one (the **F** scale) was designed to measure the person's trying to look worse on the test than he/she really is. The **?** scale measures how many questions the client left unanswered on the test, and thus can show the person's resistance to the test, confusion, or the fact that he/she did not have time to finish. These Validity scales can be interpreted either individually or in combinations.

In reality, the ? scale does not usually have to be interpreted because it rarely has enough raw score points to be scored on the profile sheet. Similarly, the L scale is only rarely above a T-score of 60, therefore the interpretation of this scale usually uses only the low end of the scale (the person is not trying to look good on the test). Only the F and K scales vary considerably therefore the various interpretations of them are considered carefully.

Greene (1980) has developed a method of assessing the validity of the MMPI profile by looking at the ? and F scales' elevations plus the TR scale (the number of the 16 repeated items on the MMPI that are marked inconsistently), the Carelessness scale (Greene, 1978), the Dissimulation scale (Gough, 1954), and the difference between the T-scores on the Weiner and Harmon (1948) subtle and obvious scales. He first determines the consistency with which the test taker has endorsed the MMPI items by using the TR and Carelessness scales. If these scales indicate consistency, then the other scales are examined to see if the test taker has been accurate in his/her item endorsement. Greene makes the point that only after determining that the test taker has answered both consistently and accurately can the Validity and Clinical scales be interpreted. We highly recommend using Greene's method of determining consistency and accuracy, especially for profiles with highly elevated F scales and for those cases where accuracy of interpretation is of the utmost importance. Greene's book should be consulted for full details concerning the scales he uses and his method of assessing consistency and accuracy.

? SCALE
(Cannot Say Scale)

The ? scale raw score is simply the number of items the client has left unanswered. Omission of items is largely dependent upon the subject's response set, which in turn is usually influenced by the instructions given. If the instructions call for all items to be answered, they usually are. MMPI's are usually given with these instructions, and most people leave few, if any, questions unanswered.

The usual number of items omitted is from 0 through 6, with a mode of zero and a median of one. When more than six items are not answered, the interpreter should look at the items omitted to see if a pattern exists. If a pattern occurs, it may indicate an area which the client does not want to consider, or about which confusion exists. This knowledge can be useful in counseling the person.

Elevations on this scale are rare. As a matter of fact, the omission of more than twelve items is very unusual. In the last 1,000 profiles we have evaluated, only two persons omitted a substantial number of items. One person omitted the last 100 items because she was stopped before she had finished. The second person omitted 57 items without knowing it because he was mentally confused. In no other situation were more than 12 items omitted.

GENERAL INFORMATION

1. The ? scale raw score is the number of test questions a person does not answer.

2. Normal people decline few items on the MMPI (Gravitz, 1971). Thus, this scale tends to be highly skewed, with 0-6 being the usual number of unanswered items. The modal value for this scale is zero, and the median value is one question unanswered.

3. The number of items omitted is largely dependent upon the subject's response set, which is usually influenced by the testing instructions given. If the instructions are for all items to be answered, they usually are.

Dahlstrom, Welsh, and Dahlstrom (1972) feel that some problems may result from giving the instruction to answer all items because people may resent having to answer all of the questions. We have found this rarely to be the case.

4. Most researchers feel this scale should not be considered or interpreted until a raw score of 30 (T = 50) or more is obtained. We feel however that even when fewer than this number are left unanswered, it might be useful to see if a certain pattern exists to the unanswered items, that is, they may all be related to a certain topic such as sex or family. This topic may be an area of concern for the client.

5. The reason people leave items unanswered may range from lack of knowledge about a subject to defensiveness. See the high score section of this scale for the various reasons for omissions.

6. The effect of a high ? score (T = 70 or above), if the omissions are scattered throughout the test, can be a general lowering of the entire profile without much distortion of the pattern, except for the women's scale 5. For this one scale, the more items that are omitted, the higher the T-score becomes.

The presence of a high ? scale score however does not always mean that the profile is too low to interpret because the motivations leading the subject to omit items also may lead him/her to choose an unusual number of deviant responses (Dahlstrom et al., 1972).

7. If the high ? score is the result of the person not finishing the test and leaving items unanswered at the end, the Validity and Clinical scales are relatively unaffected if the first 400 items have been answered. However, the Research scales are affected by the item omissions and should not be interpreted.

8. Gravitz (1967) found that ? items are a reflection of resistance on the part of subjects. Omissions appear to reflect a disinclination to respond openly to test content which patently probes personal and private feelings.

9. Considerable consistency over time is prevalent for this scale. That is, a person will have approximately the same score on it if the test should be given a second time (Dahlstrom et al., 1972).

? 34

HIGH SCORES
(T = 70 or Above)

1. High scores may indicate the following:

   a. Indecision about the question and not wanting to be incorrect in answering either way.

   b. Indecision or obsession with the "right" answer.

   c. Defensiveness (wanting to look good). These people do not know what answer would be the most favorable one for them to choose. Therefore, they do not answer the question.

   d. Not wanting to answer the question, but also not wanting to say "no" to the tester. Therefore, the client takes the test but leaves many questions unanswered.

   e. Distrust of the tester's motives.

   f. Lack of ability to read or comprehend all items.

   g. Not enough time to finish the test as would be shown when only items toward the end of the test are omitted. This situation may occur because an obsessive compulsive person might take a considerable amount of time to answer each item.

   h. A seriously depressed patient who finds the items beyond his/her capacity for decision (Carkhuff et al., 1965).

   i. Aggression toward the test or tester.

   j. Mental confusion whereby the person does not realize he/she has omitted questions.

2. In some research studies, MMPI tests with a ? scale T-score above 70 are considered invalid.

LOW SCORES
(T = 50 or Below)

1. Low scores are more likely to be obtained when the testing instructions call for answering all the items.

2. Even when only 6 items are omitted, a review of the omissions may reveal a pattern.

3. People may not answer questions in certain areas for the following reasons:

    a. because they are not sure what they feel or believe about an area,

    b. because they cannot face their feelings about an area,

    c. because they do not trust the counselor to keep the test answers confidential, and/or

    d. because the items pertain to one or more areas of life that these people have not experienced.

COMBINATIONS

The Validity scales, **?, L, F,** and **K,** in these combinations are at a T-score of 60 or above, whereas the Clinical scales, **1** through **0,** are at a T-score of 70 or above and are the highest Clinical scales on the profile.

?-L

1. The person may be trying to place himself/herself in a highly favorable light but is using rather crude methods to distort the test record (Dahlstrom et al., 1972).

?-L-F-K

1. When all the Validity scales are elevated, intense and highly generalized negativism is suggested (Carkhuff et al., 1965).

?-F

1. The profile may be invalid because of mental confusion or reading difficulties. Further testing may be necessary to distinguish which of these two hypotheses is correct.

?-K

1. The person may be very defensive (Hovey & Lewis, 1967).

?-5 See the **5-?** combination, p. 171.

SUMMARY OF ? SCALE INTERPRETATIONS

Number of Items Omitted	Interpretations
0 thru 6	This is the typical number of items omitted.
7 thru 12	The subject would prefer not answering questions about one or more areas.
13 thru 67	Scores in this range are rarely seen. Reasons for scores in this range may be in the categories above (7 thru 12) or below (67 or above).
67 or above	Scores in this range may indicate lack of time to complete the test, indecision, defensiveness, not wanting to answer the questions, distrust, lack of reading ability, aggression, depression, or confusion.

—NOTES—

L SCALE
(Lie Scale)

This scale is usually measuring the degree to which a person is trying to look good in an obvious way. The higher the scale, the more the individual is claiming socially correct behavior. The lower the scale, the more the person is willing to own up to general human weaknesses.

Our experience indicates that the L scale is nearly always below a T of 50 and is rarely above a T of 60. People scoring at a T of 55 or above on this scale may be presenting themselves as morally righteous, although this in fact may not be true. Job applicants, for example, tend to have an elevated L because they wish to impress the person doing the hiring.

In mental health centers, an elevation on this scale frequently indicates a rather naive person who has not thought deeply about human behavior, particularly his/her own. In a college setting, an elevated L, particularly with a slightly elevated 3 scale, frequently indicates people who like to look on the bright side of life and do not like to think bad thoughts about themselves or others. Thus, the exact inference to be construed from an elevated L depends upon the person's background, setting, and purpose for taking the inventory.

Scores at the low end of this scale indicate a person who is not socially naive, at least to the extent of claiming social virtues he/she does not have.

GENERAL INFORMATION

1. The 15 items of the L scale attempt to identify people who will not admit to human foibles, such as telling white lies or not reading newspaper editorials. Such persons may wish to be seen as perfectionistic (Carson, 1969), or they may be naive.

2. The L scale items are seen as positive attributes in our culture. However, most people, excepting the most conscientious or naive, do not see such attributes as being true of themselves (Carson, 1969).

3. The **L** scale may indicate the following:

   a. The way the person actually sees himself/herself, that is as morally straight.

   b. The degree to which a person may be attempting to "look good" by choosing the response that is more socially acceptable.

   c. The person's tendency to cover up and deny undesirable personal faults.

4. Caldwell (1977) believed this scale may measure a person's fears of shame and moral judgment. If a person has these fears, he/she will deny moral fault and therefore score high on this scale.

5. The **L** scale is not a subtle scale. The items are seen by most people to be fairly obvious "trap" items, and elevations on this scale above a T-score of 55 are infrequent. See the high score section of this scale for the types of people who score in this direction.

6. The mean raw score for this scale is close to zero, and the modal raw score is 4.

7. The **L** scale tends to be higher for older people, a finding that suggests greater feelings of conservatism among older age groups (Colligan et al., 1984).

8. Mexican-Americans score higher on the **L** scale than whites. Hibbs et al. (1979) feel this may be due to cultural factors.

9. The **L** scale is negatively correlated with education. That is, the more education the subject has, the more likely the **L** scale is to be low (Colligan et al., 1984).

10. Test-retest reliabilities vary considerably. These variable correlations may be an artifact of the brevity of the scale (15 items) (Dahlstrom & Welsh, 1960).

11. Although most people do not score high on this scale, in one study (Gravitz, 1970b) using normal subjects, four items of this scale (items 15, 135, 165, 255) were endorsed in the scorable direction by more than half of the subjects, while just under one-half answered

four other items in the scorable direction. Thus, eight of the 15 items in this scale were answered in the scorable direction by almost one-half of the subjects.

12. Under instructions to present oneself in the most favorable light, the **L** scale tends to elevate.

Under these instructions, the tendency is for the **L** and **K** scales to be between a T-score of 60 and 70 and for the **F** scale to be near 50. These three scales thus form a "V." See Figure 8, page 70.

HIGH SCORES
(T = 55 or Above)

Moderate and Marked Elevations

1. Persons who score high on this scale may actually see themselves as virtuous, scrupulous, conforming, and self-controlled (Hovey & Lewis, 1967).

2. Caldwell (1985) has hypothesized that an **L** scale in this range measures the fear of being judged unworthy or bad.

3. High scores on this scale in individuals with adequate intelligence may reflect the use of repression, especially rigid denial (Trimboli & Kilgore, 1983).

4. High **L** scores also may indicate

   a. Naive people.

   b. People who repress or deny unfavorable traits in themselves.

   c. People applying for jobs who want to look good on the test.

   d. People with below average intelligence.

   e. People with only elementary school education.

   f. People with rural backgrounds.

g. Ministers or people with strict moral principles.

h. People with socioeconomic or cultural deprivation—ghetto or ethnic minority backgrounds (Dahlstrom et al., 1972).

5. A high **L** score may indicate that the Clinical scales are depressed. This fact should be taken into account in reading the profile.

If the Clinical scales are elevated while the **L** scale is in this range, this means that the person's defensiveness is not working well enough to keep problems under control.

LOW SCORES
(T = 45 or Below)

1. Low scores indicate an ability to acknowledge general human weaknesses (Hovey & Lewis, 1967).

2. The person who scores low may see himself/herself as non-righteous and relaxed (Hovey & Lewis, 1967).

3. Low scores are typical of the college population. However, a socially sophisticated and/or educated person may score low on **L** and still be trying to "look good." In this instance, the **K** score may be elevated.

COMBINATIONS

The Validity scales, **?, L, F,** and **K,** in these combinations are at a T-score of 60 or above, whereas the Clinical scales, **1** through **0,** are at a T-score of 70 or above and are the highest Clinical scales on the profile.

See also the **L-F-K** profiles, pp. 69-71.

L-? See the **?-L** combination, p. 36.

L-?-F-K See the **?-L-F-K** combination, p. 36.

L-F See also the **L-F-K** profiles, pp. 69-71.
the **F-L** combination, p. 56

1. The discrepancy shown in this combination between defensiveness, such as denying socially disapproved actions and thoughts (high **L**) and acknowledgement of a number of unusual, bizarre, or atypical experiences (high **F**) may be manifested by a person exhibiting different behavior in different contexts (Dahlstrom et al., 1972).

   a. A person with this combination may be defensive in a personal interview but may show unusual experiences and thoughts in projective testing where he/she is not aware of what is being revealed.

   b. The discrepancy between defensiveness and bizarreness may be the result of poor psychological integration, which characterizes some disturbed, naive people.

L-F-K See also the **L-F-K** profiles, pp. 69-71
the **F-L-K** combination, p. 56

1. This pattern may be produced by answering all questions "false." This is called the All-False or Negative Response Set. See Figure 1, the All-False Response Profile, p. 45.

L-K See also the **L-F-K** profiles, pp. 69-71.

1. A person with this combination may be repressing and denying unfavorable traits (Blazer, 1965a).

2. This pattern may indicate deliberate faking good on the test, because high scores have been obtained in numerous studies where subjects have been asked to present themselves in the most favorable light possible (Gloye & Zimmerman, 1967; Hiner et al., 1969; Lanyon, 1967).

3. If the **L** or **K** scale is equal to or greater than 70 T-score points and **F** is not the most elevated validity scale, then Sines et al. (1979) have found

   a. if the clinical scales suggest psychosis, the person probably is psychotic; and

L

b. if the clinical scales do not suggest psychosis, the possibility is that the patient could be psychotic.

4. Marks, Seeman, and Haller (1974) noted that this Validity scale pattern occurs with their **1-3/3-1** pattern and also with their **K +** pattern. See the **1-3** pattern, p. 87, and the **K +** pattern, p. 64.

L-K-3

1. This combination may be found in highly defensive normal people. They may not even be aware of their great defensiveness.

L-1-2-3-5 See the **1-2-3-5-L** combination, p. 86.

SUMMARY OF L SCALE INTERPRETATIONS*

T-score	Interpretations
50 or below	These people are willing to admit to general human faults.
50 thru 60	These people are presenting themselves as, or may actually be, virtuous, conforming, and self-controlled.
60 or above	Scores in this range may indicate naive people, people who repress or deny unfavorable traits, or people applying for jobs who want to make a favorable impression.

*Where T-scores are listed in two categories (i.e., 50 or below and 50 through 60) and a score is obtained that is listed for two categories, use whichever interpretation seems to be most appropriate for the individual.

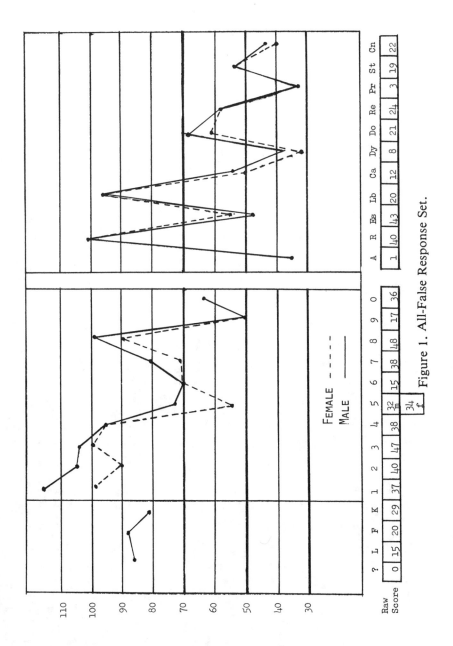

Figure 1. All-False Response Set.

Raw Score	?	L	F	K	1	2	3	4	5	6	7	8	9	0		A	R	Es	Lb	Ca	Dy	Do	Re	Pr	St	Cn
	0	15	20	29	37	40	47	38	32 m	15	38	48	17	36		1	40	43	20	12	8	21	24	3	19	22
									34 f																	

FEMALE -----
MALE ———

45

L

—NOTES—

F SCALE
(Frequency or Confusion Scale)

Experience with mental health clinic and college counseling populations suggests that the **F** scale is nearly always measuring the degree to which a person's thoughts are different from those of the general population. Only rarely is an elevated **F** indicative of purposeful faking-bad in these populations. As the elevation increases, subjects seem to be reporting an increasing number of unusual thoughts and experiences. With a college population or with creative people, different thoughts, to a mild degree, are not uncommon, and an **F** of 65 may be quite typical. When people become involved intensely in unusual religious, political, or social groups, they frequently have elevations on the scale as high as 75. However, when elevations go beyond 75, usually the person is using the **F** scale to request help by reporting many unusual thoughts and happenings.

In a mental health setting, the elevations do not have to be as high as 75 for the request-for-help interpretation to be made. For example, a T of 65 in this population may indicate that the person is having difficulty in some one area of life. As the elevation increases, the person tends to report an increasing number of problem areas and a greater degree of severity of the problems.

Elevations above 100 in either population limit the profile as an instrument for diagnosis. With an elevation above 100 on **F**, usually an elevation occurs on all of the Clinical scales. Such a profile generally indicates that the person is unable to pinpoint any one area of concern and is reacting to everything.

Low **F** scores usually indicate a person who feels he/she is relatively free from stresses and problems.

GENERAL INFORMATION

1. The **F** scale consists of 64 questions not answered in the scored direction by 90 percent of the normal population.

F

2. As the **F** scale become elevated, the person is saying more unusual things about himself/herself. This action may be for many different reasons. See the high score section for the various interpretations.

3. Greene (1980) has developed a method of determining whether an **F** scale elevation accurately reflects a person's feelings. His book should be consulted for details. See also p. 32.

4. Special comparisons are usually made with the **K** scale for diagnostic clarification. See the **F-K** Index, pp. 73-74.

5. Schenkenberg et al. (1984) have found that younger people in a psychiatric population score higher on the **F** scale than older patients.

6. The **F** scale score tends to decrease with age for low and high IQ subjects but remains relatively constant for average IQ subjects (Gynther & Shimkunas, 1965a).

7. Test-retest reliabilities are only fair. The scale is particularly sensitive to fluctuations in a person's psychological state or to treatment (Carkhuff et al., 1965).

8. Blacks tend to score high on this scale (Gynther, 1961; Gynther, 1972).

   In a prison population, Blacks tended to score higher than whites on this scale (as well as higher on scales **8** and **9**) (Holland, 1979).

9. Mexican-Americans tend to score higher than whites on this scale (as well as higher on the **L** scale). Hibbs et al. (1979) felt that this may be due to cultural factors.

HIGH SCORES

Moderate Elevations (T = 60 through 70)

1. Scores in this range may indicate one special area of concern, for example, family problems, religious problems, or health problems (Dahlstrom et al., 1972).

2. Elevations on **F** at this level, with Clinical scales above 70, may indicate that the person has become used to having the problems indicated by the Clinical scale elevations and is not too worried about them.

3. People in this range of scores may be willful, impetuous, and operating on their own schedule (Caldwell, 1985).

4. People who think differently than the general population score in this range (creative people, some college students).

5. Very compulsive people who are trying hard to be frank may score in this range (Good & Brantner, 1974).

6. Social protest or emotional commitment to a different-thinking religious and/or political movement may lead to elevations at this level. If the elevation on the **F** scale is for this reason, the Clinical scales tend not to be extraordinarily high (Carson, 1969; Dahlstrom et al., 1972).

Marked Elevations (T = 70 or Above)

T = 70 through 80

See also the **F-K** Index, pp. 73-74
See also point 3 under General Information

1. These elevations may be indicative of unusual or markedly unconventional thinking as a way of life, especially for some college students.

2. Occasionally people who are intensely anxious and want to be helped score in this range. They also may score above 80 T-score points.

3. Another cause for elevation of this scale is difficulty in reading or interpreting test statements because of poor reading ability or emotional interference. Because some of the more difficult items to read on the MMPI are on the **F** scale, it is possible for a poor reader to get an elevation on this scale (Dahlstrom et al., 1972).

4. Young people struggling with problems of identity frequently score in this range.

T = 80 through 90

See also the **F-K** Index, pp. 73-74
See also point 3 under General Information

1. Before the profile can be considered valid, it must be determined whether or not the person (1) was out of contact with reality, (2) had a low reading level, or (3) was purposely malingering (Dahlstrom et al., 1972).

   a. Once the interpreter is satisfied that these causes are not in operation, profiles with this high an **F** score can be read and interpreted.

   b. In situations where elevated **F** scale scores can be interpreted, the person's problems are such that he/she truly may have very atypical experiences which are reported in the **F** scale items (Dahlstrom et al., 1972). Occasionally people with these atypical experiences will score as high as T = 100 or above and still have a valid profile.

2. Scores this high may occur because of a "cry for help."

3. People who are severely disturbed and uncooperative subjects with behavior problems may score in this range.

4. The person may want to appear unconventional. This desire is not unusual for adolescents (Carson, 1972).

T = 90 through 100

See the **F-K** Index, pp. 73-74
See also point 3 under General Information

1. Scores in this range may indicate a random marking of the test. This random marking may be purposeful or the result of the fact that the person is illiterate and does not want to admit it. The person also may be confused, have a psychological disorder, or have brain damage (Carson, 1969). See the random response profile, Figure 2, p. 52.

2. Scores in this range also may indicate a person whose problems are such that he/she truly has very atypical experiences which are reported in the **F** scale items (Dahlstrom et al., 1972).

F   50

T = 100 or Above

See the **F-K** Index, pp. 73-74
See also point 3 under General Information

1. Scores of 100 or above may show confusion on the client's part in marking the items.

2. The person may be deliberately trying to look bad. See Figures 2, 3, and 4, the Random, All-X, and All-True Response Set Profiles.

3. These scores may reflect the severity of psychopathology the person is experiencing or highly specialized and atypical experiences in the individual's life.

4. When **L** and **K** are low (T = 45 or below), a **F** elevation of T = 100 or above may indicate an All-True Response Set. See Figure 4, the All-True Response Set Profile.

5. These scores may reflect scoring errors.

6. Gynther, Altman, and Warbin (1973a) and Gynther, Altman, and Sletten (1973) have found that white psychiatric patients with raw **F** scores greater than 26 (T = 100 or above) have higher scores on withdrawal, poor judgment, thought disorders, and reduced speech than other patients. The phrase that best describes these patients is "confused psychotic." These terms do not apply to patients generating obviously faked MMPIs. For Blacks, those scoring above an **F** score of 26 raw score were seen as no different from Blacks with scores below an **F** of 26.

7. Evans and Dinning (1983; Evans, 1984) have found that for male psychiatric inpatients, consistent responders (shown by a low **TR** score, 4 or below) with high **F** appeared to exaggerate pathology, while inconsistent responders shown by a **TR** score above 4 were indicative of random responding, perhaps due to psychotic thought disorders that made them too confused to take the MMPI conscientiously.

8. The **TR** scale also has been found useful in another study (Maloney et al., 1980) to more accurately assess high **F** scales.

The **TR** scale is reproduced in Appendices A and B.

Figure 2. Random Response Set.

?	L	F	K	1	2	3	4	5	6	7	8	9	0
0	7½	32	15	24	30	30	31	30	20	39	54	26	35

A	R	Es	Lb	Ca	Dy	Do	Re	Pr	St	Cn
19½	20	34	12½	18	28½	14	16	16	17	25

FEMALE - - - -
MALE ———

F   52

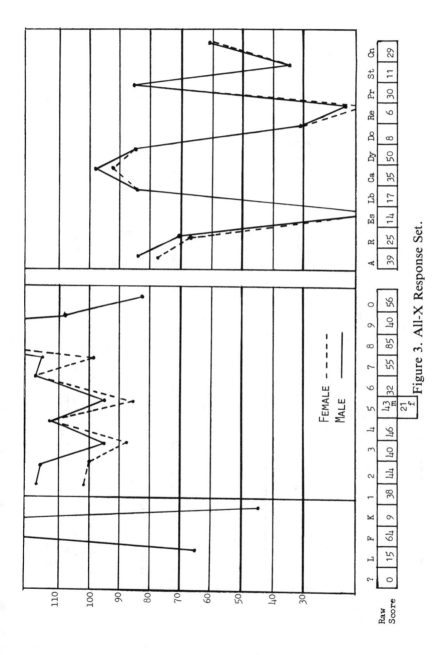

Raw Score	?	L	F	K	1	2	3	4	5	6	7	8	9	0		A	R	Es	Lb	Ca	Dy	Do	Re	Pr	St	Cn
	0	15	64	9	38	44	40	46	43 m / 21 f	32	55	85	40	56		39	25	14	17	35	50	8	6	30	11	29

FEMALE - - - -
MALE ──────

Figure 3. All-X Response Set.

53

F

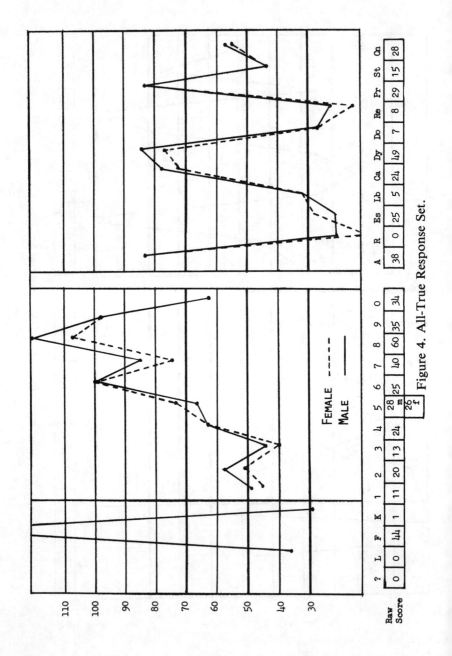

Figure 4. All-True Response Set.

Raw Score	?	L	F	K	1	2	3	4	5	6	7	8	9	0
	0	0	44	1	11	20	13	24	28 m 26 f	25	40	60	35	34

FEMALE - - - - -
MALE ————

	A	R	Es	Lb	Ca	Dy	Do	Re	Pr	St	Cn
	38	0	25	5	24	49	7	8	29	15	28

F

54

9. Maloney et al. (1980) have suggested putting the booklet form answer sheet in a manila folder with holes punched in the folder and numbered for the **TR** items. Both sides can be examined to determine if pairs of items are answered consistently.

LOW SCORES
(T = 45 or Below)

1. These scores may indicate normal persons who are relatively free from stress.

2. Adjectives which have been suggested to describe low scorers are sincere, calm, dependable, honest, simple, and conventional (Carson, 1969; Hovey & Lewis, 1967).

3. Low scores tend to indicate honestly reported records in college samples.

4. People in this range may have a high degree of social conformity (Caldwell, 1985).

5. The **F** scale score tends to reach this range after therapy.

COMBINATIONS

The Validity scales, **?, L, F,** and **K,** in these combinations are at a T-score of 60 or above, whereas, the Clinical scales, **1** through **0,** are at a T-score of 70 or above and are the highest Clinical scales on the profile.

F >25 Raw Score Points

1. If the **F** scale elevation is not the result of random marking or low reading level, the client who has this elevation usually appears to be confused. There may also be impaired judgment and delusions of reference and hallucinations (Gynther et al., 1973).

F-? See the **?-F** combination, p. 37.

F-?-L-K See the **?-L-F-K** combination, p. 36.

F-L See also the **L-F** combination, p. 43;
the **L-F-K** profiles, pp. 69-71.

1. This combination suggests the response set pattern where the person selects the most deviant answers (Blazer, 1965b). See Figure 3, the All-X Response Set Profile, p. 53.

F-L-K See also the **L-F-K** combination, p. 43
the **L-F-K** profiles, pp. 69-71.

1. When the **L** and **K** are moderately elevated and the **F** is markedly elevated, a random marking of the test may be indicated (Dahlstrom et al., 1972). See Figure 2, the Random Response Set Profile, p. 52.

F-K See the **L-F-K** profiles, pp. 69-71

1. This combination involves a contradiction in that the person reports self-enhancement and self-depreciation at the same time. This contradiction seems to be the result of lack of insight, confusion, or difficulties in grasping the nature of the test (Dahlstrom et al., 1972).

F-4-8 See the **4-8-F** combination, p. 155.

F-8-6 See the **8-6** combination, point 8, p. 210.

F-8

1. A person with the **F-8** combination may have tendencies toward withdrawal (Marks, 1961).

2. Blacks in rural, isolated area had this profile pattern (Gynther, Fowler, & Erdberg, 1971).

F-8-6-4-9 See the **8-6-4-9-F** combination, p. 211.

F-8-9-6 See the **8-9-6-F** combination, p. 214.

F-9

1. This combination may indicate manic behavior (Blazer, 1965b).

SUMMARY OF F SCALE INTERPRETATIONS*

T-score	Interpretations
50 or below	Scores in this range may indicate a normal person relatively free from stress.
50 thru 60	The majority of people score within this range.
60 thru 70	The person may have concerns about one area of life, such as religion or health, but is not too worried about it.
	The person may be involved in an atypical political or social organization or in an unusual religious group.
70 thru 80	This person may be upset and asking for help.
	A person with a score in this range may have had difficulty in reading or interpretating the test.
	The person may think somewhat differently than the general population. This is especially true if the **8** scale is above 70.
	College students with identity problems may score in this range.
80 thru 90	At this level, before interpreting the MMPI, check that the person was not out of contact with reality, did not have a low reading level, or did not have reason to malinger.
	If the elevation is not because of any of these reasons, then the person's problems are such as to give him or her a long list of bizarre, peculiar, and atypical experiences.
	This may be a person who is anxious (check the **7** scale) and asking for help.
90 thru 100	This may be a random marking of the test. It may or may not be deliberate.

F

If this is not a random marking of the test, then the person's problems may have produced a long list of bizarre, peculiar, and atypical experiences.

100 or above   A score in this range may indicate confusion in marking items.

The confusion usually is not deliberate at this level.

This score may indicate that the person's deliberately trying to look bad.

It may reflect the severity of psychopathology of the person.

With low **L** and **K** (T = 45 and below), an **F** score in this range may indicate an All-True Response Set. See Figure 4.

---

*Where T-scores are listed in two categories (i.e., 50 or below and 50 through 60) and a score is obtained that is listed for two categories, use whichever interpretation seems to be most appropriate for the individual.

K SCALE

(Correction Scale)

This scale measures defensiveness and guardedness. Therefore, it evaluates some of the same behavior as the **L** scale but much more subtly.

In order to evaluate the **K** scale properly, the specific population, college or mental health center, must be noted. In addition, the **K** scale interpretation must be modified for special groups of people within the population. In this introduction are discussed the usual interpretations for the two major populations with whom this book is concerned and, when appropriate, modifications are noted.

In a college population, a T-score on this scale between 55 and 70 is typical. People scoring in this range are indicating that their lives are satisfactory, that they are basically competent, and that they can manage their lives. Such scores are usual for people coming for counseling about an academic major or for students taking the MMPI as part of some experiment. When T = 70 or above for the **K** scale, these people are indicating not only that they are competent people and can manage their own lives, but also that they are being a bit cautious about revealing themselves. Such scores are usually attained when a person is defensive, and/or when the test administrator does not fully explain the reason for the test, the use to which it will be put, or the confidentiality of the results.

When **K** is below 45 and the **F** scale is elevated above 60 T-score points, the college student may be experiencing some stress. The **K** scale score usually elevates to the 55 through 65 range when the stress is alleviated.

When **K** is below 45 and the **F** scale is below 60 score points, the college student may be feeling that life has been rough, that he/she has had fewer advantages than most people.

In a mental health setting, if the client is having difficulties, he/she usually scores below 45 on the **K** scale. The severity of the problem is usually indicated by how low the **K** score is (the lower the score, the more severe the problem). Below a T-score of 35, the prognosis for successful therapy is poor. A score in this range does not indicate that the person will or should be hospitalized for his/her problem, but more that the person is unable to improve at this time. Scores between 35 and 45 typically reflect situational difficulties, such as marriage, family, or job problems.

Elevations over 55 are unusual in the mental health population and for people who do not have some college education and/or are unsuccessful in business. Typically such scores are attained by persons who blame others for their situation, e.g., the other mate in marriage counseling. A person in this range also may be bringing someone else in to be counseled, such as a parent who brings a child in with school difficulties. As the **K** goes above 60, defensiveness is usually present. When the person has a T score over 70, the prognosis for the person recognizing problems he/she may have is poor. Marks, Seeman, and Haller's (1974) "**K + **" profile should be studied for further information concerning this pattern. See point 7 under the marked elevations.

College counseling and mental health centers personnel frequently evaluate persons for other agencies. In these instances, the above rules for interpretation of the **K** scale do not always hold since the person may have an ulterior motive for taking the test, rather than just taking it to tell how he/she is at the moment. Persons applying for jobs and students being screened for specific programs (doctoral admissions, for example) may have a T-score of approximately 70. Conversely persons applying for such things as disability pensions (where the person wishes to look bad) tend to have unusually low **K** scores and elevated **F** scores.

Persons under scrutiny by the courts may have either high or low **K** scores, depending upon their situations. If the person is seeking parole or wishes to win custody of his/her child, a high **K** score may be obtained. If the person is seeking to avoid a sentence by appearing to be mentally ill, a low **K** score may result. Therefore, in these special instances the examiner must know the purpose of the examination and what the person expects to gain from it.

When the **L** scale (T = 60 or above), the **3** scale (T = 70 or above), and/or the **R** scale (T = 60 or above) are elevated with the **K** scale (T = 65 or above), the diagnosis of defensiveness is reinforced. The person not only does not want to look bad to others (**L** and **K** elevations), he/she does not want to think badly of others (**3** scale elevation), and he/she also does not want to look or talk about certain areas of life (**R** scale elevation).

K   60

GENERAL INFORMATION

1. The **K** scale of 30 items was chosen as a correction factor to sharpen the discriminatory power of certain Clinical scales, specifically scales **1, 4, 7, 8,** and **9.**

2. The **K** scale was developed after the other Validity scales when it was noted that there was no correction for defensiveness on the test.

3. The **K** scale was developed to measure how much the examinee wished to "look good" on the test. The higher the **K** score the more the indication was that the person desired to look good and thus a portion of the **K** score was added to five Clinical scales (**1, 4, 7, 8,** and **9**) to correct for this attitude. The five Clinical scales were the only ones seemingly affected by this "looking good" attitude; therefore, the correction is applied only to them.

4. In spite of the **K** correction additions to Clinical scales, high scores on **K** are usually associated with *lower* profile elevations, whereas low scores on **K** are usually accompanied by *higher* profile elevations (Dahlstrom et al., 1972).

5. This is a subtle scale. The items are not as obvious as those on the **L** scale. The **K** scale is thus intended to detect defensiveness in psychologically sophisticated people.

6. This scale may measure the intactness of the individual's psychological defenses.

7. Caldwell (1977) has hypothesized that the **K** scale may measure a fear of emotional intensity and an avoidance of intimacy when it goes over 65 T-score points for non-college populations and above 70 T points for college populations.

   He also has hypothesized (1985) that elevations on this scale are associated with a marked constriction of affective responsiveness.

8. Some authors (Adams, 1971; Dahlstrom et al., 1972) have suggested that **K** scores in the 60 through 70 range do not always mean covering up more subtle atypical psychological characteristics, but may at least in part, reflect a true assertion of psychological health,

K

especially for females, for college students, and for people from higher socioeconomic levels. When the **K** scores go above a T of 70, however, the authors feel the scores do seem to reflect defensiveness for these groups.

9. Generally speaking, therapy prognosis tends to be poor with extremely high (T = 70 or above) **K** scale scores (Carson, 1969).

10. The higher values of **K** have not been used for discarding a profile as invalid as has been the case with higher values on the other Validity scales.

11. Test-retest reliabilities are fair to good (between .60 and .80) (Dahlstrom & Welsh, 1960).

12. Hibbs et al. (1979) have found that older women score higher on this scale.

13. In one study of a normal population, the women's mean score was 55 on this scale (Colligan et al., 1984).

14. A fairly high negative correlation occurs between the **K** and **F** scales and between the **O** and **K** scales.

15. Under ideal self-instructions ("take this test trying to look as good as possible"), the **K** scale tends to become elevated to between 60 and 65 score points.

16. Post therapy profiles tend to show an increase in **K** (Cottle, 1953).

AVERAGE SCORES
(T = 45 through 60)

1. An average score on the **K** scale is an indication of a balance between self-disclosure and self-protection.

2. Adults with elementary school education and lower middle-class socioeconomic status generally will score in this range (Dahlstrom et al., 1972).

3. Occasionally, people with higher socioeconomic status (including college students) will score in the range between 45 and 50. In such cases these people may be undergoing some stress and thus do not feel as good about their lives as others of their socioeconomic level usually do (Dahlstrom et al., 1972).

HIGH SCORES

Moderate Elevations (T = 60 through 70)

1. Scores of moderate elevation are typical for people in the upper-middle class and lower-upper class, and for college students.

2. These people tend to have good mental health. They are independent and are easily capable of dealing with their day-to-day problems. The generally favorable view they show of themselves on the K scale is correct and therefore appropriate (Dahlstrom et al., 1972).

   Contrary to the conclusions of the response set studies, these people seemingly are not merely describing themselves favorably to achieve social acceptance. Their lives actually are under control and well managed.

3. If someone from the lower socioeconomic class has this elevation, it is more likely to reflect some defensiveness or a set toward looking socially desirable.

4. Job applicants may appear at this elevation because they wish to make a good impression.

Marked Elevations (T = 70 or Above) See also Figure 1, the All-False Response Set Profile, and Figure 5, the All-0 Response Set Profiles.

1. The usual reason for this elevation is that the person is impelled to present a psychologically healthy appearance to others.

   Limits do exist to this defensiveness however so that it does not usually include the obvious items of the L scale. Thus, extremely

K

high elevations on the **K** scale are not usually accompanied by high scores on the **L** scale (Dahlstrom et al., 1972).

2. The person tends to restrict his/her emotions and appears calm and even-tempered.

3. Elevations on this scale may reflect the use of repression and rationalization as defense mechanisms (Tromboli & Kilgore, 1983).

4. Because women tend to judge themselves more harshly than do men on a test such as the MMPI, a high **K** score by a woman is likely to reflect psychological effectiveness rather than defensiveness (Dahlstrom et al., 1972).

5. A high **K** score is associated with the low probability of delinquency, especially with females (Carson, 1969).

6. A very high **K** score with accompanying Clinical scale elevations may indicate an unwillingness or inability to look at problem areas. In fact, the person may not perceive self as having problems at all.

7. Marks, Seeman, and Haller (1974) found a **K** + pattern (only the **K** scale elevated above 70) in their university hospital and clinic population. People with this pattern tended to be shy, inhibited, and defensive. They also tended to be uninvolved in activities. The Marks, Seeman, and Haller book should be consulted for further information concerning this pattern.

8. A high **K** score with low **L** and **F** scores may indicate an "All-0" (all normal) Response Set. See Figure 5, the All-0 Profile.

LOW SCORES

Low Range (T = 35 through 45)

1. People may have scores in this range for one of two reasons.

   a. They may have problems which they are quite willing to admit. This interpretation is likely to be true if the **F** scale is elevated *above* 60 T-score points. If they do have problems, they are often sarcastic and caustic concerning themselves and the world (Carson, 1972).

1) These people tend not to feel good about themselves and often feel that they lack the skills to deal with their problems (Hovey & Lewis, 1967). If this is so, the **Es** scale usually is below 45 T-score points.

b. They believe life has been rough for them and that they have not had some of the advantages that others have had. This interpretation is likely to be true if the **F** scale is *below* 60 score points.

1) This belief may be an accurate perception because people scoring in this range frequently have had a deprived family background and/or limited income (Dahlstrom et al., 1972).

Markedly Low Range (T = 35 or Below)

1. A person with a score in this range is too willing to say uncomplimentary things about self and tends to exaggerate his/her faults (Carson, 1972).

2. The person has answered items on the test so as to create the impression that he/she is undergoing a serious emotional problem (Dahlstrom et al., 1972).

3. Scores below a T of 35 may arise from any of the following (Dahlstrom et al., 1972):

a. Special pleading for help or attention.

b. A general state of panic in which the person believes that his/her world or the control over his/her destiny is rapidly disintegrating.

c. Deliberate malingering.

4. When the **K** score is in this range, the **F** scale and the Clinical scales usually are high (Dahlstrom et al., 1972).

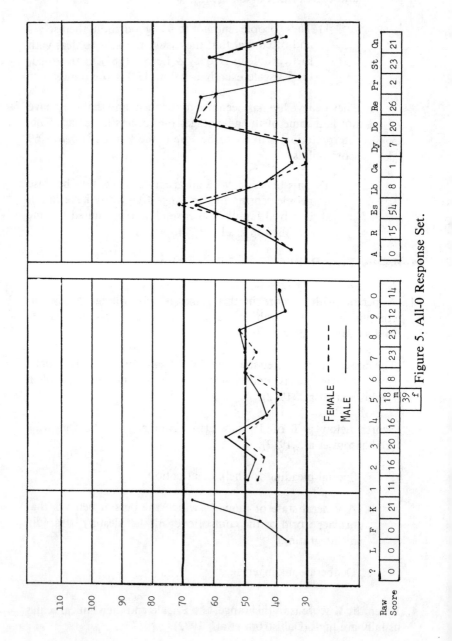

Figure 5. All-0 Response Set.

COMBINATIONS

The Validity scales, **?, L, F,** and **K,** in these combinations are at a T-score of 60 or above, whereas the Clinical scales, **1** through **0,** are at T-score of 70 or above and are the highest Clinical scales on the profile.

K-? See the **?-K** combination, p. 37.

K-?-L-F See the **?-L-F-K** combination, p. 36.

K-L See the **L-K** combination, p. 43.
the **L-F-K** profiles, pp. 69-71.

K-L-F See the **L-F-K** combination, p. 43
the **L-F-K** profiles, pp. 69-71.

K-L-3 See the **L-K-3** combination, p. 44.

K-F See the **F-K** combination, p. 56.

K-1-3 See the **1-3-K** combination, p. 89.

K-3-F-8

1. Persons with this combination tend to be conventional persons who are joiners and overly concerned about being accepted and liked by others (Carson, 1969).

2. They have difficulty expressing and receiving anger, and they also have difficulty making decisions unpopular with their group (Carson, 1969).

3. They tend to be unrealistically optimistic even when the facts indicate otherwise (Carson, 1969).

K-9

1. This combination indicates a person who is hypomanic but organized and efficient (Caldwell, 1974).

SUMMARY OF K SCALE INTERPRETATIONS*

T-score	Interpretations
35 or below	The client may have deep emotional difficulties and feel quite bad about them. He or she also may be deliberately malingering or pleading for help.
35 thru 45	People with this range of scores feel they are not as well off as most people. This appraisal may be accurate.
	People in this range may be having some situational difficulties. If they are, the **F** scale will be above 60.
45 thru 60	The majority of people score in this range.
60 thru 70	A person in therapy with this score tends to blame others for his/her problems or feels that it is the other person who needs counseling.
70 or above	The client may be defensive (as the T-score increases the client is more defensive), and does not wish to look at difficulties. The likelihood of the client recognizing the need for him/her to change or for his/her life to change is poor.

Relation to Research Scales

Es scale—If the **K** scale is below 45 T-score points and the **Es** scale is also below 45 T-score points, the person may be feeling bad about self as well as his/her life situation.

---

*Where T-scores are listed in two categories (i.e., 35 or below and 35 through 45) and a score is obtained that is listed for two categories, use whichever interpretation seems to be most appropriate for the individual.

L-F-K SCALE

In addition to looking at the Validity scales separately, the patterns produced by three of them (**L, F,** and **K**) also should be reviewed. The **?** scale is omitted from these patterns, because it is rarely high enough to be scored. Six validity patterns are presented in this section. The last two are less common than the others, but are still seen occasionally, usually in the mental health center setting.

1. The solid line pattern (Figure 6) is the one usually obtained with clients who admit emotional difficulties and request help. The **L** and **K** are typically below a T of 50 and the **F** is above a T of 60. The higher the **F** scale (dashed line), the more the person is saying he/she feels bad. When the **F** scales gets above 80 in this profile, possibly the client is exaggerating his/her symptoms, perhaps to be helped sooner. It is important in this profile that **L** and **K** are below 50 and that **F** is above 60.

Figure 6. **L-F-K** Profile
(elevated **F** scale).

Figure 7. **L-F-K** Profile
(elevated **K** scale).

2. Figure 7 is a typical Validity scale profile for a job applicant, for those in counseling for vocational and/or educational help, and for those coming to counseling to help someone else. These interpretations hold true even when the **K** scale is above 70 and the **L** and **F** scales are lower than indicated.

The Validity scale profile in Figure 7 is usually accompanied by Clinical scales below 70 except perhaps for scales **5** and **9**. For a profile with this Validity scale pattern, see Figure 5, All-0 Response Set Profile, p. 66.

L-F-K

3. People with the pattern shown in Figure 8 are presenting themselves in the best possible light. They feel very good about themselves and tend to deny common human foibles. They also tend to be simplistic and to see their world in extremes of good and bad. This profile is frequent for naive job applicants, public office holders, and strict, moralistic clergy. Important considerations for the Figure 8 profile are that the **L** is above 50, the **K** scale is above 60, and the **F** scale is the lowest point in the profile.

4. People with the profile shown in Figure 9 (solid line) tend to have long standing problems to which they have become adjusted to the extent that they feel good about themselves (elevated **K**) while still admitting to some bad feelings, usually about their situations (elevated **F**). As the **F** scale becomes elevated (dashed line), these people still feel rather secure about themselves, but they are more worried about their problems. Important considerations in the Figure 8 profile are that the **F** scale is above 60 and the **K** scale is above 50 and the L scale is 50 or below.

Figure 8. **L-F-K** Profile
(elevated **L** and **K** scales).

Figure 9. **L-F-K** Profile
(elevated **F** and **K** scales).

5. Figure 10 is an unusual profile, but still found frequently enough to be included in this section. The solid line is usually associated with a naive, unsophisticated person who is feeling bad. The person with this pattern is saying many of the same things as someone with the Figure 6 profile, but he/she has in addition a lack of sophistication. Even when the **F** scale is greatly elevated (dashed line), the person still shows the same behavior as long as the L scale is near 60 and the **K** scale is below 50.

Figure 10. **L-F-K** Profile
(elevated **L** and **F** scales).

Figure 11. **L-F-K** Profile
(all scales elevated).

6. The total profile accompanying this Validity scale pattern (Figure 11) should be compared with the all-false response set profile. The possibility is that the person with this validity pattern has answered the test from a response set of marking false to questions, rather than from his/her own feelings. The All-False Response Set Profile is illustrated in Figure 1, p. 45.

—NOTES—

F MINUS K INDEX

[Also called the Dissimulation Index by Gough (1956)]

The **F** minus **K** index was developed to detect faking bad and faking good profiles. The index number is obtained by subtracting the *raw score* of **K** from the *raw score* of **F**. If the resultant number is positive and above 11, the profile is called a "fake bad" profile. The person is trying to look worse than he/she really is. If the resultant number is negative, the profile is called a "fake good" profile. The person is trying to look better than he/she really is.

We do not use this index very much in our work with university and mental health clients. The "fake good" part of the index is usually grossly inaccurate for these populations, and the "fake bad" part can have another very dissimilar interpretation. In addition to the person scoring positively on this index because he/she is faking bad, a second interpretation can be made that the person really is feeling bad, and the scales are accurately reflecting this fact.

We tend to suspect that the faking bad interpretation is the correct one when the client is seeking some disability compensation, is wanting to be judged insane by a court and thus escape some punishment, or if he/she is standing to gain by seeming to be extremely mentally ill.

GENERAL INFORMATION

1. This index is found by subtracting the *raw* score on the **K** scale from the *raw* score on the **F** scale. Positive scores are in the symptom-exaggeration direction ("fake bad"), and minus scores are in the defensive direction ("fake good"). However, the index is much more successful in detecting the former test-taking attitude than the latter.

2. The problem with detecting "fake good" profiles is that college students and people with good mental health tend to get elevated **K** scores and low **F** scores which, while accurately reflecting their

psychological health, are incorrectly read as "faking good" by this index.

3. Because of these problems for the "fake good" direction of the index, the recommendation is that this index be used only for detecting "fake bad" profiles, and then only when the person is suspected of having something to gain by looking bad. If the person is not trying to look bad, then an **F - K** raw score difference of 9 or more usually is an indication of actually feeling bad.

4. In one study of a normal population, the fake bad index worked best if **F - K > 7** or **F > 15.** The fake good index worked best if **F -K ≥ - 11,** but this index was not as accurate as the fake bad index (Grow et al., 1980).

5. In the same study, for clinical populations, faking bad was best discovered with an **F - K** index **>7** or **F > 15.** The fake good index worked best when **F - K < - 11.**

CHAPTER **5**

CLINICAL SCALES

A history of the MMPI Clinical scales development and construction is available in the *MMPI Handbook: Vol. 1* by Dahlstrom, Welsh, and Dahlstrom (1972). Presently the Clinical scale section of the MMPI profile is composed of ten scales, each with a number, abbreviation, and formal name. These scales are as follows:

1 Hs   Hypochondriasis
2 D   Depression
3 Hy   Conversion Hysteria
4 Pd   Psychopathic Deviate
5 Mf   Masculinity-femininity
6 Pa   Paranoia
7 Pt   Psychasthenia
8 Sc   Schizophrenia
9 Ma   Hypomania
0 Si   Social Introversion

In actual practice, the formal names and abbreviations are not usually used. The names are long and in many instances do not convey a clear picture of what is being measure by the scale. We prefer to use the numbers for the scales because they are neutral and the way the scales are usually reported in the research literature.

Most practitioners tend to view the Clinical scales as giving some indication of problem areas for a client. We feel such a viewpoint is incomplete because these scales also can, in some instances, indicate strengths and/or coping behaviors for the person.

For example, an elevation above 70 on scale 5 is fairly typical for college educated males in the arts (music, drama, literature, and art). An elevation on this scale shows aesthetic interests, and as such would be quite advantageous to an arts major. However, engineers with such an elevation on scale 5 may have a problem because their great interest in aesthetics may conflict with the demands from the engineering professional for "scientific rigor." Therefore, elevations on the Clinical scales must be elevated in terms of the person's situation.

In all of these clinical scales, the behavior or emotion mentioned as being the meaning of that scale is most clearly seen when that scale is the highest one in the clinical section of the profile, otherwise the behavior or emotion may be partially masked or modified by the higher scale(s).

The term "elevation" as used with the Clinical scales usually indicates that a scale score is above 70 T-score points. We have noted trends in behavior at lower T-score levels. Consequently, we have devised two categories of elevations: Moderate Elevation refers to T-scores of 60 thru 70, and Marked Elevation refers to T-scores of 70 and above. This division of elevations into categories is a convenience and should not be taken as absolute. This is particularly true with T-scores of 69 through 71. In these cases, the judgment of the tester must be used to determine if the Moderate or Marked Elevation interpretation is most appropriate.

We also have included information on Clinical scale low point scores of below 45 T-score points. The information about the low end of the scales is scanty because little is written or researched about persons receiving such scores. Nevertheless, we do see some trends in these areas that can be useful.

Two other terms for some of the Clinical scales with which the reader should be familiar are the neurotic triad and the neurotic tetrad. The first term refers to scales 1, 2, 3, and the second term refers to scales

1, 2, 3, and **7.** The use of these two terms can be misleading because the implication is that with these three or four scales one can diagnose neurotics. In fact, these scales do not do so with any degree of accuracy. Consequently, we prefer to use the terms triad and tetrad without the adjective "neurotic." In reality, we do not use the tetrad combinations at all because they have not been found to be very useful in diagnosis. However, the various combinations formed by the triad scales have been found to be very useful, and therefore, a section on them is included in this chapter after scale **3.**

—NOTES—

78

SCALE 1

(Hs, Hypochondriasis Scale)

Scale 1 is a straightforward scale which measures the number of bodily complaints claimed by a person and whether these complaints are used to manipulate others. This scale does not distinguish actual from imagined physical difficulties.

When the T-score of the scale is below 45, the person is generally seen as an alert, capable person who tends to deny bodily complaints. This T-score is the normal level of the scale for persons in the medical profession and related areas (nurses, physical therapists, etc.). Others who also may receive a scale score at this level are the children of those in the medical profession, the children of hypochondriacs, and student nurses. These people have been around illness a lot and have seen others use it as a manipulative device. They do not wish to be classified with these manipulators, and therefore, they deny they have illnesses and tend not to seek medical help in the early stages of real somatic complaints.

In recent years we have been seeing people with low scale 1 scores who do not fit the above categories. For these people, what seems to be the common reason for the low scores is that they have negative feelings toward illness and see it as a sign of some weakness. Frequently, joggers and health food enthusiasts score in this range.

Most people score in the 45 through 60 range on this scale which indicates they have the usual number of physical complaints. T-scores of 60 through 70 are common for person who are physically handicapped. Persons with this elevation who do not have such a physical disability may be suffering from a cold or flu and thus may be feeling slightly "under the weather."

As the elevation on this scale increases, and it is the highest scale elevated, people tend to use bodily complaints (either real or imagined) to avoid dealing with psychological difficulties and to manipulate those around them. When the manipulation does not work, particularly with physicians and counselors, clients may shop around until a physician or counselor is found who can be manipulated. Thus, the higher the elevation, the less likely the person is to stay in productive counseling.

1

When this scale is elevated above 70 and is not the highest scale, it may indicate that the person is having physical problems related to the emotion or behavior shown by the highest scale. For example, if the 7 scale is the highest scale and the 1 scale also is elevated but lower than the 7 scale, the person would be having physical problems that he/she most likely would see as the result of the high anxiety that is present.

Kunce and Anderson (1976, 1984) posit that the underlying dimension on this scale is conservation. When the characteristics measured by a scale 1 are working in the positive direction as shown by a moderate elevation (60-70) in a psychologically normal person, the individual will be conscientious, careful, considerate, and sincere. These individuals seem to be unusually responsive to their environment and tune not only into changes in their bodies but also into the immediate environment around them, e.g., heat and light. A person with a moderate elevation thus may be interested in both personal health and ecological problems. Even in a person who is otherwise well adjusted, stress may turn these positive characteristics into transitory irritability, dependence, and bodily preoccupations.

When scale 1 is moderately elevated along with scale 3 and scale 2 is relatively low Hovey and Lewis (1967) have found the following traits: the individual is socially skillful, confident, fluent, talkative, and relatively free of depression and tensions. In addition the person is quite open to others about what he/she is thinking.

Elevations above 70 on scale 1 are rare in college population but are found frequently in mental health clinic populations. We have found about 10% of the people is our mental health clinic populations scoring above 70 on this scale. This elevation is more likely to be on a man's profile than a woman's. However, when either one has an elevation on this scale and it is the highest scale, it usually indicates behavior of long standing.

GENERAL INFORMATION

1. The 33 items of this scale are fairly obvious questions having to do with bodily problems (Carson, 1972).

2. We believe this scale to be "characterological," that is, elevations on the scale tend to reflect long-term behavior.

1   80

3. Caldwell (1985) has hypothesized that people with this scale as their highest elevation are concerned about their bodily functions because of conditioning experiences of having their physical health seriously threatened.

4. When the person is actually physically ill and this scale is markedly elevated, the person is likely to be using the physical illness in a manipulative way to control others.

5. When no physical illness exists and this scale is elevated, the person tends to be using vague somatic complaints in a manipulative way to control others around him/her.

6. Although this scale may rise somewhat with physical disease, more likely scale 2, depression, would be affected by the illness rather than scale 1 (Carson, 1972).

7. The 1 scale tends to be higher for older people from a normal population, perhaps reflecting greater somatic concern (Colligan et al., 1984). Schenkenberg et al. (1984) have also found that older people from a psychiatric population score higher on the 1 scale.

8. Hibbs et al. (1979) have found that men score significantly higher than women on this scale (as well as scale 9). They suggest that this may be due to a sex-role sanctioning of somatizing behavior.

9. Blacks and/or people from lower socioeconomic backgrounds tend to have higher scores on this scale (McDonald & Gynther, 1963; Nelson, 1952; Perlman, 1950).

10. Test-retest reliabilities are high, ranging between .80 and .90 (Dahlstrom and Welsh, 1960). Scale 1 is one of the most stable sales for clinic populations (Carkhuff et al., 1965).

HIGH SCORES

Moderate Elevations (T = 60 through 70)

1. Physically ill persons may score in this range.

1

2. Kunce and Anderson (1976) have hypothesized that when this scale is in the moderate range (and there are no Clinical scales above 70 T-score points except perhaps the 5 scale for men), it may measure a constructive concern for one's own and others' physical well-being.

Marked Elevations (T = 70 and Above)

The behaviors mentioned for this elevation are most clearly seen when this scale is the highest of the Clinical scales.

1. People with scores in this range tend to see themselves as having some physical problems. If this is the highest Clinical scale, they may be using the problems to manipulate others.

2. People in this range tend to complain a great deal and are whiny (Carson, 1969).

3. People with scale 1 scores in this range may be very cynical and defeatist, especially toward those who are helping them (Carson, 1969).

4. The following adjectives frequently are used to describe these people: unambitious, stubborn, and egocentric (Carson, 1969).

5. Elevations on this scale tend to reflect the use of displacement to cope with anxiety (Trimboli & Kilgore, 1983).

6. The higher the score on this scale:

   a. The more manipulative the client is with his/her physical complaints.

   b. The more unable he/she is to cope with life.

   c. The more he/she has the attitude "you must take care of me."

   d. The more the person uses his/her somatic complaints to get out of responsibility and to gratify dependency needs.

   e. The more immaturely he/she behaves.

1

7. This scale may measure dependency needs which are channeled into claims of physical illness (Carson, 1972). These people force others to take care of them, and thus, the dependency needs are met.

8. People with scale 1 scores in this range tend to "shop" for physicians and may see one after another, or several at one time (Carson, 1969).

9. In therapy, persons with high 1 scores tend to frustrate the therapist in any efforts toward psychological change. This elevation is associated with poor progress in psychotherapy.

10. In one study of medical patients, people who had high scale 1 scores did not have successful lower back surgery (Long, 1981).

11. For individuals in a weight reduction program, Scale 1 was negatively correlated, -.43, with significant weight loss (Wadden & Lucas, 1980).

LOW SCORES
(T = 45 or Below)

1. These scores may indicate people who have been closely associated with others who have used illness in a manipulative way. Because they do not want to appear hypochondriacal themselves, they reject even admitting a normal amount of aches and pains.

2. These people may also take pride in their good health and do not like to see themselves as ill even to the point of ignoring illness until it becomes quite severe.

3. People with these scores are described as alert, capable, and responsible (Carson, 1969; Hovey & Lewis, 1967).

4. They seem to be free from hampering inhibitions and undue concern about the adverse reactions of others (Dahlstrom et al., 1972).

COMBINATIONS

All scales in the combinations are at a T-score of 70 or above and are listed in order from the highest to the lowest peaks. The scales in the combinations must be the highest Clinical scales on the profile.

1-2 See also point 1a in the **1-2-3** Triad profile, p. 133.

1. People with the **1-2** combination tend to see themselves as ill and are typically depressed about this illness.

2. They tend to have medical symptoms, pain, fatigability, and over-evaluation of minimal complaints (Lachar, 1974).

3. Graham (1977) has found that people with this combination complain about pain and somatic discomfort, especially in the digestive tract. They tend to react to stress with physical symptoms and resist psychological explanations for their discomfort.

4. Caldwell (1974) has hypothesized that this combination possibly indicates a phobic fear of death.

5. State hospital and mental health clinic inpatients with this pattern **1-2/2-1,** were found to have multiple somatic complaints, insomnia, and physical problems. However, they seemed to be less disturbed than other state hospital patients. Older males tended to have histories of alcoholism. These findings may not apply to females (Gynther, Altman, Warbin, & Sletten, 1973).

6. In another study (Gynther, Altman, & Sletten, 1973), this pattern was found to be similar to Gilberstadt and Duker's (1965) **1-2-3-4** code type, p. 86.

7. Adolescents in treatment with this **1-2/2-1** pattern (Marks et al., 1974) were referred to treatment because of being shy and overly sensitive. They were also excessively fearful. The Marks, Seeman, and Haller book should be consulted for further information about this profile.

8. For internal medicine patients with the combination, males had two different sets of symptoms. One group of men complained of

1

marked epigastric distress, usually of the upper gastro-intestinal tract. The other group complained of tension and depression. Both groups of men were competitive and industrious but immature and dependent. Though they dreaded increased responsibilities, they maintained their normal level of efficiency in spite of their worries (Guthrie, 1952).

9. Male college counselees with these scores tend to have tension, insomnia, insecurity in heterosexual relationships and other social situations, worry, and introversion.

10. Female college counselees with these scores (especially with a low **5** scale) tend to have headaches, depression, worry, anxiety, shyness, social insecurity, and indecisiveness (Drake & Oetting, 1959).

1-2-3 See also the 1-2-3-5̄ pattern, p. 86
and point 1b in the **1-2-3** Triad pattern, p. 134

1. People with this pattern are depressed, and have loss of interest, apathy, and tension (Lachar, 1974).

2. A person with this pattern (called the **1-2-3** slope) usually is male, tends to be in declining health, and feels "over the hill." He usually had poor health in childhood. Also, he does not tend to take risks or to change jobs frequently. He may feel a profound sense of loss of body functioning (Caldwell, 1972).

3. Some persons with valid physical disabilities that result in declining health also have this pattern. However, in this instance not all three scales are above 70.

4. Gilberstadt and Duker (1965) found this **1-2-3** pattern in a VA hospital male population. Men with this pattern usually reacted to stress with physiological symptoms. They tended to lack aggressiveness and sexual drive. The Gilberstadt and Duker book should be consulted for further information concerning this profile.

5. In contrast to patients with high **1, 1-3,** and **1-3-4** profiles, patients with **1-2-3** combinations in one study tended to have successful lower back surgery (Long, 1981).

1

1-2-3-4

1. Gilberstadt and Duker (1965) found this **1-2-3-4** pattern in a VA hospital male population. Men with this pattern tended to be demanding and dependent. They developed somatic symptoms, especially ulcers and gastrointestinal disturbances. They tended toward alcoholism, which appeared to be associated with physiological hyperactivity of the gastrointestinal tract. The Gilberstadt and Duker book should be consulted for further information concerning this pattern.

2. Fowler and Athey (1971) also have found the same behavior as Gilberstadt and Duker for this code type: general psychological discomfort, depression, hostility, and heavy drinking.

3. Gynther (1974) reported Gilberstadt and Duker's (1965) description of persons with this pattern also is accurate for the populations he has studied.

4. This person may have a history of gastrointestinal difficulty. He or she may be prone to ulcers (Caldwell, 1974).

1-2-3-$\overline{5}$ (5 scale T = 45 or Below) See also point 1b in the **1-2-3** Triad profile, Figure 12, p. 134.

1. Women with this combination tend to have masochistic behavior with self-depreciation, long-suffering sacrifice, and unnecessary assumption of burdens and responsibilities (Dahlstrom et al., 1972).

1-2-3-$\overline{5}$-L (L scale T = 60 or Above)

1. This pattern may be found in women who are characterized by one of the following (Blazer, 1965a):

    a. Having marital difficulties.

    b. Feeling sexually frigid.

    c. Complaining about infidelity or drinking by their husbands.

    d. Having menopausal difficulties.

e. Having hysterical attacks (fear, palpitation, sweating, insomnia, and abdominal pain).

f. Complaining of fatigue.

g. Feeling conscientious about their work.

h. Being easily hurt by criticism or rebuff.

1-2-3-7

1. To properly evaluate disability clients who have this pattern, an important procedure is to take a thorough medical history and to look at scores on the Dependency scale (**Dy**) and the social responsibility scale (**Re**). If no long history of previous illnesses is present and the individual has a normal **Dy** scale (below 50) and a high **Re** scale (above 50), most likely the person has a disability with multiple symptoms which has developed recently with concomitant reactive depression and anxiety.

2. Gilberstadt and Duker (1965) found this **1-2-3-7** pattern in a VA hospital male population. Men with this pattern tended to have physical complaints that may or may not have been real. They usually were weak, fearful, and unable to take ordinary stresses and responsibilities. The Gilberstadt and Duker book should be consulted for further information concerning this profile.

3. In an internal medicine population, very few of the men with this pattern had demonstrable physical problems. Women with this profile combination had a varied set of physical complaints, including epigastric distress. They complained of tension, depression, lack of energy, occasional attacks of dizziness, and fear. These women were willing to accept a chronic level of maladjustment and therefore showed poor response to treatment (Guthrie, 1952).

1-3 See also the **1-3-K** combination, p. 89
the **1-3-2** combination, p. 89
the **3-1** combination, p. 126
point 1a for the **1-3-2** Triad profile, Figure 12, p. 134.

1

1. A person with this combination tends to convert his/her psychological difficulties into physical problems.

2. Pain is a frequent complaint, especially in the extremities (Lachar, 1974).

3. Gastrointestinal problems are common (Carson, 1972). In highly disturbed patients, severe eating problems may be present, such as anorexic vomiting (Drake & Oetting, 1959).

4. This combination is more frequent with women and older persons. Physical symptoms tend to increase in times of stress. People with this combination are very difficult to deal with in psychotherapy because they see their problems as physical in origin, and they expect definite answers to their problems from the therapist (Graham, 1977).

5. The high scale 3 seems to temper the pessimistic complaining attitudes shown by the high 1 scale (Carson, 1969).

6. The lower the 2 scale, so that it is not above 70, the more likely the person has become adapted to his/her physical problems.

7. Elevations on these two scales cannot be used reliably to distinguish functional disorders from actual physical disorders (Schwartz & Krupp, 1971).

8. Marks, Seeman, and Haller (1974) found this 1-3/3-1 pattern in a university hospital and outpatient clinic. This tended to be a female profile. A woman with this pattern usually had a somatic complaint. Her behavior could best be described as agitated, depressed, and confused, with periods of weakness, forgetfulness, and dizziness. The Marks, Seeman, and Haller book should be consulted for further information concerning this pattern.

9. In one sample of psychiatric inpatients, people with a 1-3 pattern showed significantly more somatic concern than other patients (Lewandowski & Graham, 1972).

10. Gynther, Altman, and Sletten (1973) also have found that psychiatric inpatients with this pattern, 1-3/3-1, have an unusual amount of bodily concern.

11. Adolescents in treatment with this **1-3/3-1** pattern (Marks et al., 1974) were referred for treatment because of attention seeking behavior and somatic concern. They saw themselves as physically ill. The Marks, Seeman, and Haller book should be consulted for further information concerning this pattern.

12. Thirty-nine percent of all MMPI **1-3/3-1** patterns in one study had organic diagnoses. Thirty-four percent of all patterns had psychological diagnoses. However, 66 percent of the psychological diagnoses were found in the group members who were under 40. In other words, the older people with **1-3/3-1** patterns in the study tended to have organic problems, whereas the younger people with this pattern had psychological problems (Schwartz, Osborne, & Krupp, 1972).

13. In one study (Long, 1981), patients with this combination did not have successful lower back surgery.

14. Wiltse and Rocchio (1975) have found that for patients treated by chemonucleolysis and laminectomy for low back syndrome, the relative elevations of the **1** and **3** scales on MMPIs administered before the treatment were predictive of successful recovery.

When both scales were 85 or above   10% had good recovery
When both scales were 75 to 84   16% had good recovery
When both scales were 65 to 74   39% had good recovery
When both scales were 55 to 64   72% had good recovery
When both scales were 54 or below   90% had good recovery

When patients were high (above 70) on only one of the scales, the patient had a 39% chance of good recovery.

1-3-K

1. With the **1-3-K** combination if the person has had surgery, the individual may have intractable post-operative pain (Caldwell, 1974).

1-3-2 See also point 1c in the **1-3-2** Triad pattern, p. 135.

1. Gilberstadt and Duker (1965) found this **1-3-2** pattern in a VA hospital male population. Men with this pattern tended to be extroverted, sociable, and highly conforming. Under stress, they

tended to develop psychosomatic illnesses. The Gilberstadt and Duker book should be consulted for further information concerning this profile.

1-3-$\overline{2}$ (scale 2 T = 45 or Below) See also the 1-3 pattern, and point 1b in the 1-3-2 Triad pattern.

1. This person tends to talk a lot about his/her physical complaints, but does not seem to be either depressed or anxious about them (Hovey & Lewis, 1967).

2. This person tends to believe that he/she does not have any emotional problems (Hovey & Lewis, 1967).

3. A history of hysteric pain which suddenly goes away often is present (Caldwell, 1972).

4. When the **K** score is also high with this pattern, intractable post-operative pain may exist (Caldwell, 1972).

5. A high incidence of overeating and odd eating habits may be present (Caldwell, 1972).

1-3-4

1. In one study (Long, 1981), patients with this combination did not have successful lower back surgery.

2. Caldwell (1985) has found that when patients have this profile they are more likely to sue their doctors for malpractice.

1-3-7

1. Gilberstadt and Duker (1965) found this **1-3-7** pattern in a VA hospital male population. Men with this pattern tended to have severe anxiety attacks and were clinging people. Under stress they developed psychosomatic illnesses. The Gilberstadt and Duker book should be consulted for further information about this profile.

1-3-8

1. A person with this profile tends to have strange ideas and/or bizarre sexual and religious beliefs. He/she often may be depressed and changeable (Caldwell, 1972).

2. Usually a family background of psychosis and/or childhood deprivation exist (Caldwell, 1972).

3. This type of person seems to need structure. He/she tends to do well in school when the school is structured. However, when this structure or a significant relationship is gone, bizarre symptoms may be seen (Caldwell, 1972).

4. Gilberstadt and Duker (1965) found this **1-3-8-(2)** pattern in a VA hospital male population. The **2** scale is elevated above 70, but it is not necessarily the next highest scale after the **8.** Men with this pattern tended to have confused thinking, suspiciousness, and jealousy. These researchers hypothesize that these men may have somatic illnesses to defend against their schizophrenic tendencies. The Gilberstadt and Duker book should be consulted for further information concerning this profile.

1-3-8-2 See the **1-3-8** pattern, point 4, above.

1-3-9

1. Gilberstadt and Duker (1965) found this **1-3-9** pattern in a VA hospital male population. Men with this pattern tended to have chronic organic illnesses, frequently with organic brain dysfunction. Temper outbursts were seen at times, and occasionally these people became combative and disruptive. The Gilberstadt and Duker book should be consulted for further information concerning this pattern.

1-4

1. This combination is not found frequently, but when present is more likely a male's profile rather than a female's. There may be severe hypochondriacal symptoms, especially headaches. People with this combination may be rebellious but not express this directly (Graham, 1977).

2. The person may be pessimistic, grouchy, bitchy, and dissatisfied (Lachar, 1974).

3. Gynther, Altman, and Sletten (1973) have found that psychiatric inpatients with this pattern, **1-4/4-1,** may have a drinking problem. These researchers found almost no females with this pattern.

4. Adolescents in treatment with the **1-4/4-1** pattern (Marks et al., 1974) were referred, typically by the courts because they were defiant, disobedient, and impulsive. They were seen as aggressive, outspoken, resentful, and self-centered. The Marks, Seeman, and Haller book should be consulted for further information about this profile.

1-5

1. Men with this pattern may have passivity, and a fussy, complaining attitude (Lachar, 1974).

2. For men, this combination may suggest multiple surgeries. For women, the **1-$\overline{5}$** would also suggest the same (Trimboli & Kilgore, 1983).

3. Adolescents in treatment with this **1-5/5-1** pattern (Marks et al., 1974) were referred because of their hyperactivity. They tended to be impulsive and effeminate. They presented themselves as physically ill and had had significant amounts of illness as children. The Marks, Seeman, and Haller book should be consulted for further information concerning this pattern.

1-6

1. Adolescents in treatment with this **1-6/6-1** pattern (Marks et al., 1974) were referred for emotional overcontrol. Family disruption was frequent for these adolescents. They were defensive and evasive, egocentric, self-centered, and self-indulgent. They did not report physical complaints however. The Marks, Seeman, and Haller book should be consulted for further information concerning this pattern.

1-7

1. With this pattern, chronic, mild anxiety often exists (Hovey & Lewis, 1967).

1-8

1. These people tend to be remote from people and to feel inadequate socially (Hovey & Lewis, 1967).

2. People with this combination tend to have feelings of hostility and aggression which they either inhibit altogether or show in a belligerent way. Psychiatric patients may complain about somatic symptoms that are so bad as to seem delusional (Graham, 1977).

3. Adolescents in treatment with the **1-8/8-1** pattern (Marks et al., 1974) presented themselves as physically ill. As children they had been seriously ill and currently only one-half of them were in good health. They were seen as insecure, unambitious, and constantly demanding attention. The Marks, Seeman, and Haller book should be consulted for further information concerning this pattern.

1-9 See also the **9-1** combination, p. 224.

1. This person is usually quite tense and may be distressed by an inability to attain high goals (Lachar, 1974).

2. He/she tends to be very anxious, tense, and restless. On the surface the person appears to be extroverted, verbal, and aggressive, but underneath he/she is usually a passive, dependent person. These people tend to be ambitious but lack definite goals (Graham, 1977).

3. This person tends to be one who has coronary attacks (Caldwell, 1972).

2-1-3 See the **2-3-1** combination, point 3, p. 102.

2-1-3-7 See the **2-3-1-(7)** combination, p. 102.

2-3-1 See p. 102.

2-3-1-7 See p. 102.

2-7-3-1 See p. 108.

2-8-1-3 See p. 113.

3-1-2 See the **3-1-2** pattern in the Triad section, p. 136.

3-2-1 See p. 127.

8-1-2-3 See p. 208.

1

8-2-1-3 See the **2-8-1-3**, p. 113.

SUMMARY OF 1 SCALE INTERPRETATIONS*

T-score	Interpretations
45 or below	With a score in this range, a person is denying bodily complaints. This is typical of people in the helping professions, children of these people, and people with hypochondriacal parents. Runners and health conscious individuals also may score in this range.
45 thru 60	The majority of people score in this range.
60 thru 70	This level is usual for persons with valid bodily complaints.
70 or above	With this score, the person tends to use bodily complaints to avoid emotional situations and also tends to use these complaints as a way of manipulating others. If this is the highest Clinical scale, the person may be whiny, complaining, and makes others miserable. As the scale is elevated, these people tend to be defeatist, to solicit help from others, and then to sabotage this help. They may "shop" for physicians and/or counselors.

*Where T-scores are listed in two categories (i.e., 45 or below and 45 through 60) and a score is obtained that is listed for two categories, use whichever interpretation seems to be most appropriate for the individual.

SCALE 2

(D, Depression Scale)

Two observations should be noted in evaluating scale **2**. First of all, this is a mood scale. It measures the degree of pessimism and sadness the person feels at the time the MMPI was administered. Thus, a change in mood will lower or raise this scale. Second, scale **2** is rarely elevated by itself; usually at least one or two other scales also are elevated. These other scales can be helpful in determining how the depression is shown.

Most people are below the 60 T-score point on this scale. When the T-score is between 60 and 70, a mild dissatisfaction with life may exist, but either the dissatisfaction is not enough for the person to be really concerned or the dissatisfaction is of long standing and the person has learned to live with it. When the **2** scale is at 60 and the **9** scales at 45, possibly the person took the inventory at the bottom of a mood swing (for example during a post-exam let-down), at the end of a long work day, or when he/she had a cold. In these situations the person's real pattern is usually an elevated scale **9** (T = 60 to 65) and a lowered scale **2** (T = 45 to 55).

As the elevation increases, the person's attitude changes from sadness (T = 70) to gloom (T = 80) to all pervasive pessimism about self and the world (T = 90 or above).

Low scale **2** scores (45 or below) indicate that the person is cheerful, optimistic, and easy going. However, these attitudes should be checked in terms of their appropriateness for the person's situation, particularly if a tragedy has occurred recently.

Kunce and Anderson (1976, 1984) posit evaluation as the underlying dimension on this scale, that is, the person has an inclination for sorting out good from bad, right from wrong. A moderately high elevation on scale **2** (60 to 70) in an individual who has good mental health would indicate a person who is realistic and objective. In addition he/she is likely to be deliberate and contemplative. When placed under stress this same individual will show transitory worry and anxiety with feelings of guilt connected with an overly critical attitude toward his/her own behavior.

Scientists such as mathematicians, physicists, engineers, and chemists tend to have moderately high scores on this scale (Kunce & Callis, 1969; Norman & Redlo, 1952) which is consistent with the realistic and objective dimension of this scale. Hovey and Lewis found that when scale 2 is elevated along with 3 these individuals are ambitious, conscientious, industrious, and take responsibilities seriously.

Scale 2 is one of the most frequent high points on a profile for clients in college counseling centers and mental health clinics. It usually indicates a reaction to problems that are pressing on the person. Very rarely is this elevation an indication of chronic depression.

GENERAL INFORMATION

1. This 60-item scale concerns poor self-concept, sadness, pessimism, and a lack of hope (Carson, 1969).

2. Harris and Lingoes (1955) have subjectively divided the 2 scale into 5 subscales: subjective depression, psychomotor retardation, physical malfunctioning, mental dullness, and brooding.

3. Scale 2 is the most frequent high point in psychiatric profiles.

4. This scale measures people's present attitudes about themselves and their relationships with others (Carson, 1969).

5. Scale 2 is the best scale for measuring a person's present feelings of contentment and security (Carson, 1969).

6. Caldwell (1985) has hypothesized that people who have this scale as one of their highest have a fear of irretrievable loss or a fear of hope.

7. Trimboli and Kilgore (1983) have found that the relative elevation of the 2 scale is the best single index of the extent to which an individual's typical defenses are being breached.

8. This scale quickly reflects changes in a person's day-to-day feelings (Carson, 1969). Therefore, it tends to be a fairly changeable scale.

Scale **2** is less reliable in a test-retest situation than the other Clinical scales (Carkhuff et al., 1965; Dalhstrom & Welsh, 1960).

9. An accurate interpretation of scale **2** relies on the rest of the profile (Carson, 1969). Therefore, high point combinations should be considered carefully.

10. This scale tends to decrease in elevation on a retest, even without intervening therapy.

11. Women who have an elevated **2** scale tend to report depression significantly more often (2 to 1) than men who have an elevated **2** scale (Gravitz, 1968).

12. The **2** scale tends to be higher for older people, perhaps reflecting greater dysphoric emotional tone (Colligan et al., 1984).

13. This scale is negatively correlated with education (Colligan et al., 1984).

14. Burkhart et al. (1980) have found that the obvious items on the **2** scale (Weiner, 1948) are the best predictors of depression. Inclusion of the subtle items adds nothing to the predictive power of the scale and indeed decreases the overall utility of the scale.

HIGH SCORES

Moderate Elevations (T = 60 through 70)

1. A person with a score in this range may have a feeling that something is not right, but he/she does not always recognize this feeling as depression.

2. Kunce and Anderson (1976) have hypothesized that when this scale is in the moderate range (and there are no other Clinical scales above 70 T-score points except perhaps the **5** scale for men), it may measure a penchant for sorting out what is right and wrong, what is good and bad. An existential questioning may occur about life and its meaning.

3. College freshmen with this elevation tend to report more homesickness than freshmen without elevations on this scale (Rose, 1947).

4. With a scale 2 score approximately at a T of 60 and a 9 scale score on or near a T of 45, possibly the MMPI was taken when the person had had a long hard work day, had a cold, or was at the bottom of a mood swing.

Marked Elevations (T = 70 or Above)

The behaviors mentioned for this elevation are most clearly seen when the scale is the highest of the Clinical scales.

1. A person with a 2 scale score at the lower end of this range (T = 70 to 80) may be withdrawn but may not show the typically tearful depression associated with higher elevations.

2. People with high 2 scales frequently rate themselves as nervous or upset. They also report a decreased amount of time sleeping in bed (Bieliauskas & Shekelle, 1983).

3. A person with a 2 scale elevation above a T of 80 tends to be self-deprecating, withdrawn, and may be feeling guilty. If the person is feeling guilty the Es scale also will be below 45 T-score points. The higher the 2 scale becomes, the more these symptoms are seen, together with an over-riding feeling of hopelessness.

4. Marked elevations on this scale may reflect a lack of psychic energy (confirmed by scale 9 below 50 or the lowest point on the Clinical scales) and social withdrawal (confirmed by an elevated scale 0). This combination of lethargy and interpersonal isolation may make traditional psychotherapy inappropriate prior to chemotherapy (Lachar, 1974).

5. Other high scales should be checked to determine how the depression is being felt and/or shown; for example, a high 7 with the high 2 usually means the person is in an agitated, depressed state.

6. Suicide risk tends to be greater when the 2 scale is elevated with scale 4 and/or scale 8 or scale 9 (Trimboli & Kilgore, 1983).

2   98

7. When the **2** scale is elevated by itself, a **2** spike, it usually indicates a clearcut, uncomplicated reactive depression (Lachar, 1974).

8. Kelly and King (1979a) have found that college counseling center clients with a spike **2** profile (the only elevation above 70) were reactive depressives. They were tense, nervous, and indecisive. They also had a great deal of rage.

9. Anderson et al. (1979) have found a **2-4** profile (**2** = 70, **4** = 67) as one of three sex offender profiles (the others were **F-6-8** and **4-9**). These people had a greater incidence of serious crimes than the other sex offenders. They also tended to be older and less well-educated. Two-thirds of these men had a history of alcohol abuse and one-half of them had served time for previous crimes.

10. With college counselees, this elevation may reflect situational problems rather than long term depression (Mello & Guthrie, 1958).

    a. When it does, Mello and Guthrie have found that these people tend to remain superficial in therapy and resist efforts to go deeper.

    b. When the situational pressure lessens, these clients usually discontinue treatment.

11. In a study done with short term patients in a university health center, the following formula helped eliminate a false diagnosis of depression, when (10 x **2** scale raw score) minus (5 x **4** scale raw score) plus (4 x **6** scale raw score) minus (4 x **8** scale raw score) plus (2 x **0** scale raw score) equals more than 190 then label depressed (Post & Lobitz, 1980).

12. When the **2** scale is the only one above 70 and scale **9** is the low point of the profile, the depression is usually mild, but the person may complain of fatigue and loss of energy. These complaints tend to yield readily to supportive therapy (Guthrie, 1949).

LOW SCORES
(T = 45 or Below)

1. People with this level of scale **2** tend to be optimistic, gregarious, and alert (Carson, 1969).

2

2. These people seem to have a naturalness, buoyancy, and freedom of thought and action.

3. The lack of inhibition seen in a person with a low scale **2** score may sometimes lead to negative reactions from others (Carkhuff et al., 1965).

4. These scores tend to be seen more often with younger people, because scale **2** tends to become elevated with age.

COMBINATIONS

All scales in the combinations are at a T-score of 70 or above and are listed in order from the highest to the lowest peaks, unless otherwise noted. The scales in the combinations must be the highest Clinical scales on the profiles.

For all the combinations involving scales **1, 2,** and/or **3,** also see the Triad profiles, pp. 133-137.

1-2-3 See p. 85.

1-2-3-4 See p. 86.

1-2-3-5 See p. 86.

1-2-3-5-L See p. 86.

1-2-3-7 See p. 87.

1-3-2 See p. 89.

1-3-2 See p. 90.

1-3-8-2 See the **1-3-8** combination, point 4, p. 90.

2-1 See the **1-2** combination, p. 84;
also point 1b in the **2-1-3/2-3-1** Triad profile, p. 135.
2-1-3 See the **2-3-1** combination, point 3, p. 102;
also point 1a in the **2-1-3/2-3-1** Triad profile, Figure 14, p. 135

1. This pattern was found in a group of male alcoholics. Also found were the **2-4-7, 4-9,** and **8-7-6** patterns (Conley, 1981).

2-1-3-7 See the **2-3-1-(7)** combination, p. 102.

2-3 See also point 1c in the **2-1-3/2-3-1** Triad profile, Figure 14, p. 135.

1. People with the **2-3** combination typically are seen as over-controlled. They may be unable to start things or to complete them once they are started (Guthrie, 1949). They lack interest and involvement in life (Graham, 1977).

2. They are insecure persons who keep things inside themselves and are unable to express their feelings (Dahlstrom et al., 1972).

   a. They lack interest or involvement in things and feel constantly fatigued, exhausted, nervous, and inadequate.

   b. They are frequently described as inadequate and immature.

   c. Their troubles are typically of long standing.

   d. Their response to treatment is poor.

3. These two points elevated together indicate ineffective use of repressive and hysteroid defenses (Lachar, 1974).

4. This combination is much more common for women than for men. It indicates a lowered standard of efficiency for prolonged periods of time (Graham, 1977).

5. Gynther, Altman, and Sletten (1973) found that a group of psychiatric inpatients with the **2-3/3-2** pattern, showed depressed mood and decreased activity. A person with the **2-3** pattern also had feelings of helplessness and multiple somatic complaints.

   a. Men may complain of lack of recognition on their jobs or of not being promoted when they should be, but they are adequate on their jobs. (Dahlstrom et al., 1972).

   b. Women frequently have family or marital maladjustments, but divorce is rare (Dahlstrom et al., 1972).

6. Adolescents in treatment with the **2-3/3-2** pattern (Marks et al., 1974) were referred because of poor relationships with their peers. They were lonely people with long histories of personal isolation. They tended to overcontrol their impulses. The Marks, Seeman, and Haller book should be consulted for further information concerning this pattern.

7. Lewandowski and Graham (1972) have found that patients with the **2-3** pattern have significantly less conceptual disorganization, unusual mannerisms and postures, suspiciousness, hallucinatory behavior, and unusual thought content than patients with other patterns.

8. Internal medicine patients have the same symptoms as **1-2/2-1** patients (Guthrie, 1952).

2-3-1 See point 1a in the **2-1-3/2-3-1** Triad profile, Figure 14, p. 135.

1. People with this pattern tend to be smiling depressives. They smile while they cry, and they do not know why. They deny aggression and hostility, and usually are inhibited. This profile is frequent for people with deteriorating neurological diseases (Caldwell, 1972). Fifty percent of the people with this pattern in one population had lost their parents when they were young (Caldwell, 1985).

2. People usually have at least moderate distress and multiple somatic complaints. They tend to have learned to tolerate the unhappiness and therefore may have poor motivation for treatment (Lachar, 1974).

3. Marks, Seeman, and Haller (1974) found this **2-3-1/2-1-3** pattern in a university hospital and outpatient clinic. People with this pattern tended to show a combination of depression and somatic complaints. They saw themselves as physically sick. The Marks, Seeman, and Haller book should be consulted for further information concerning this profile.

2-3-1-(7)

1. In this pattern, the **7** scale is also elevated above 70, but is not necessarily the next highest scale. People with this pattern tend to be older than patients in general. They feel they cannot get things done

and are pessimistic. Their somatic complaints are secondary to their depression (Caldwell, 1972).

2-4 See also the **4-2** combination, p. 147.

1. People with this pattern are impulsive and unable to delay gratification. They feel frustrated by their own lack of accomplishment and are resentful of demands placed on them by others (Graham, 1977).

2. They tend to have behavioral difficulties which have developed over time (Hovey & Lewis, 1967).

3. They may be remorseful after acting out but not seem sincere about this remorse (Graham, 1977).

4. They tend to run from people's expectations for them and from their own problems.

5. The person cannot take pressure in therapy, and if it is applied, he/she will leave. Prognosis for change is poor.

    a. He/she will change jobs or leave town but will not confront the therapist directly.

    b. If the person cannot run from therapy, he/she will tend to have a "spontaneous" recovery.

    c. He/she will be superficially deferent to the therapist.

6. If these scales are both highly elevated, suicidal ideation and attempts may occur. The attempts are usually to get other people to feel guilty (Graham, 1977).

7. Lewandowski and Graham (1972) found in one study that patients with this pattern were significantly more sociable than patients with other patterns.

8. Gynther, Altman, and Warbin (1972) and Gynther, Altman, and Sletten (1973) have found psychiatric patients with this pattern, **2-4/4-2,** are apt to show less psychotic pathology and fewer defects in judgment and orientation than the typical state hospital inpatient. Both males and females are more likely to be diagnosed as alcoholic

2

than patients with other MMPI patterns. *Females* are more likely to show depressive symptoms and *males* are more likely to have had a job loss than the average patient. There may be a recent history of suicidal behavior.

9. Adolescents in treatment with the **2-4/4-2** pattern (Marks et al., 1974) were referred for treatment because of difficulty concentrating. They tended to resent authority figures, were argumentative, and afraid of involvement with others. They had a history of drug usage and tended to escape their problems by running away, using drugs, or attempting suicide. The Marks, Seeman, and Haller book should be consulted for further information concerning this profile.

10. Megargee and Bohn (1979) found a group of incarcerated criminals (Group George) with the **2-4/4-2** code type predominating (53% of the group). They did not have extensive criminal records, were bright, and well educated. Many of the men were drug pushers but did not use drugs themselves. They seemed to be career criminals and in spite of making a good prison adjustment had a high recidivism rate.

11. In one study, this code type was consistently found in profiles of DWI offenders and alcoholics (Sutker et al., 1980).

12. In another study, the **2-4/4-2** profile occurred most frequently in four alcoholism treatment centers. It accounted for 12 to 21% of the profiles in any one facility (Schroeder & Piercy, 1979).

13. Kelley and King (1979a) found the **2-4/4-2** code type in a college counseling center. Clients with this profile were depressed, impulsive, and had a history of physical problems. Females were usually seen to have a personality disorder and to be in situational distress. Males had many characterological symptoms such as impulsivity, drug abuse, and criminal records, yet they were guilt ridden, depressed, and unable to sleep.

14. Clients in another college counseling center with this code were difficult clients with whom to work because they dropped out of therapy when pressure was put upon them to improve. Their main symptoms included depression, disturbed home life, few friends, and sexual problems. Therapists who used a supportive, nondemanding approach made more progress than therapists who used confrontive or uncovering therapies (Anderson & Bauer, 1985).

2-4-7 See the **2-7-4** combination, point 3, p. 109.

1. Caldwell (1985) found that people with this pattern tend to get into trouble with alcohol even when the MAC scale (p. 309) is not elevated. They drink to relieve their depression. They may have episodic bouts of drinking.

2. This pattern was found in a group of male alcoholics. Also found were the **2-1-3, 4-9,** and **8-7-6** patterns (Conley, 1981).

2-4-8

1. Persons with this pattern have a high incidence of sexual difficulties (Caldwell, 1972).

2. This pattern is found frequently in people with suicidal ideation and multiple suicide attempts (Caldwell, 1985).

2-4-8-9

1. Women with this pattern may have many affairs with men, but typically do not enjoy them (Caldwell, 1972).

2-5

1. Adolescents in treatment with the **2-5/5-2** pattern (Marks et al., 1974) were referred because of poor relationships with their siblings. They tended to be indecisive, shy, hypersensitive, suspicious, and negative. They were seen as unmasculine and rarely dated. They also had anti-social activities such as breaking and entering and stealing. The Marks, Seeman, and Haller book should be consulted for further information concerning this profile.

2. College students with this profile combination are usually anxious and have a history of physical complaints and difficulties. They also have a history of dating infrequently (King & Kelley, 1977b).

2-6

1. These people are touchy, take offense easily, and become tired and depressed quickly (Guthrie, 1949).

2. A great deal of other directed anger exists along with fatigue and depression (Lachar, 1974).

3. They tend to induce rejection by others.

4. This profile is of an agitated, depressed person who gets others involved in his/her problems (Caldwell, 1974).

5. Little change is likely in therapy over time and prognosis is poor (Guthrie, 1949).

6. Kelley and King (1979a) found the 2-6/6-2 profile code in a college counseling center. The clients were all women who came to counseling following a recent breakup with a boyfriend. They had numerous physical complaints and were dependent, moody, tearful, and had recently lost weight. They had suicidal thoughts and indeed had made suicide attempts in the past. They used alcohol to excess and had a high frequency of alcoholic relatives. They were diagnosed as latent schizophrenics in spite of their depressive features.

2-7 See also the **7-2** combination, p. 195.

1. These people tend to be very anxious and depressed and have feelings of worthlessness. They also tend to be agitated and obsessed about their problems (Hovey & Lewis, 1967).

2. They tend to have distress, neurasthenia (weakness), and lack of self-esteem and self-confidence (Lachar, 1974).

3. They usually anticipate problems before they occur and overreact to minor stress. Somatic problems are typically seen (Graham, 1977).

4. A person with this elevation usually has been an achiever in the past and with lower **2-7** elevations may be an achiever still. Generally, the person has been successful in his/her field. Then something goes wrong and the person reverts to child-like behavior and cannot do anything. This is especially true when scale **3** is also elevated (Caldwell, 1972).

5. This combination reflects acute distress. More severe deterioration is shown by an accompanying rise on scale **8** (Trimboli & Kilgore, 1983).

6. Suicidal preoccupation may be present with these people (check MMPI item #339). The possibility of suicide is greater when the person does not act depressed than when he/she appears deeply depressed (Good & Brantner, 1961).

7. This person is usually a good candidate for psychotherapy, because he/she is hurting so much. However, with extreme elevations, the agitation and worry may be so excessive that the person cannot sit still for therapy (Carson, 1969). Consequently, these people may need medication to quiet them so that they can participate in therapy.

8. Marks, Seeman, and Haller (1974) found the **2-7** pattern in a university hospital and outpatient clinic. These people tended to be seen as depressed and anxious. They also tended to be perfectionistic and compulsively meticulous. Because they felt they must live up to their own high expectations, they tended to be self-punishing and felt hopeless. The Marks, Seeman, and Holler book should be consulted for further information concerning this profile.

9. Gilberstadt and Duker (1965) found the **2-7-(3)** pattern in a VA hospital, male population. The parentheses around the **3** are to indicate that the **3** scale elevation is above 70, but it is not necessarily the next highest scale in the profile. A man with this pattern was usually a chronically anxious, ambitious person. When he was unable to tolerate stress, he tended to become depressed, self-deprecating, inadequate, and clinging. The Gilberstadt and Duker book should be consulted for further information concerning this profile.

10. In one study, patients with the **2-7** pattern were found to be feeling blue and depressed. They did not tend to get angry or annoyed easily, were less irritable, and socially were more competent than other patients in the study (Lewandowski & Graham, 1972).

11. Gynther, Altman, and Warbin (1973c) and Gynther, Altman, and Sletten (1973) have found psychiatric in-patients with the **2-7/7-2** pattern to have more suicidal thoughts and feelings of worthlessness than patients in general. When a patient had the **2-7** pattern, he/she had a "loss of interest" as well. They were less evasive, unrealistic, angry, hostile, deluded, and antisocial than patients in general. These researchers found this code pattern to be quite similar to the

2

2-7-8 pattern, and questioned the need for a separate three-point code type.

12. Adolescents in treatment with the **2-7/7-2** pattern (Marks et al., 1974) were tearful, restless, nervous, and anxious. They were also depressed, passive, and nonassertive. The Marks, Seeman, and Haller book should be consulted for further information concerning this profile.

13. Kelley and King (1980) found the **2-7/7-2** profile code in a college client population, however, too few females were found to analyze. Males had many neurotic features typical of an obsessive-compulsive individual such as perfectionism, rumination, and meticulousness.

14. These people tended to have test anxiety in college with obsessive thinking and rigidity connected with this anxiety. They were also introverted, dependent, self-conscious or insecure. They had conflicts at home usually with their mothers or siblings. They also tended to be nonverbal (Drake & Oetting, 1959).

15. More husbands from the general population have either **2-7** or **7-2** code types than do husbands in marriage counseling (Arnold, 1970; Ollendick et al., 1983).

2-7-3 See also the **2-7** pattern, points 4 and 5, p. 106.

1. People with this pattern are likely to be easily led and dependent. They usually encourage others to come to their aid, particularly therapists (Carson, 1969).

2-7-3-1

1. These people may be socially dependent, but they are not typically a member of any group (Caldwell, 1972).

2. They tend to have much self pity and self blame (Caldwell, 1972).

2-7-4 See also the **2-7-4-5** pattern, p. 109.

1. This pattern tends to indicate a situational depression (Caldwell, 1972). However, Lachar (1974) has found the depression may be

chronic and expressed as feelings of inadequacy and lack of self-confidence. A person with this combination may be passive-aggressive and response to treatment may be quite poor.

2. Gilberstadt and Duker (1965) found the **2-7-4-(3)** pattern in a VA hospital male population. The parentheses around the **3** are to indicate that the **3** scale is elevated above 70, but it is not necessarily the next highest scale after the **4** scale. A patient with this profile tended to be a hostile, passive-aggressive, anxious, immature person who also had feelings of inferiority. Chronic alcoholism also was Found with this pattern. The alcoholism tended to be associated with the anxiety and tension. The Gilberstadt and Duker book should be consulted for further information concerning this profile.

3. Marks, Seeman, and Haller (1974) found this **2-7-4/2-4-7/4-7-2** pattern in a university hospital and outpatient clinic. People with this pattern tended to be depressed and have many worries. They were usually described as passive aggressive, generally tearful, full of fear, nervous, and irritable. The Marks, Seeman, and Haller book should be consulted for further details concerning this profile.

4. If a person with this combination is an alcoholic and stops drinking and then his/her life situation gets better, the person may become depressed and revert back to alcohol (Caldwell, 1972).

5. A man with this profile may have been a mama's boy, and his mother always came to his rescue. He often marries a woman similar to his mother, and if the wife also tries to rescue her husband and is unsuccessful, she may become sick (Caldwell, 1972).

6. Women with this profile tend to be daddy's girls. They may have long affairs with married men. They may have problems because of poor relationships with others and want to be rescued (Caldwell, 1972).

7. Females with this combination and a low **5** scale tend to show the same behavior as men with the **2-7-5-(4)** pattern.

2-7-4-3 See the 2-7-4 pattern, point 2, above.

2-7-(4)-$\overline{5}$ (5 Scale T = 45 or Below)

1. In this pattern, the **4** scale is elevated above 70, but it is not necessarily the next highest scale after **7**. Females with this pattern tend to show the same behavior as men with the **2-7-5-(4)** pattern.

2-7-5-(4)

1. In this pattern the **4** scale is elevated above 70, but it is not necessarily the next highest scale after **5**. Males with this combination usually try to look weak and submissive (Carson, 1969).

    a. They are self-effacing and try not to show any strength.

    b. They seem to ask others to act superior to them and are usually most comfortable when others act this way toward them.

2. Males with this combination tend to be ambivalent and have a sense of failure (Caldwell, 1972).

2-7-8 See also the **2-7** pattern, point 8, p. 107.

1. This is one of the most frequent profile patterns found in a psychiatric population. Likely long standing distress and obsessional features exist (Lachar, 1984).

2. The person with this pattern has the greatest risk of completing suicide of any other code type (Caldwell, 1985).

3. Gilberstadt and Duker (1965) found this **2-7-8-(4-0-1-3-5-6)** pattern in a VA hospital male population. Scales **4, 0, 1, 3, 5,** and **6** are elevated above a T of 70, but they are not necessarily the next highest scales in the profile after **2, 7,** and **8**. A man with this pattern tended to be depressed, shy, quiet, withdrawn, and anxious. He usually felt inadequate in all areas of his life. He may have had bizarre thinking and flat affect. The Gilberstadt and Duker book should be consulted for further information concerning this pattern.

4. Marks, Seeman, and Haller (1974) found this **2-7-8/8-7-2** pattern in a university hospital and outpatient clinic. A person with this pattern was typically described as tense, anxious, and depressed with confused thinking and much self-doubt. The Marks, Seeman, and Haller book should be consulted for further information concerning this pattern.

5. Kelley and King (1979b) found the **2-7-8/7-2-8** profile in a college mental health clinic. Only males reported difficulty concentrating. They also tended to complain of affective or eating problems. Females with this profile type had many neurotic symptoms. They were tense, nervous, and had respiratory somatic complaints. They also had crying spells, appetite and weight loss, sleep disturbance, fatigue, and feelings of inferiority.

6. For women with a low scale **5** (T = 45 or below), the deep anxieties, depression, study problems, and lack of skills with the opposite sex, seen in the **2-7-8** pattern are intensified (Drake & Oetting, 1959).

2-7-8-(0)

1. In this combination the **0** scale is elevated, but it is not necessarily the next highest scale after **0.** For people with this pattern there usually is chronic depression, introversion, and shyness (Caldwell, 1972).

2. Over a period of time, the psychomotor responses in these clients may slow up. The clients appear to have mood swings, but in reality they have been steadily slowing down with occasional bursts of energy (Caldwell, 1972).

3. This person may report waking early in the morning (Caldwell, 1972).

4. He/she usually is negative concerning his/her achievements (Caldwell, 1972).

5. A person with this profile is a problem in therapy. He/she tends to intellectualize endlessly (Caldwell, 1972).

6. A person with this profile may report incidents of teasing in early childhood. The person may feel that he/she is the inferior member in the family (Caldwell, 1972).

2-8

1. A person with this profile tends to be withdrawn because of feelings of worthlessness.

2. He/she tends to have severe depression with anxiety and agitation and a fear of loss of control (Lachar, 1974).

3. The individual is usually confused and may have difficulty concentrating.

4. He/she also tends to be agitated, tense, and inefficient. Such persons are likely to say they are physically ill and have such symptoms as dizziness, blackouts, nausea, and vomiting (Graham, 1977).

5. Usually a history of repeated hurts in childhood exists. The person now fears being hurt more and therefore runs from closeness (Caldwell, 1972).

6. Caldwell (1985) has found that if the **4** scale is not significantly elevated, psychotropic medicines work well with these people. If the **4** scale is also elevated, people do not respond well.

7. If both scales are highly elevated, this combination may indicate serious pathology.

8. Marks, Seeman, and Haller (1974) found the **2-8/8-2** pattern in a university hospital and outpatient clinic. People with this pattern were usually anxious, depressed, and tearful. They tended to keep people at a distance and were afraid of emotional involvement. They tended to fear loss of control and reported periods of dizziness and forgetfulness. The Marks, Seeman and Haller book should be consulted for further information concerning this profile.

9. Gynther, Altman, and Sletten (1973) and Warbin, Altman, Gynther, and Sletten (1972) also found that psychiatric inpatients with this **2-8/8-2** pattern showed symptoms of depression such as suicidal thoughts or attempts. The suicidal ideation may be in the form of a specific plan. For this code type, different diagnostic implications are associated with the **2-8** and the **8-2** codes.

   a. With a **2-8** profile, somatic delusions may be present.

   b. For the **8-2** profile, one or more symptoms of schizophrenia, i.e., hallucinations or delusions of persecution, may be present.

10. However, Lewandowski and Graham (1972) have found that patients with this pattern in comparison to other patients tend to be

more grandiose and less likely to be anxious or to say they feel blue or depressed.

11. Adolescents in treatment with the **2-8/8-2** pattern (Marks et al., 1974) were referred to therapy because of being emotionally inappropriate. They were also nervous, anxious, and timid. They appeared fearful of emotional involvement and had inner conflicts about sexuality and emotional dependency. Almost half of these adolescents had made suicide attempts. They were frequent truants. The Marks, Seeman, and Haller book should be consulted for further information concerning this profile.

12. Kelley and King (1980) found the **2-8/8-2** profile in a college client population. These people had disruptive thoughts, and social withdrawal. They tended to be diagnosed as schizophrenic. Females had more affective features and were diagnosed schizoaffective. They also abused many types of drugs. Males were more flat and apathetic and had more somatic symptoms and motor peculiarities such as tics.

2-8-1-3

1. People with this profile tend to have somatic complaints, chronic tension, and dramatic tremors. They also may have intellectual confusion (Caldwell, 1972).

2. They may attempt to promote rescue by their therapists but will back off when the therapists try to help them. This type of person often sets the therapist up with the result that the therapist gets angry at him/her (Caldwell, 1972).

3. If these people are older than 40, they may complain of having thinking and recall problems. They may show organic deficits in testing, but they are not really as bad as the tests indicate. Their slowness causes the low scores on these tests (Caldwell, 1972).

2-8-7

1. Kelley and King (1980) found the **2-8-7/8-2-7** profile group in a college client population had suicidal ideation. In addition, males had disruptive and tangential thought processes, inappropriate affect, and were disoriented, all suggestive of psychosis. However, they did

not display overt psychotic symptoms. They were also depressed, had difficulty in concentration, and loss of interest. Females were seen as neurotic. They had difficulty concentrating and had made suicide attempts. They had no thought disorder but had derealization, la belle indifference, perfectionism, and alcohol abuse. Thus men and women with this profile were quite different.

2-9 See also the **9-2** combination, p. 224.

1. This is a rare profile but may be seen in older populations. It can indicated a brain lesion or deterioration (Lachar, 1974).

2. This person tends to be agitated (Hovey & Lewis, 1967).

3. He/she may show agitated depression with the depression sometimes masked by activity.

   The person with the **2-9** combination is different from the person with the **2-7** combination in that less obsessive thinking and rigidity is seen, and more motor activity is evident.

4. Alternating periods of activity and fatigue may occur (Graham, 1977).

5. A feeling of pressure for the client without euphoria and grandiosity may be observed in people with high **2** and **9** scale scores. This pressure usually alternates with fatigue. The prognosis is good for these people (Caldwell, 1972).

6. Graham (1977) has hypothesized that this code may be found primarily for people who have feelings of inadequacy and worthlessness but are trying to deny them.

7. This person, when a child, may have had to be emotional to get attention (Caldwell, 1974).

8. Heavy drinking may be present for men with this pattern.

9. Aggressive and antagonistic behavior is found in college counselees with this pattern. They also tend to rationalize a great deal (Drake & Oetting, 1959).

2

114

10. Test anxiety is seen in college students with this pattern (Oetting, 1966).

2-0 See also the **0-2** combination, p. 232.

1. This combination may indicate a socially withdrawn and introverted person with a mild but chronic and characterological depression. This depression may be related to poor human relations and inadequate social skills. He/she tends to be inhibited, shy, and timid (Webb et al., 1981).

2. VA males with this profile code were found to be socially insecure and withdrawn. They were unhappy, tense, lacked effective social skills, and tended to have insomnia (Hovey & Lewis, 1967).

3. Adolescents in treatment with the **2-0/0-2** pattern (Marks et al., 1974) were nervous and anxious, listless, apathetic, shy, and overly sensitive. They had few friends, and did not enjoy social gatherings. They felt inferior and were viewed by their therapists as schizoid. The Marks, Seeman, and Haller books should be consulted for further information concerning this profile.

4. College students with this profile combination frequently seek counseling (especially men). They are unhappy, introverted, and lack social skills.

   With a low **1** scale score, women college students may feel physically inferior (Drake & Oetting, 1959).

5. Kelley and King (1979a) have found college clients with the **2-0/0-2** profile tend to have academic problems and an inability to choose a career. They were described as indecisive by the counselors.

3-1-2 See the **3-1-2** pattern in the Triad Section, p. 136.

3-2-1 See p. 127.

4-6-2 See p. 152.

4-7-2 See p. 153.

4-8-2 See p. 156.

4-8-9-2 See the **4-8-9** combination, point 4, p. 156.

6-4-2 See the **4-6-2** pattern, p. 152.

8-1-2-3 See p. 208.

8-2-4 See p. 208.

8-2-4-7 See the **8-2-4** combination, point 2, p. 209.

8-4-2 See the **8-2-4** pattern, point 1, p. 208.

8-6-7-2 See the **8-6** combination, point 6, p. 210.

8-7-2 See the **2-7-8** combination, point 4, p. 110.

SUMMARY OF 2 SCALE INTERPRETATIONS*

T-score	Interpretations
45 or below	This person is cheerful, optimistic, and outgoing. For all persons with this score, their attitude should be checked as to whether or not it is appropriate for their situations.
45 thru 60	The majority of people score in this range.
60 thru 70	With this range of scores, a mild dissatisfaction with life may be present, or a long-term situation exists with which the person has learned to live. The person with a 2 scale in this range may not be aware of the dissatisfaction until questioned about it.
70 thru 80	At this level, usually a general sadness either about life or the world exists. This sadness tends to be situationally specific or temporary in nature. If the person is feeling guilty or self-deprecating the **Es** scale will be below 45 T-score points.
80 thru 90	At this level, gloom is usually the theme. Not much exists about which to feel good. If the person is feeling guilty or self-deprecating, the **Es** scale will be below 45 T-score points.
90 or above	An all-evasive pessimism is present. Nothing is positive in the person's world. All is dark. If the person is feeling guilty or self-deprecating, the **Es** scale will be below 45 T-score points.

*Where T-scores are listed in two categories (i.e., 45 or below and 45 thru 60) and a score is obtained that is listed for two categories, use whichever interpretation seems to be most appropriate for the individual.

—NOTES—

SCALE 3

(Hy, Conversion Hysteria Scale)

One way many people avoid facing difficulty and conflict is to deny such situations exist. Scale **3** measures the amount and type of such denial. This characteristic tends to be a way of life and may be so ingrained that the person is not even aware that such a defense mechanism is being utilized. These people are extremely difficult in therapy, because they may adamantly refuse to recognize obvious realities. For example, in two recent situations, women with elevations above 70 on this scale refused to recognize that they were divorced. One became angry when the newspaper notice of her divorce was shown to her, and she claimed the notice referred to someone else with the same name. The second verbally acknowledged her divorce but went back home to her ex-husband every day where she did the cooking and housework, going to her own place only at bedtime.

Interpretation of scale **3** is a bit complicated and involves at least three parts. First, evaluate the position of scale **3** itself to determine what information it gives about the client. A low scale **3** score (45 or below) indicates a person who tends to face reality head-on in a tough, realistic manner. He/she may be caustic and questioning and believe that people in general see others in a too trusting and optimistic way. Scores between 45 and 60 are where the majority of people score and are not interpreted. As the scale elevates from 60 to 70, the person tends to "think positively" and to prefer not to think about unpleasant things. Above a T of 70, the person is probably not able to see unpleasantness and "bad things" (except as qualified in the next paragraph). In addition, people with scale **3** scores above 70 are usually very social but quite shallow in their relationships. Women with an elevated **3** also tend to have a sensuous, flirtatious quality about them.

Second, the actual areas of denial can be determined by comparing the elevation of scale **3** with the elevations on the other Clinical scales. Generally, symptoms indicated by scales with scores above scale **3** are seen and acknowledged by the client, while those indicated by scales with elevations below scale **3** are denied or not seen. For example, if scale **3** is at a T of 80, scales **2** and **8** at a T of 90, and scales **4** and **7** at a T of 70, the person is usually aware of being depressed (scale **2**) and confused (scale **8**), but will probably deny or not see the fighting (scale **4**) and agitation or anxiety (scale **7**) shown by the two scales lower than scale **3**.

Third, if the elevation on this scale is above 60, it should be compared with scales **1** and **2** (see Triad Profiles). These other two scales influence the interpretation of scale **3** and therefore also have to be considered. Figures 12 through 16 are illustrations of the Triad Profiles, pp. 133-137.

Kunce and Anderson (1976, 1984) posit expression as the underlying dimension on this scale. Individuals with moderate elevations where a positive interpretation is called for are emotional, sensitive, generous, affectionate, optimistic, and friendly. People who work with this person are likely to find him/her enthusiastic, enterprising, and clever. This individual is likely to be in touch with his/her emotions and can readily show pleasure and displeasure. Stress may turn these virtues into psychomatic reactions or denial.

Individuals in art, music, and business administration are likely to have moderately high scores (e.g., Normal & Radlo, 1952; Kunce & Callis, 1969). These individuals profit readily from reassurance or advice. When the **3** scale is moderately elevated with the **2** scale, individuals are ambitious, conscientious and take their responsibilities seriously. With a moderately elevated **4** they may have some socially unacceptable impulses but their ability to inhibit and control are good. Finally a moderately elevated **9** gives the individual a flare for the dramatic and an openness with others.

Scale **3** is more typically elevated on women's profiles than it is on men's. The behavior measured by scale **3** is much more likely to be considered "good" behavior for women than it is for men, because the person tends to be passive and agreeable even though not quite accurately seeing other people's behavior or her own.

In college populations, an elevated scale **3** (T = 70 or above) is rare, but elevations between 60 and 70 for women are seen more frequently. In mental health clinic populations however women do show elevations above 70.

GENERAL INFORMATION

1. This scale consists of 60 questions which are divided into two different categories, one centering around bodily problems and one

rejecting the possibility that the person is in any way maladjusted or has problems (Carson, 1969).

2. For most people who take the inventory, these categories tend to be mutually exclusive. However, for some people who have elevated scale 3 scores, the categories do fit together so that these people acknowledge many physical problems but deny that they are worried about them.

3. Harris and Lingoes (1955) have subjectively divided the 3 scale into 5 subscales: hysteria; denial of social anxiety; need for affection and reinforcement from others; lassitude-malaise, and somatic complaints; and inhibition of aggression.

4. When scale 3 is moderately elevated (60 to 70), a denial of problems (a "Pollyanna" attitude) may be all that is seen. When scale 3 becomes markedly elevated (70 or above), however, physical complaints and denial become more prominent.

5. People with even moderate elevations on this scale, if this is one of the highest on the profile, tend to inhibit direct expression of anger (Trimboli & Kilgore, 1983).

6. Caldwell (1974, 1985) has hypothesized that a profound fear of emotional pain may exist with these people. To be rejected by or to lose a loved one is painful, and these people have a high incidence of such loss of love in childhood. The only way to deal with the pain is to shift attention away from it, and deny that it exists.

7. Women with an elevated scale 3 (70 or above) tend to have an underlying sensuality and sexuality which become more obvious and denied as the scale is elevated and the scale 5 scores become lower (45 or below).

8. This is considered a character scale. (Trimboli and Kilgore, 1983).

9. A large sex difference exists in respect to the frequency of scale 3 peaks. For women, scale 3 elevations are common, but for men such peaks are unusual (Dahlstrom et al., 1972).

   Yet in a recent study of a normal population, the men's mean score was 57 on this scale (Colligan et al., 1984).

3

10. Test-retest reliabilities are low (Carkhuff, 1965):

    a. The low reliabilities may be a result of the many different kinds of items that make up the scale.

    b. The tendency to phrase items in the present tense and the use of ambiguous modifiers such as "often" also may reduce the test-retest reliability.

11. In a recent study (Wilson, 1980) comparing the subtle and obvious items of this scale (Weiner, 1948), the obvious items were more predictive than the subtle ones.

12. Hibbs et al. (1979) have found the **3** scale to be higher for both younger and older subjects, perhaps reflecting heightened sensitivity to physiological processes for the adolescent and preoccupation with physical vulnerability for the older subjects.

13. Schenkenberg et al. (1984) also have found that older people from a psychiatric population score higher on scale **3**.

HIGH SCORES

Moderate Elevations (T = 60 through 70)

1. People with moderate elevations on scale **3** tend to be optimists and to think positively about people.

2. Kunce and Anderson (1976) have hypothesized that when this scale is in the moderate range (and there are no other Clinical scales above 70 T-score points except perhaps the **5** scale for men), it may measure being in touch with one's positive emotions and an ability to show these emotions readily.

Marked Elevations (T = 70 or Above)

The behaviors mentioned for this elevation are most clearly seen when the scale is the highest of the clinical scales for the profile.

1. People with elevations this high tend to have much denial, suggestibility, and functional physical complaints. They may have anxiety attacks when they are under pressure, with heart palpitations (Hovey & Lewis, 1967).

2. They tend to be naive and self-centered (Carson, 1969).

3. They also are likely to be exhibitionistic, extroverted in their relations with others, and superficial (Carson, 1969).

4. They tend to have a great lack of insight into their own and other's motivations and actions (Carson, 1969).

5. Classical conversion symptoms may not be seen until the 3 scale is 80 or above (Trimboli & Kilgore, 1983).

6. Elevations on the 3 scale may reflect the use of the defense mechanism of repression (Tromboli & Kilgore, 1983).

7. When a person has a high scale 3, the individual is not likely to be diagnosed as psychotic, even when other Clinical scales are high (Carson, 1969).

8. Elevations of 3 and K, when scales F and 8 are low, may indicate a constricted, over-conventional person (Lachar, 1974).

9. People with this elevation initially express enthusiasm about psychological treatment, because they have a strong need to be liked and accepted (Carson, 1969).

   a. However, they cannot stand questioning of their way of looking at the world.

   b. They can make inordinate demands of the counselor or therapist.

   c. They tend to want concrete solutions from the therapist while they resist developing insight into their problems.

   d. College males with this elevation tend to come in for only one interview. They want specific answers to their problems (Drake & Oetting, 1959).

10. College counselees with a scale **3** this high tend to present problems rooted in an unhappy home situation (Mello & Guthrie, 1958).

   a. The prominent pattern seen involves a father described as rejecting, to which women react with somatic complaints and men with rebellion or covert hostility.

   b. Their specific worries are concerned with scholastic failure, difficulties with authority figures, and lack of acceptance by their social group.

11. The behavior seen in point 10b with college students also is seen in clinic populations with work failure substituting for scholastic failure.

12. With scale **0** low, male college counselees tend to show aggressiveness and generally extroverted behavior (Drake, 1956).

13. College women with this scale elevation are described by their peers in rather uncomplimentary terms such as irritable and having many physical complaints. However, they see themselves as trustful, alert, friendly, and loyal (Black, 1953).

14. For individuals in a weight reduction program, scale **3** was negatively correlated (-.41) with significant weight loss (Wadden & Lucas, 1980).

LOW SCORES
(T = 45 or Below)

1. People with these scores may be caustic, sarcastic, and socially isolated (Carson, 1972).

2. They tend to feel that life is hard and tough (Carson, 1972).

3. They may have narrow interests.

COMBINATIONS

All scales in the combinations are at T-scores of 70 or above and are listed in order from the highest to the lowest peaks. The scales in the

3   124

combinations must be the highest ones on the profile. For all combinations using scales **1, 2,** and **3,** see the Triad profiles, p.

1-2-3 See p. 85.

1-2-3-4 See p. 86.

1-2-3-5 See p. 86.

1-2-3-5-L See p. 86.

1-2-3-7 See p. 87.

1-3-K See p. 89.

1-3-2 See p. 89.

1-3-2 See p. 90.

1-3-4 See p. 90.

1-3-7 See p. 90.

1-3-8 See p. 90.

1-3-8-2 See the **1-3-8** combination, point 4, p. 91.

1-3-9 See p. 91.

2-1-3 See the **2-3-1** combination, point 3, p. 102.

2-1-3-7 See the **2-3-1-(7)** combination, p. 102.

2-3-1 See p. 102.

2-3-1-7 See p. 102.

2-7-3 See p. 108.

2-7-3-1 See p. 108.

2-7-4-3 See the **2-7-4** combination, point 2, p. 109.

3

2-8-1-3 See p. 113.

3-L-K See the **L-K-3** combination, p. 44.

3-K-F-8 See the **K-3-F-8** combination, pp. 67.

3-1 See also the **1-3** combination, p. 87;
the **3-1-2** Triad profile, p. 136.

1. In contrast to the **1-3** combination, people with a **3-1** pattern tend to have symptoms that are relatively specific and of a somewhat more episodic nature. They tend to have a long history of insecurity and immaturity. They also tend to develop physical symptoms when stresses increase (Guthrie, 1952).

2. Because people with a high scale **3** tend to deny that things are going badly, the whining and complaining about physical problems typically seen in persons with high scale **1** scores is modified when the **3** scale is higher than the **1** scale (Carson, 1969).

   People with this scale combination tend to try to charm people into taking care of them with their illnesses rather than coercing people as those with a **1-3** combination tend to do.

3. The lower the **2** scale, the more adapted the person has become to his/her problems.

4. Marks, Seeman, and Haller (1974) found this **3-1/1-3** pattern, in a university hospital and outpatient clinic. This profile tended to be of a female. A woman with this profile usually had a somatic complaint. Her behavior could best be described as agitated, depressed, and confused, with periods of weakness, forgetfulness, and dizziness. The Marks, Seeman, and Haller book should be consulted for further information concerning this profile.

3-1-K See the **1-3-K** combination, p. 89.

3-1-2 See the **3-1-2** pattern in the Triad section, p. 136.

3-2 See also the **2-3** combination, p. 101;
the **3-2-1** Triad pattern, point 1a, p. 137.

1. Women with the **3-2** combination tend to have a history of marital difficulties, but no divorces (Guthrie, 1949).

    a. They frequently are sexually frigid and not interested in sexual activity with their husbands.

    b. They tend to complain about the infidelity and drinking of their husbands.

    c. They tend to be conscientious and easily hurt by criticism.

2. Men with this pattern tend to be ambitious and conscientious (Dahlstrom et al., 1972; Guthrie, 1949).

    a. They may have much anxiety and show the physical effects of prolonged tension and worry. One of the main areas of concern for these men is their work.

    b. They may have stomach problems which could result in ulcers.

3. Internal medicine patients with this combination tended to see the physician for only one visit. For those who did continue treatment, their physical symptoms did not change. Even though the **2** scale is elevated, little depression was evident. They seemed to be insightless, non-introspective people who were very resistant to psychotherapy (Guthrie, 1952).

3-2-1 See also **3-2-1** Triad profile, point 1b, p. 137.

1. Patients with this pattern may have periodic hysterical attacks with palpitations, sweating, fear, and exhaustion (Lachar, 1974).

2. For a woman, this pattern tends to be a hysterectomy or gynecological complaint profile. Typically, she has had a life-long history of ill health. Women with this pattern rarely date and usually are sexually inhibited. If they do marry, they may be sexually frigid (Caldwell, 1972).

3. Women with this profile may be quite involved with their parents in a symbiotic fashion. Frequently, these women report that their mother has physical problems about which the mother does not complain (Caldwell, 1972).

3

4. Marks, Seeman, and Haller (1974) found this **3-2-1** pattern in a university hospital and outpatient clinic. The pattern usually was for a woman who was described as anxious, tense, depressed, and tearful with somatic complaints. These researchers also found a high probability of hysterectomy and gynecological complaints. The Marks, Seeman, and Haller book should be consulted for further information concerning this profile.

3-4 See also the **4-3** combination, p. 148.

1. Scale **4** shows the amount of aggressive or hostile feelings the person has, while scale **3** indicates the controls the person has available (Dahlstrom et al., 1972). In this **3-4** pattern, since scale **3** is higher than scale **4,** the aggressions and hostilities shown by the **4** scale would tend to be masked and only shown indirectly, most likely passive-aggressively, because of the denial and controls shown by the higher **3** scale.

2. These people tend to be very immature. They may satisfy their own aggressions and hostilities in an indirect manner by having friends who are acting out (Carson, 1969).

3. In a VA hospital, men with this combination tended to have many socially unacceptable impulses with a fairly effective inhibitory or suppressive control. They tended to be passive aggressive (Hovey & Lewis, 1967).

4. Adolescents in treatment (Marks et al., 1974) with the **3-4/4-3** pattern were referred for sleep difficulties and sometimes suicidal thoughts. They tended to resent their sisters. The majority were heavy drug users and one third had made suicide attempts. The Marks, Seeman, and Haller book should be consulted for further information concerning this pattern.

5. Internal medicine patients with this profile code and the **3-6** code tend to show some of the same behavior. They typically are women who have a superficial outlook on life and an inability to recognize the shortcomings of either themselves or their friends. In spite of this, the interpersonal relations of these women are tenuous and many experience well-rationalized hostility toward their immediate family (Guthrie, 1952).

6. Kelley and King (1979a) found only female clients in a college counseling center with a **3-4/4-3** profile. They were coming in to therapy for marital problems, particularly sexual difficulties. They were excitable and complained of hostile feelings and aggressive outbursts. They also had many physical complaints. These women tended to overcontrol their anger and express it in irrational outbursts of rage.

3-4-5

1. These men are typically immature and sexually inadequate. Exhibitionism, voyeurism, and a need for more than usual sexual stimulation is possible (Lachar, 1974).

3-6 See the **6-3** combination, p. 182.

1. This individual tends to deny his/her own hostilities, aggressions, and suspicions (Carson, 1969).

2. He/she may be hard to get along with because the underlying hostility and egocentricity of this person are likely to be apparent the closer you get (Carson, 1969).

3. When these two scales are elevated, the person's anger is usually easily seen by others, but the individual typically is unaware of it (Carson, 1969).

4. A person with this pattern may tend to have deep and often unrecognized feelings of hostility toward family members (Hovey & Lewis, 1967). These feelings, when awareness of them exists, are unusually rationalized away. See the **3-4** combination, point 5.

5. He/she may report moderate tension and anxiety, but these do not seem to be acute or incapacitating. The person may be mildly suspicious and resentful of others as well as self-centered (Graham, 1977).

6. Adolescents in treatment with the **3-6/6-3** pattern (Marks et al., 1974) were referred for a variety of reasons. One-third had attempted suicide. They were suspicious, obsessional, and resentful. The Marks, Seeman, and Haller book should be consulted for further information concerning this pattern.

3

3-7

1. Some chronic physical symptoms resulting from mental stress is likely with these people (Hovey & Lewis, 1967).

2. Women with this combination together with a low scale **0**, usually lack academic drive, are anxious, and have insomnia (Drake & Oetting, 1959).

3-8

1. These people complain of problems in thinking clearly (Hovey & Lewis, 1967).

2. Possibly they may have delusional thinking (Hovey & Lewis, 1967).

3. They may have much psychological turmoil and have difficulty making even minor decisions (Graham, 1977).

4. People with this combination may have brief, highly sexualized psychotic episodes, for which they are amnestic (Trimboli & Kilgore, 1983).

5. Marks, Seeman, and Haller (1974) found this **8-3/3-8** pattern in a university hospital and outpatient clinic. This profile tended to be of a woman who was having difficulties thinking and concentrating. She usually was seen by others as apathetic, immature, and dependent. The Marks, Seeman, and Haller book should be consulted for further information concerning this profile.

6. College students with this pattern tend to be indecisive, confused, worrying, and report a lack of knowledge or information (Drake & Oetting, 1959).

3-9

1. These people may be dramatic, superficially open, and highly visible in social situations (Hovey & Lewis, 1967).

2. They may have episodic attacks of acute distress (Dahlstrom et al., 1972; Guthrie, 1949; Hovey & Lewis, 1967).

3. The physical problems of this group usually are not severe and tend to be easily treated (Hovey & Lewis, 1967). They may develop medically atypical or medically impossible symptoms which yield to superficial treatment.

4. Kelley and King (1979a) found the **3-9/9-3** profile code in a college counseling center. Female clients typically had come in because of difficulty with an instructor (to whom some of them were sexually attracted). They were seen by their counselors as defensive and were diagnosed frequently as hysterical in spite of having depression and disturbed thought processes. These women seemed to be in acute distress precipitated by the interpersonal conflict with their instructors.

4-3-5̄ See p. 87.

8-1-2-3 See p. 208.

8-2-1-3 See the **2-8-1-3** combination, p. 113.

SUMMARY OF 3 SCALE INTERPRETATIONS*

T-score	Interpretations
45 or below	These people tend to be caustic and tough. They may believe that others are too optimistic about life.
45 thru 60	The majority of people score in this range.
60 thru 70	These people tend to look on the "bright side" of life, are optimistic, and prefer not to think about unpleasant things. This does not mean that they cannot consider reality if it is unpleasant, only that they prefer not to do so.
70 or above	Persons at this level tend to be naive, lack insight, and deny psychological difficulties. They also tend to be uninhibited and visible in social situations (particularly with a low scale 2). There may be some irritability and somatic complaints (especially when scale 1 is also elevated). When people with this scale as their highest elevation have their way of thinking questioned, the questioning usually meets with denial and hostility. If they are in counseling, although they may claim they are interested in working and say they need therapy, they are in fact usually looking for simplistic, didactic answers which do not require them to evaluate their emotions realistically. If they are required to evaluate their emotions, they tend to terminate counseling prematurely. Women with this elevation tend to be sensual and flirtatious.

*Where T-scores are listed in two categories (i.e., 45 or below and 45 through 60) and a score is obtained that is listed for two categories, use whichever interpretation seems to be most appropriate for the individual.

THE TRIAD PROFILES

Traditionally scales **1, 2,** and **3** are called the "neurotic triad." However, we feel this choice of terms is unfortunate for many reasons, not the least of which is that these scales do not differentiate neurotics from other groups of people. Consequently, we prefer to call these scales "The Triad," which eliminates the negatively loaded and ambiguous adjective, "neurotic." Interpretations of some selected Triad patterns follow.

1-2-3

1. In this pattern, scale **1** must be higher than scale **2,** and scale **2** must be higher than scale **3.** This pattern is usually associated with males, and generally indicates a concern about physical problems. This concern is used frequently as a means of not facing emotional problems.

Figure 12. **1-2-3** Triad Profile.

a. At lower elevations (solid line) (scales **1** and **2** above 70 and scale **3** lower than 70), mental health clients tend to be irritable, to overevaluate minor dysfunctions, and to use physical complaints seemingly to avoid thinking about psychological problems. College counselees with such a profile are usually anxious, insecure in social situations, and have insomnia or headaches. (See also the **1-2** combination, pp. 84-85).

b. An elevated **1-2-3** profile (dashed lines) (scales **1, 2,** and **3** all above 70) is called a "declining health" profile. A person with this pattern is usually over age 35 and feels "over the hill" (see also the **1-2-3** combination, p. 85). This pattern is common in VA populations, male welfare and social security claimants, and long-term alcoholics. Females rarely have this elevated pattern; however, those who do and who also have a low **5** scale tend to be masochistic (see the **1-2-3-5̄** combination, p. 86).

1-3-2

1. This is one of two patterns known as the "conversion V" (See the **3-1-2** pattern for the other). For this pattern, scale **1** must be at least 5 T-score points greater than scale **3**. The general meaning of the **1-3-2** pattern is that persons with it convert psychological stress and difficulties into physical complaints. The wider the T-score spread between scale **2** and scales **1** and **3**, the more severe, long standing, and resistant to change are the physical complaints as shown by the fact that the person is no longer depressed about them.

Figure 13. **1-3-2** Triad Profile.

a. When scales **1** and **3** are above 70 and scale **2** is between 50 and 60 (solid line), people tend to be somewhat pessimistic and complaining. They also may have gastrointestinal complaints. With this pattern, there may or may not be valid physical complaints. The interpretation is that the real or imagined complaints are used to avoid facing up to emotional difficulty. (See also the **1-3** combination, p. 87.)

b. When scales **1** and **3** are above 70 and scale **2** is below 45 (dashed line), the interpretation of the pattern is similar to the one provided in the previous paragraph. The primary difference is that the person does not exhibit genuine concern about the physical difficulties. Also existing are more denials of emotional difficulties, histories of hysteric-like pain which suddenly abates, plus unusual eating patterns. (See also the **1-3-2̄** profile, p. 90.)

c. When scales **1, 3,** and **2** are all above 70 (dotted line), the person can be described as similar to the person discussed in paragraph "a," except that he/she is also depressed. (See the **1-3-2** combination, p. 89.)

2-1-3/2-3-1

1. These two patterns generally are considered to be interchangeable at the higher elevations (scales **1, 2,** and **3** all above 70). However, at the lower levels each should be dealt with separately.

Figure 14. **2-1-3/2-3-1** Triad Profile.

a. Persons with elevations above 70 on all three scales tend to be anxious and depressed with long-standing physical problems and gastrointestinal difficulties. (See the **2-3-1** combination, p. 102.)

b. When scales **1** and **2** are above 70 and scale **3** is below 70 (solid line), refer to the lower elevation interpretation of the **1-2-3** profile, point 1a, p. 133.

1-2-3

c. When scales **2** and **3** are above 70 and scale **1** is below 70 (dotted line), people usually are defined as overcontrolled with bottled-up emotions. They frequently are fatigued, nervous, and filled with self-doubt, which prevents them from doing anything. Their difficulties are generally of long standing, and they frequently are described as inadequate and immature. (See also the **2-3** combination, p. 101.)

3-1-2

1. This is one of the two patterns known as the "conversion V" (the other is the **1-3-2** pattern). Interpretation of this pattern is similar to the **1-3-2** pattern with some modifications. When the **3** scale is higher than the **1** scale, the person tends to be optimistic about his/her physical symptoms, instead of pessimistic about them as people with the **1-3-2** pattern are. These people play down their physical complaints, and they also deny that the physical complaints may have a psychological basis. Thus, they tend to be difficult in therapy. The physical complaints of this group in general are more specific and less global, in contrast to the **1-3-2** pattern. (See also the **3-1** combination, p. 126.)

Figure 15. **3-1-2** Triad Profile.

3-2-1

1. The **3-2-1** slope in general is associated with females and is commonly called the "hysterectomy profile." As its name implies, females with such a pattern usually present gynecological complaints.

Figure 16. **3-2-1** Triad Profile.

a. At the lower levels (solid line) (scales **3** and **2** above 70 and scale **1** below 70) women may report marital difficulties such as frigidity, lack of sexual desire, and husbands with infidelity and drinking problems. (See the **3-2** combination, pp. 126-127.)

b. At the higher elevations (dashed line) with all three scales above 70, a history of female operations is quite common. These women may be aversive to sex, have a life-long history of ill health, and may have symbiotic relationships. (See also the **3-2-1** combination, p. 127.)

2. Males rarely have this profile. However when they do, the scores are usually at the lower levels. Such men usually have physical problems as the result of prolonged stress and worry.

—NOTES—

SCALE 4

(Pd, Psychopathic Deviate Scale)

The key phrase for an elevation on this scale is "fighting something." The exact nature of the conflict and its appropriateness depends upon the target (parents, friends, spouse, society, or school), the amount of confusion connected with the fighting out (particularly as indicated by scale 8), and the context in which it occurs. Thus value judgments (for example, high 4 behavior is bad) are inappropriate to apply to elevations of this scale without some awareness of the person's situation. At the lower elevations of this scale, the fighting out may not be overt but rather a covert feeling that something or someone other than the client needs to be changed. Others with this elevation may be having situational stress such as marital problems and a gradual decline in this scale is observable as the problem is resolved.

Kunce and Anderson (1976, 1984) posit an underlying dimension, assertiveness for this scale. In individuals with good ego strength, an elevation between 60 to 70 on scale 4 can reflect positive personality traits; enterprising, assertive, frank, and adventurous. These individuals adjust rapidly to new situations and show initiative and drive. A fair number of occupations have members who show moderate elevations on scale 4, for example, authors, editors, commercial artists, athletic coaches, and physicians (e.g., Daniels & Hunter, 1949). When frustrated these positives can turn to aggression and maladaptive social behavior.

Hovey and Lewis (1967) see the positive traits of people with elevated scale 4 as adventurousness, sociability, and energy. When coupled with a moderately high 3 the individual has some socially unacceptable impulses but also fairly effective controls.

T-scores of 60 to 70 are quite common in both the mental health clinic and college counseling center populations. This range is more typically seen in men than in women, but both may have elevations in this range. This range of scores is frequently seen for college students concerned with peaceful societal change, and persons in helping professions such as social work or psychology.

As the elevation on this scale increases, the degree of fighting intensifies and becomes more noticeable. As the scale exceeds 70, clients may frequent places where trouble occurs, or hang around with people who get into trouble.

The permanence of such a fighting-out pattern appears to be correlated with age. An elevated **4** is common with adolescents particularly those in difficulty with family, school, or the law. In most cases, the **4** scale elevation disappears as the person becomes older. However, if the **4** scale is still above 70 by the age of 40, it usually is indicative of long-standing antisocial behavior. Fighting out at this age may be shown by alcoholism or confidence rackets and bad check writing. Although this trait probably is unchangeable, vocational counseling may channel the antisocial behavior into more socially acceptable pursuits, by helping the person find a job where the behavior can be beneficial.

An interesting relationship exists between the **4** and **5** scales. When the **4** scale is elevated above 70 *and* the **5** scale is elevated above 60 for males or below 40 for females, then the fighting out shown by the **4** scale is tempered in such a way that the fighting tends to be more covert than overt.

Persons with a low scale **4** can be described as conventional and concerned with correct social appearances. They are basically non-fighters and prefer a quiet, uneventful life. This non-fighting may have come about because of one of two reasons:

1. The person may have been born with a very easy-going nature.

2. He/she at one time might have been a fighter but because this behavior was so painful or nonproductive, the person switched to being a non-fighter.

As Carson (1972) has noted, these people may have a great capacity for tolerating a dull, boring life. One peculiarity noted by Meehl (1951) which we also have found in the mental health clinic and college counseling center populations is that persons with scale **4** scores in this range may be uninterested in sexual activity.

The **4** scale is frequently a high point for college student profiles and for people coming into mental health clinics who are in trouble with the law.

GENERAL INFORMATION

1. This scale consists of 50 items which concern social imperturbability and a lack of general social adjustment, such as family or authority problems, and social alienation (Carson, 1969).

2. Harris and Lingoes (1955) have subjectively divided the **4** scale into four subscales, one of which is divided into two. The five subscales are familial discord, authority conflict, social imperturbability, social alienation, and self alienation.

3. This scale may measure a continuum ranging from inhibited over-conformity on the low end to rebellious, anti-social acting out of impulses on the high end. (Lachar, 1974)

4. The major features of a person with a high **4** scale may be as follows:

   a. A tendency to see others as needing to change their behaviors.

   b. An emotional shallowness toward others, especially sexually (Dahlstrom et al., 1972).

   c. An inability to profit from experiences, both good and bad (Carkhuff et al., 1965; Dahlstrom et al., 1972).

   d. A revolt against family and/or society (such as school, religion or politics) (Carson, 1969). If this is true, the **Re** scale will be below 50 T-score points. For the **Re** scale, see pp. 279-285.

5. Trimboli and Kilgore (1983) consider this a character scale.

6. Caldwell (1985) has hypothesized that people with this scale as one of their highest, have a fear of caring. They have come from a home where they felt no caring and they have shut down their own caring as a defense against hurting.

4

7. Often the person with the **4** scale as the highest Clinical scale above 70 goes undetected until he/she is in a situation demanding responsibility, loyalty, and an appreciation of social mores (Dahlstrom et al., 1972).

8. The older a person is with a high **4,** the less likely the scale will decline in elevation with time.

    a. At approximately age 40, this elevation on scale **4** most likely reflects long-standing antisocial behavior.

    b. At age 65 or above, this elevated score more likely reflects social alienation, apathy, absence of pleasure, and lack of involvement, rather than antisocial behavior (Good & Brantner, 1974).

9. The **4** scale is a frequent peak point for males and often appears in a variety of high point combinations. Other scales suppress (scale **5**) or activate (scale **9**) the behavior seen in scale **4.**

    a. When scales **1, 7,** or particularly **2** are high with scale **4,** the delinquency rate is reduced below the level expected for boys in general (Dahlstrom et al., 1972).

    b. When scales **8** and **9** are high with scale **4,** the delinquency rate is greatly increased (Dahlstrom et al., 1972).

10. Gynther et al. (1979) have found that the obvious items on this scale (Weiner, 1948) are better predictors than the subtle and neutral items. However, the subtle items make a small but unique contribution.

11. Snyder and Graham (1984) have also found that the obvious items are the most useful.

12. Scale **4** scores tend to be lower for older people in a non-psychiatric population, perhaps reflecting fewer feelings of impulsivity and rebelliousness (Colligan et al., 1984).

13. Hibbs et al. (1979) have found the **4** scale to be higher for younger people.

4   142

14. Schenkenberg et al. (1984) have also found that younger people in a psychiatric population score higher on this scale than older people from this population.

15. High **4** scores tend to characterize Blacks more than whites (Hokanson & Calden, 1960; Mitler, Wertz, & Counts, 1961).

16. Test-retest reliability is fair (Carkhuff et al., 1965). Scale **4** tends to be subject to maturational changes as well as shifts because of psychological treatment.

17. Anderson and Holcomb (1983) found one of their 5 groups of murderers had an MMPI pattern with the highest scale **4** at 67. These murderers had the highest IQ and were the oldest of the five groups. They were more likely to kill a friend or relative. Sixty percent of the crimes they committed had a sexual element. Their profiles resembled Megargee and Bohn's (1979) Item group.

18. In a study of heroin addicts (Craig, 1984a) 44% of the cases had the **4** scale as one of the highest points. Twenty-one percent of the cases were **4-9/9-4**, 14% were **4-2/2-4**, and 9% were **4-8/8-4**.

19. The **4** scale is more prominent in profiles of husband and wives in marriage counseling than in profiles of husbands and wives from the general population (Arnold, 1970; Ollendick et al., 1983).

20. Separate college norms have been advocated, because college students average significantly higher than the original norming sample on scale **4** (Murray, Munley, & Gilbert, 1965).

HIGH SCORES

Moderate Elevations (T = 60 through 70)

1. Kunce and Anderson (1976) have hypothesized that when this scale is in the moderate range and no other Clinical scales are above 70 T-score points except perhaps the **5** scale for men, the **4** scale may measure a readiness to assert oneself and to express one's physical energy and drive. People scoring in this range may adjust rapidly to new situations and show initiative and drive.

2. For college students with the **4** scale in this range and good ego strength (**Es** above 50), the individual may be energetic, enterprising, venturesome, and social (Munley & Gilbert, 1965).

3. Marks, Seeman, and Haller (1974) found that the mean score for this scale for their adolescent populations in counseling was a T of 68.

Marked Elevations (T = 70 or Above)

The behaviors mentioned for this elevation are most clearly seen when the scale is the highest of the Clinical scales.

1. Elevations on this scale tend to reflect hostility toward social sanctions, authority figures, and a variety of parental surrogates. The focus of the anger is diffuse and well-rationalized (Dahlstrom et al., 1975).

2. This elevation often indicates a resentment for rules and regulations.

   Depending upon other high peaks, the resentment and asocial feelings may be shown many different ways. See the combination section for further information.

3. People with **4** scale elevations as the highest Clinical scale score above 70 tend to make good first impressions, but after longer acquaintance their unreliability and self-centeredness becomes apparent (Carson, 1969).

4. Many people at this elevation seem unable to plan ahead. They tend to disregard the consequences of their actions and not profit by them (Carson, 1969).

5. Elevations on this scale reflect heavy reliance on the defense mechanisms of externalization, acting-out, and rationalization or intellectualization (Trimboli & Kilgore, 1983).

6. People in this range may be reacting to situational pressures which require them to act out against their own or others' morals; for example, getting a divorce. They may return to the normal range for the scale (T = below 70) when the situational pressure is gone.

4   144

7. Therapy seems to be less effective in changing a person with a marked elevated **4** scale than is age (Carson, 1969).

8. However, the higher the intelligence, the more likely a person with a high **4** scale can be channeled by therapy into constructive pursuits, such as finding a suitable job where the high **4** behavior can be used to advantage.

9. The following people tend to have an elevated **4** scale:

   a. Alcoholics.

   b. Drug users (Brill, Crumpton, & Grayson, 1971; Smart & Jones, 1970).

   c. People in trouble with the law, juvenile delinquents (Stone & Rowley, 1963), and convicts.

   d. Adolescents labeled as "problems," but not identified as delinquents (Davies & Maliphant, 1971).

   e. Non-achievers in high school and college (Haun, 1965).

10. A **4** scale in this range or higher with a low **2** scale (45 or below) may indicate little, if any, likelihood of significant personality change (Carson, 1969).

11. Gilberstadt and Duker (1965) found a high **4** pattern (a "spike **4**") in a VA hospital male population. A person with this pattern tended to be irresponsible, impulsive, egocentric, and emotionally unstable. He also tended to have a low frustration tolerance. The Gilberstadt and Duker book should be consulted for further information concerning this profile.

12. Anderson et al. (1979) found a spike **4** profile as one of three profiles in a group of sex offenders. (The other two profiles were **F-6-8** and **2-4**). These men had the best pre-incarceration adjustment. They also had less severe adjustment problems on the wards compared to the other sex offenders.

13. VA hospital males with this profile combination tended to be somewhat nonconforming socially and inclined to resent authority.

4

They tended to have conduct problems and poor work records. They shied away from close personal ties and had inadequate family and social relationships (Hovey & Lewis, 1967).

14. College students with a spike **4** profile were in academic and/or legal difficulties. They had a significantly higher rate of past crime than other students (King & Kelley, 1977).

15. In counseling centers, high **4** counselees may not show the classic amoral, asocial behavior, but the scale elevation may be an index of rebelliousness rather than an indication of acting out impulses (Mello & Guthrie, 1958). Typically these people will also have a low **Re** scale (see p. 279).

16. Female medical patients with this elevation may have recurrent marital difficulties and illegitimate pregnancies. Their medical symptoms tend to be mild in nature and over-shadowed by their behavioral problems (Mello & Guthrie, 1958).

LOW SCORES
(T = 45 or Below)

1. People with these scores tend to be very conventional and may be concerned with social status (Carson, 1969).

2. They may have a great capacity for a boring, routine life (Carson, 1972).

3. Low scores, especially with **3** scale elevations, may indicate decidedly repressed aggressive and assertive tendencies (Graham, 1977).

4. The low scores also may indicate people who have low sexual interest. This indication is particularly true when scale **4** is the low point of the profile (Meehl, 1951).

5. These scores tend to characterize older people (Canter et al., 1962; Swenson, 1961).

COMBINATIONS

All scales in the combinations are at a T-score of 70 or above and are listed in order from the highest to the lowest peaks. The scales in the combinations must be the highest Clinical scales on the profile.

1-2-3-4 See p. 86.

1-3-4 See p. 90.

2-4-7 See p. 105 and the **4-7-2** pattern, p. 153.

2-4-8 See p. 105.

2-4-8-9 See p. 105.

2-7-4 See p. 108.

2-7-4-3 See the **2-7-4** pattern, point 2, p. 109.

2-7-4-5̄ See p. 109.

2-7-5 -4 See p. 110.

3-4-5 See p. 129.

4-1 See the **1-4** combination, p. 91.

4-2 See also the **2-4** combination, p. 103.

1. People with the **4-2** combination may seem to be depressed and feeling guilty, but they are not always very convincing or sincere in these feelings (Dahlstrom et al., 1972).

2. People with the **4-2** pattern say one thing, but their behavior is the opposite. For example, they may be self-condemning but act out continuously (Caldwell, 1972).

3. They tend to put their problems on other people so that other people will feel guilty (Caldwell, 1972).

4

4. When a person with an elevated **4** scale gives responses that indicate difficulty with parents and family, the usual interpretation is that the client, in fact, is the difficult one, and the family often has put up with considerable disruption from him/her. However, when the **2** scale is also elevated, the family may truly have been difficult in some way such as one parent being alcoholic or emotionally explosive. The client's report may reflect a real situation rather than a psychopathic interpretation of reality.

5. The **2-4/4-2** code type occurred most frequently in four alcoholism treatment centers. It accounted for 12 to 21% of the profiles in any facility (Schroeder & Piercy, 1979).

6. In a recent study of heroin addicts (Craig, 1984a) 14% had the **4-2/2-4** profile. The only code with a higher percentage of cases was the **4-9/9-4** code.

7. Anderson and Bauer (1984) have found that college students with high **4-2** (and also elevated **7** and **8** scales) had

    a. poor relationships with the opposite sex,

    b. significantly more depression than other clients,

    c. low self-esteem,

    d. many problems with their families,

    e. rigid rules,

    f. dependency, and

    g. no improvement in therapy.

4-3 See also the **3-4** combination, p. 128;
the **4-3-5̄** combination, p. 149.

1. The elevation of scale **4** indicates the amount of aggressive or hostile feelings present, while the elevation of scale **3** indicates the repressive or suppressive controls available. Consequently, because scale **4** is higher than scale **3** in this combination, the controls seen in scale **3** are not always adequate limits. Therefore, the person tends periodically to break out into violent behavior.

a. A life-long pattern may exist of over-control, a sudden explosive episode, and then quiet again for about two years until the next episode. The pattern has been found in males and females (Davis, 1971; Davis & Sines, 1971; Persons & Marks, 1971).

b. Caldwell (1972) saw the **4-3** person as a socially correct role player who periodically breaks out into antisocial behavior.

2. Gilberstadt and Duker (1965) found the **4-3** pattern in a VA hospital male population. A person with this pattern tended to be sensitive to rejection and had poorly controlled anger with temper outbursts. Suicide attempts and alcoholism occurred when this anger turned inward. The Gilberstadt and Duker book should be consulted for further information concerning this profile.

3. However, a more recent study (Gynther, Altman, & Warbin, 1973c) has failed to replicate the findings of antisocial and violent behavior for the **4-3** pattern.

4. Megargee and Bohn (1979) found a group of incarcerated criminals with this **4-3** combination (32% of Group Easy). This pattern might have been produced by a fake good tendency. These criminals were the best adjusted and best controlled of the ten groups of prisoners. They had a relatively easy time of it in the prison and the lowest recidivism rate. The Megargee and Bohn book should be consulted for further information concerning this profile group.

4-3-5 ($\overline{5}$ scale T = 45 or Below)

1. This pattern may be found for a woman who is hostile and aggressive. She represses anger, but she is unable to prevent her feelings from being acted out. Consequently, she resorts to overt masochistic behavior, which is intended to provoke rage in others. She can then pity herself for being mistreated (Carson, 1969).

4-5 See also the **5-4** combination, p. 171.

1. Men with this pattern may be nonconforming but are not likely to act out in obviously delinquent ways. However, their low tolerance for frustration can lead to brief periods of problem behavior (Graham, 1977).

2. An elevation on scale **5** may act as a suppressor of the acting out behavior that usually would be seen from the high scale **4**.

3. Adolescents in treatment with this **4-5/5-4** pattern (Marks et al., 1974) were seen by their therapists as in better shape than the typical adolescent patient. They had greater ego-resiliency, were adaptive and organized. They also tended to be heavy drug users. The Marks, Seeman, and Haller book should be consulted for further information concerning this profile type.

4. Outpatient psychiatric males with **4-5** frequently had interpersonal problems, especially breaking up with a girlfriend (King & Kelley, 1977).

5. Male college students with this combination tend to have home conflicts, insomnia, restlessness, and worry (Drake & Oetting, 1959).

6. Professed male homosexuals tend to have a high **4-5,** whereas ideational homosexuals tend to have a high **3-5** combination (Dahlstrom et al., 1972).

4-5-7-9

1. These elevations may indicate home conflict in male college counselees (Drake & Oetting, 1959).

4-5-9

1. For men with this pattern the high **5** score may be an indication that the **4-9** behavior is suppressed. Therefore, the person may not be acting out directly.

   When the **4-5-9** pattern is present in a male college student, the under-achievement which is typically seen with the **4-9** pattern, is not manifested. The **5** scale acts as a suppressor (Drake, 1962).

4-6 See also the **4-6-5** combination, p. 152.

1. These people may be hostile, resentful, and suspicious (Hovey & Lewis, 1967).

2. People with this pattern tend to transfer blame for their problems onto others (Carson, 1969). They may be litigious and threaten to initiate law suits.

3. These two scale potentiate each other. These people typically have poor impulse control, explosiveness, and a propensity towards violence (Trimboli & Kilgore, 1983).

4. Seriously disruptive relationships with the opposite sex may exist such as divorce (Dahlstrom et al., 1972; Guthrie, 1949).

5. These people tend to have poor work records (Dahlstrom et al., 1972; Guthrie, 1949).

6. Alcoholism or poor judgment may be associated with this pattern.

7. People with this pattern tend to convert everything into anger (Caldwell, 1974).

8. They may demand a great deal of attention for themselves but resent giving any to other people (Graham, 1977).

9. They tend to be poor risks for counseling (Carson, 1969).

10. In one study of women with this profile plus low 5 scale (Walters & Solomon, 1982) the women were indecisive and demanding of love and attention.

11. Marks et al. (1974) found the 4-6/6-4 pattern in a university hospital and outpatient clinic. It tended to be found for females who were described as self-centered, hostile, tense, defensive, and irritable. They usually refused to admit their difficulties, and therefore did not deal with them. They frequently used rationalization as a primary defense mechanism. The Marks, Seeman, and Haller book should be consulted for further information concerning this pattern.

12. VA hospital males with this profile tended to be socially maladjusted with women. They were confused, resentful, and evasive (Hovey & Lewis, 1967).

13. Adolescents in treatment with this 4-6/6-4 pattern (Marks et al., 1974) were referred because they were defiant, disobedient, tense,

restless, and negative. Their relationships with their parents were poor. They demanded attention and undercontrolled their impulses. About one-half of the group were involved with drugs. The Marks, Seeman, and Haller book should be consulted for further information concerning this profile.

14. For college students with this profile, men tended to be aggressive and belligerent with conflicts with their fathers. Women were rebellious towards their homes, restless, and lacking skills with the opposite sex (Drake & Oetting, 1959).

4-6-2

1. Hostility and depression often form a cyclical pattern with this profile. The expressions of hostility often lead to guilt, then anger reoccurs because of resenting the guilt feelings (Lachar, 1974).

2. Marks et al. (1974) found the **4-6-2/6-4-2** pattern in a university hospital and outpatient clinic. The pattern was primarily found for females. A woman with this pattern tended to be acting out, depressed, critical, and skeptical. The Marks, Seeman, and Haller book should be consulted for further information concerning this profile.

4-6-$\bar{5}$ See **4-6** point 10.

1. Wives who are in marriage counseling have a higher proportion of this profile pattern than do wives from the general population (Arnold, 1970; Ollendick et al., 1983).

4-6-8

1. A person with a **4-6-8** pattern may be brought in for help by someone else. He/she usually has symptoms of seething anger. Prognosis is poor because the person tends to want his/her problems solved by having other people change (Caldwell, 1972).

2. This is an adverse pattern for most short-term therapy.

3. Anderson and Holcomb (1983) have found this pattern as one of five in a group of accused murderers. This group of murderers had paranoid personalities or were sociopaths with bad judgment. They

were also the group with the highest intelligence. They resembled Megargee and Bohn's (1979) Foxtrot pattern.

4-6-9

1. This is one of the most dangerous profiles for the potential to act out against others (Tromboli & Kilgore, 1983).

2. This pattern is found in people who suddenly are violent (Carson, 1969). This is especially true if scale **8** is elevated also.

4-7

1. People with this pattern tend to have repeated patterns of acting out and then being sorry for the acting out (Hovey & Lewis, 1967).

2. While they may be very remorseful about acting out, this remorse is not usually sufficient to prevent them from acting out again (Dahlstrom et al., 1972).

3. These people have both excessive insensitivity and excessive concern about their actions. This may be cyclical (Lachar, 1974).

4. These people may respond to therapeutic support, but they are unlikely to make long term changes in their personality (Graham, 1977).

5. Adolescents in treatment with this profile **4-7/7-4** (Marks et al., 1974) acted out, were provocative, resentful, and basically insecure. They had many friends but few close ones. The Marks, Seeman, and Haller book should be consulted for further information concerning this pattern.

6. Kelley and King (1979a) found the **4-7/7-4** profile code in a college counseling center. Clients with this profile were immature, moody, and reported feelings of inferiority, ruminations, and gastrointestinal problems.

4-7-2

1. Marks et al. (1974) found the **2-7-4/2-4-7/4-7-2** pattern in a university hospital and outpatient clinic. People with this pattern tended

to be depressed and to have many worries. They were likely to be described as passive-aggressive, generally tearful, full of fear, nervous, and irritable. The Marks, Seeman, and Haller book should be consulted for further information concerning this profile.

4-8 See also the **8-4** combination, p. 209.

1. People with this pattern may be unpredictable, impulsive, and odd in appearance and behavior (Dahlstrom et al., 1972; Hovey & Lewis, 1967).

2. People with this pattern tend to distrust others and have problems with close relationships (Caldwell, 1972).

3. These people tend to see the world as threatening, and they respond by either withdrawing or lashing out in anger. They may have serious concerns about their masculinity or femininity (Graham, 1977).

4. They tend to get into trouble because they have poor judgment as to when and how to fight out, rather than because they crave the excitement of trouble as people with the **4-9** pattern do.

5. One study (Lewandowski & Graham, 1972) has found that hospitalized psychiatric patients with this pattern have more unusual thoughts than other psychiatric patients and also are younger than the other patients.

6. This pattern is found frequently in people with suicidal ideation (Caldwell, 1972).

7. The person with the high **4** and **8** scales and a low **9** scale may be the black sheep of the family and constantly in trouble (Caldwell, 1972).

8. Gynther et al. (1973) found that psychiatric inpatients with the **4-8/8-4** pattern had a history of antisocial behavior such as promiscuity or deserting their families.

9. VA hospital males were likely to be argumentative, unpredictable, odd, delinquent, and asocial (Hovey & Lewis, 1967).

10. Adolescents in treatment with the **4-8/8-4** pattern (Marks et al., 1974) were immature and extremely narcissistic. Only 16% showed

4   154

any improvement in therapy. These adolescents were argumentative, resentful, and acting out. Those with the **4-8** pattern were more deviant and difficult in therapy than those with the **8-4** pattern. The Marks, Seeman, and Haller book should be consulted for further information concerning this pattern.

11. Crimes committed by persons with this profile often are senseless, poorly planned, and poorly executed. They may include some of the more savage and vicious forms of sexual and homocidal assault (Pothast, 1956).

12. Anderson and Holcomb (1983) found this pattern as one of five in a group of murderers. Men with this pattern were most clearly identified by others as having severe mental problems. They tended to kill as the result of insults or slights. They were least likely to be drunk when they killed. Their profile pattern resembles Megargee and Bohn's (1979) Howe pattern.

13. In a recent study (Craig, 1984a), 9% of the heroin addicts had the **4-8/8-4** pattern, 21% had the **4-9/9-4** code, and 14% the **4-2/2-4** code.

14. In another study of drug abusers (Patalano, 1980) this was the most frequent two point code for Black abusers. The **4-9/9-4** code was the most frequent code for whites.

15. Caldwell (1972) found in one MMPI study of prostitutes and call girls that all of them had the **4-8** combination.

16. College men with this pattern tended to be indecisive, unhappy, worrying, and confused. They had conflicts with their fathers and were aggressive and belligerent.

   Females also had conflicts at home, were depressed, and had headaches. They also lacked skills with the opposite sex (Drake & Oetting, 1959).

4-8-F

1. These elevations tend to be obtained by potential juvenile delinquents (Hathaway & Monachesi, 1958).

2. They also are found in emotionally disturbed adolescents.

4

3. When these elevations occur with a low **2** scale, the person is usually an aggressive, punitive individual who likes to arouse anxiety and guilt in others (Carson, 1969).

   Such people may end up in jobs where their behavior is socially approved, e.g., law enforcer, school disciplinarian, or over-zealous clergyman.

4-8-2

1. This profile indicates a person who is distressed while at the same time hostile and distrustful. The person tends to be isolated and potentially suicidal (Lachar, 1974).

2. Marks et al. (1974) found the **4-8-2/8-4-2/8-2-4** pattern in a university hospital and outpatient clinic. A person with this profile tended to be distrustful of others, keeping them at a distance. The person usually was described as depressed, tense, irritable, and hostile. The Marks, Seeman, and Haller book should be consulted for further information concerning this profile.

4-8-9

1. A person with a **4-8-9** profile may have a history of repeated aggression in situations where others get hurt. These people typically do not realize how they hurt others (Caldwell, 1972).

2. When a male has this profile, he may be violent but has charisma and vitality (Caldwell, 1972).

3. Highly aggressive males have the **4-8-9** scales as high points (Butcher, 1965).

4. When the **2** scale also is elevated (but not necessarily the next highest scale after the **4, 8,** and **9**), people talk about depression and tend to manipulate others so that they can get their own way (Caldwell, 1972).

4-8-9-2 See the **4-8-9** combination, point 4, above.

1. Caldwell (1985) has found this to be a profile for people who are homicidal. The greater the difference between the **7** and **8** scales (the

7 scale being lower), the greater the potential for marked asocial behavior.

4-9 See also the **9-4** combination, pp. 224-225.

1. People with their highest scale elevations on the **4** and **9** scales tend to be arousal seekers. They must maintain excitement and will stir things up to get it (Carson, 1969, 1972). In contrast to people with high **4-8** scales (when poor judgment may get the person into trouble), the high **4-9** person seems to be seeking the excitement of the trouble.

   The **9** scale activates and energizes the feelings shown by the **4** scale.

2. The person with an elevated **4-9** profile may be self-defeating.

3. A marked disregard for social standards and values may exist (Graham, 1977). If this is true, the **Re** scale also will tend to be low.

4. The **4-9** pattern tends to characterize the following people:

   a. Juvenile delinquents.

      1) However, accompanying high scores on scale **2, 5, 7,** and **0** act as inhibitors of the delinquent behavior (Carkhuff et al., 1965).

      2) This pattern may disappear with age.

   b. Convicts.

      1) Habitual criminals are higher on **4** and **9** than first offenders of the same age (Panton, 1962).

      2) With male adults, this tends to be a chronic fixed pattern.

   c. Heroin addicts (Craig, 1984a). In a recent study 21% had the **4-9/9-4** profile.

   d. School and college under-achievers (Brown & Dubois, 1974). This is especially true for males if the **5** scale is low, whereas high **5** acts as a suppressor to the under-achievement tendency of the **4-9** pattern (Drake & Oetting, 1959).

  e. Students in trouble for college misconduct (Nyman & LeMay, 1967).

  f. Female college students with interpersonal difficulties but fewer intrapsychic problems (King & Kelley, 1977).

5. Lewandowski and Graham (1972) found that patients with an elevated **4-9** profile were younger at their first hospitalization than other patients. They also were irritable, angry, and easily annoyed. They became upset quickly if things did not suit them.

6. Gilberstadt and Duker (1965) found the **4-9** pattern in a VA hospital male population. A man with this pattern tended to be self-centered, moody, and irritable. He tended to be superficially friendly, but he had a low frustration tolerance. The Gilberstadt and Duker book should be consulted for further information concerning this profile.

7. In another study of VA hospital males, patients with this pattern were energetic, ambitious, and lively. They were emotionally unstable with asocial tendencies. They were impulsive and had difficulty controlling their impulses (Hovey & Lewis, 1967).

8. Marks et al. (1974) found the **4-9** pattern in a university hospital and outpatient clinic. A person with this pattern tended to be self-centered, under-controlled, insecure, irritable, and hostile. The Marks, Seeman, and Haller book should be consulted for further information concerning this profile.

9. Two recent studies (Gynther et al., 1973a; Gynther et al., 1973) also have found antisocial behavior such as excessive fighting and attempts to harm others for this pattern **4-9/9-4**. Men with this pattern also tended to have a history of alcoholic benders. This description may not apply to Blacks who have a **4-9** profile.

10. Adolescents in treatment with the **4-9/9-4** pattern (Marks et al., 1974) were referred because of being defiant, disobedient, provocative, and truant from school. They usually had constant conflict with parents. However, they had many friends and were well liked by them. They were typically drug users. The Marks, Seeman, and

4   158

Haller book should be consulted for further information concerning this pattern.

11. Megargee and Bohn (1979) found four profiles with this code type for a group of incarcerated criminals. Their book should be consulted for classification rules to distinguish among the profiles and for descriptions of the behaviors associated with them.

    This was the most common two point code for Group Able (83% of the group). The men in this group were happy-go-lucky and outgoing. They were charming, popular, and manipulative. They created a popular impression but were likely to get into trouble again when they got out of prison.

    Group Foxtrot also had this **4-9/9-4** combination (69% of the group) but also tended to be elevated on the **8** scale. Their criminal behavior seemed to be symptomatic of pervasive psychopathology. They had extensive criminal records and were one of the most violent groups. They had poor prison adjustment and the highest recidivism rate.

12. This pattern was found in a group of male alcoholics. Also found were the **2-1-3**, **2-4-7**, and **8-7-6** combinations (Conley, 1981). In contrast to the other combinations, the **4-9** profile did not change with treatment.

13. College students with high points on these scales have lower grade point averages and higher dropout rates than would be expected according to their ability (Barger & Hall, 1964).

14. College counselees with these high points were rated difficult to deal with (aggressive and opinionated) by their counselors (Drake, 1954).

    Male clients also had conflicts with their fathers. Female clients had home conflicts, vague goals, lacked academic drive and were socially extroverted (Drake & Oetting, 1959).

4-9-6

1. With this profile, explosive outbursts of aggression may occur, especially if **8** is also elevated (Carson, 1969).

4-0

1. Adolescents in treatment with the **4-0/0-4** pattern (Marks et al., 1974) were suspicious and distrustful. They were resentful and prone to acting out. They were also shy and had few friends. The Marks, Seeman and Haller book should be consulted for further information concerning this pattern.

6-4-2 See the **4-6-2** pattern, p. 152.

8-2-4 See p. 208.

8-2-4-7 See the **8-2-4** pattern, point 2, p. 209.

8-4-2 See the **4-8-2** pattern, p. 156.

8-6-4-9-F See p. 211.

SUMMARY OF 4 SCALE INTERPRETATIONS*

T-score	Interpretations
45 or below	Persons with these scores tend to be conventional. They usually are able to tolerate routine and like to be peaceable. They may lack interest in heterosexual activity.
45 thru 60	The majority of people score in this range. People scoring at this level seldom show dissatisfaction with authority figures, and they tend to go along with society as it is presently constituted.
60 thru 70	With college educated persons, this level usually indicates concern about the social problems of the world. It is a common level for social workers, psychologists, and others in the helping professions. People with scores in this range tend to be appropriate in their use of anger.

70 or above   Persons at this level tend to be angry and fighting out. If the **5** scale is above or within the **5** T-score points of the **4** scale for men, this fighting out will be more covert than overt. People at the lower end of this elevation (70 to 80) may have a situational crisis such as marital discord. In this latter instance, the elevation tends to go down after the problem is resolved. Other people with scores above 70 may be unable to profit from their experiences, both good and bad. These people may not be in actual trouble with authority figures, but instead may associate with persons who are. Adolescents usually outgrow this difficulty, but at age 40, such an elevation, if it is one of the highest scales, can be considered a long-standing trait and is probably very difficult to change. The key to success with these people is to try to channel the drive indicated by the high **4** into socially acceptable behavior.

Relation to Research Scales

Do scale—if the **4** scales is above 70 T-score points and the **Do** scale also is above 70 T-score points, the person frequently will be seen as domineering.

Re scale—if the **4** scale is above 70 T-score points and the **Re** scale is below 50, the person may be rebellious.

---

*Where T-scores are listed in two categories (i.e., 45 or below and 45 through 60) and a score is obtained that is listed for two categories, use whichever interpretation seems to be most appropriate for the individual.

—NOTES—

SCALE 5

(Mf, Masculinity-Femininity Scale)

Scale 5 is probably the most misunderstood of all the Clinical scales for three reasons. The first reason is the scale's name, "Masculinity-Femininity." The implication is that this scale can determine if one is more or less masculine or feminine. The problem in today's society is that the definitions of masculinity and femininity are changing rapidly, and the current ones may not be very much like the original definitions used when this scale was constructed.

A second difficulty with the scale is the frequent assumption that it can detect males who are actual or latent homosexuals. Such an assumption is not warranted. Some males with homosexual preferences do receive elevations on this scale, but many false positive and false negatives exist. This scale just does not do an adequate job of identifying male homosexuality.

The third difficulty with this scale is purely mechanical. Actually two 5 scales exist, one for males and one for females, and each scale has its own interpretations.

Males

Kunce and Anderson (1976, 1984) posit role-flexibility as the underlying dimension of scale 5. When this scale is elevated for males, it indicates an individual who can enjoy a wide range of interests and who will be perceived as interesting, complex, tolerant, and insightful. This scale tends to be moderately elevated among adjusted members of many occupational groups, among them: social scientists (including psychologists), authors, physicians, artists, ministers, and teachers. Under stress the individual with a moderately high score may show role adjustment difficulties.

Hovey and Lewis (1967) found that individuals with moderate elevations on scale 5 were sensitive, curious, socially perceptive, and tolerant. They were unlikely to show delinquent behavior and understood themselves and others fairly well.

Scores between 45 and 55 on this scale indicate that a man is interested in traditional masculine activities. Between 50 and 55 seems to be the typical range for non-college educated males and for college educated males interested in majors such as engineering and agriculture. When this score goes lower than a T of 45, the man tends to adopt the attitudes of the legendary he-man, particularly in the treatment of females (examples: "love them and leave them" and "a woman's place is in the home"). In fact, some of these men appear to score conquests by carving notches on the bedpost (particularly so if their 4 scale is elevated).

As the elevation on this scale increases to above 60, one of two types of behavior may be observed. One is an interest in aesthetics such as art, music, and literature. This interest tends to increase with education (a score in the 60 thru 70 range is the norm for college graduates). The second type of behavior that can emerge is passivity. By passivity, we mean a preference for working through things in a covert and indirect manner, rather than in an overt and direct manner. the question of which of the two behaviors is indicated by the 5 scale score is best determined by consulting other scales (particularly the Research scales **Dy** and **St**). High **Dy** (dependency) plus high 5 usually indicates passivity. High **St** (status) plus high 5 usually is indicative of aesthetic or achievement interests. When both the **Dy** and **St** scales are elevated above 60 T-score points, the relative heights of the two scales can indicate how much passivity and/or aesthetic or achievement interests are being shown by the 5 scale.

Above a T of 80, both an appreciation for aesthetics and passivity usually are present. With persons actively involved in the arts however the passivity may not be present until a T-score of 85 is reached.

While the 5 scale is the most frequent high point on male college student profiles, with scale 9 a close second, for male non-college clients this is not a frequent high point. They rarely score above 60 on this scale; in fact, their typical score is around 55.

Females

In the counseling center and mental health clinic populations, the usual maximum scale 5 score for women is 50; very rarely do we see scores above this level. Those few women we have seen who do score above 50 tend to be uninterested in being seen as feminine. They may or may not have masculine interests, but they definitely are not interested in appearing or behaving as other women do. They usually like to think of themselves as unique or different from women in general.

Another group of women who score in this range are teen age girls who are in some kind of trouble with the law or their families. They frequently seem to be unsure of what they are like as females and therefore score above the usual range of T-scores for females.

Scores between 35 and 50 are typical and indicate interest in traditional feminine pursuits. This does not mean that the woman has no interest in a career outside the home, but, instead, that she may prefer both a career and the traditional activities connected with being a woman. As the score on this scale goes below 35, a seductive, helpless, coyness usually begins to emerge if the **Dy** scale (see pp. 269-272) is also above 50 T-score points. As the **Dy** scale goes above 50 and the **5** scale goes below 35, the amount of helplessness typically increases. The woman with these scores is not always actually helpless, but she may be using this approach to get others to help her, particularly males.

GENERAL INFORMATION

1. The **5** scale of 60 items contains questions concerning aesthetic interests, vocational choices, and passivity (Carson, 1969).

2. The same scale is used for both sexes, but high raw scores are elevations for men and low points for women.

3. This scale is highly correlated with education (Colligan et al., 1984).

   However, Gulas (1973) has indicated that the **5** scale may be more correlated with IQ, educational aspiration, and/or socio-economic status than with years of education, *per se.*

4. The **5** scale frequently is elevated for men, but not for women.

5. Scale **5** is considered a character scale by Trimboli and Kilgore (1983). They consider mild to moderate elevations in the feminine direction to reflect the capacity for sublimation, an adaptive defense mechanism. With high elevations (low scores for women), the use of suppression is more likely.

6. Caldwell has hypothesized that the 5 scale may measure caring for others on the feminine end of the scale (high 5 for men, low 5 for women) with relationships meaning a great deal, and practical, survival, self-caring on the masculine end of the scale (low 5 for men, high 5 for women). People at the feminine end value emotions, feelings, and aesthetics, and are introspective. People at the masculine end value action and pragmatism (Caldwell, 1985).

7. Volentine (1981) has found that the femininity measures of the Bem Sex Role Inventory were more strongly related to scale 5 than the masculinity measures. Scale 5, therefore, may be interpreted more accurately as a measure of femininity rather than a measure of masculinity.

8. For males, high 5 tends to negate the overt acting out behavior indicated by elevations on certain scales such as 4, 6, and 9. Passive-aggressive behavior may be seen instead.

9. A high 5 scale may indicate homosexuality for men. However, this cannot be assumed without evidence from other sources.

Male homosexuals are able to score in the typical range on this scale if they wish to, because obvious sex-oriented items can be avoided easily.

10. With females, if a large number of questions are left unanswered, the scale is elevated.

11. In a study of a normal population, scores on scale 5 were lower for older men and higher for older women, perhaps reflecting somewhat lower educational levels for the older age groups (Colligan et al., 1984).

12. For a normal population, the mean score on this scale was 46 for women and 58 for men (Colligan et al., 1984).

13. Test-retest reliabilities are good (Carkhuff et al., 1965; Dahlstrom & Welsh, 1960). Indeed this scale frequently remains the same even when the rest of the profile changes dramatically.

14. VA hospital males with this scale as a high point were likely to be peaceable and not show any delinquent behavior. They also tended to be sensitive, dependent, and submissive (Hovey & Lewis, 1967).

5   166

HIGH SCORES

Moderate Elevations—Male (T = 60 through 70)

1. This elevation is characteristic of males having a wide range of interests, especially aesthetic ones.

2. Kunce and Anderson (1976) have hypothesized that when this scale is in the moderate range, it may measure role-flexibility. A person who is role-flexible can enjoy a wide range of interests and may be perceived as interesting, colorful, complex, inner-directed, insightful, tolerant, and possibly dramatic.

3. Trimboli and Kilgore (1983) have expressed the belief that moderate elevations on this scale for men may reflect some capacity for sublimation, an adaptive defense mechanism.

4. Males scoring in this range on the scale are not necessarily passive, but they do tend to dislike physical violence (Caldwell, 1985).

5. High **5** tends to be more characteristic of college males then of college females.

6. The **5** scale tends to be one of the two most frequent high points for male college students. The other frequent high point is scale **9.**

7. Gulas (1973) found that the two most frequently elevated scales (two-point code groups) in a study of 609 college males were (from most frequent to least frequent) **3-5/5-3, 5-9/9-5, 2-5/5-2, 5-7/7-5, 5-8/8-5,** and **5-6/6-5.** These two-point patterns were *not* necessarily above a T-score of 70.

Moderate Elevations—Female (T = 50 through 55)

1. Women with this elevation on the **5** scale may enjoy sports and/or outdoor activities.

2. They also tend to be uninterested in being considered feminine.

5

3. They may prefer mechanical, computational, and scientific pursuits, and tend not to prefer literary pursuits (Carkhuff et al., 1965).

4. Scale 5 moderate elevations are frequent for females who drop out of school (Barger & Hall, 1964).

5. This elevation may be shown by girls in their late teens and by women from atypical cultural backgrounds (Carson, 1969).

6. Scale 5 is frequently elevated for girls in trouble with their families or the law.

Marked Elevations—Male (T = 70 or Above)

The behaviors for this elevation are most clearly seen when the scale is the highest of the Clinical scales.

1. As elevations increase, the likelihood that passive behavior will be seen in men increases.

2. Trimboli and Kilgore (1983) have expressed the belief that men with elevations at this level will tend to use the defense mechanism of suppression.

3. This elevation is characteristic of college males having a wide range of interests, especially aesthetic ones (Hathaway & Meehl, 1951).

4. Scores in this range for blue collar men tend to indicate passivity rather than aesthetic interests.

5. A high score suggests that the man does not identify with the culturally prescribed role for his sex (Carson, 1969).

6. Men with this elevation may tend to care too much about relationships.

7. Male homosexuals may show marked elevations on the 5 scale (Manosevits, 1971). However, since this is an obvious scale, males with same-sex preferences also can produce scores in the typical ranges by avoiding these obvious sex-oriented items.

Marked Elevations—Females (T = 55 or Above)

1. As the elevation increases, the likelihood that aggressive behavior will be seen in women increases (Carson, 1969).

2. A high score suggests that the woman does not identify with the culturally prescribed role for her sex (Carson, 1969).

3. High scores in this range also may mean that the person is having trouble identifying with the feminine role.

4. Women with this elevation may become anxious if they are expected to adopt a feminine sexual role (Carson, 1969).

5. Trimboli and Kilgore (1983) have hypothesized that women with scores in this range may have difficulty appropriately channeling aggressive impulses.

LOW SCORES

Male (T = 50 or Below)

1. Low scores suggest strong identification with the prescribed masculine role (Carson, 1969).

2. Males with scores in this range may be described as easy going, adventurous, and "coarse" (Carson, 1969).

3. Some males with low 5 scores may appear to be compulsive and inflexible about their masculinity (Carson, 1969).

4. Trimboli and Kilgore (1983) have hypothesized that men with scores in this range may have difficulty appropriately channeling aggressive impulses.

Female (T = 35 or Below)

1. Low scores suggest strong identification with the prescribed feminine role (Carson, 1969).

2. Females with very low **5** scale scores may be passive, submissive, yielding, and demure, at times living caricatures of the feminine stereotype (Carson, 1969).

3. Caldwell (1985) has found that women with **5** scales this low are not caricatures of traditional femininity. They dress self-expressively to fit their mood. They are attracted to sensitive men with whom they can communicate.

4. Trimboli and Kilgore (1983) have hypothesized that women with **5** scales at this level will tend to use the defense mechanism of suppression.

5. These women tend to care too much about relationships. That may account for some lack of self-assertiveness in interpersonal relationships.

COMBINATIONS

All scales in the combinations are at T-score of 70 or above and are listed in order from the highest to the lowest peaks. The scales in the combination must be the highest Clinical scales in the profile.

5   170

4-5-9 See p. 150.

4-6-5̄ See p. 152.

5-?

1. An elevation on the **5** scale for females can result from the omission of items (elevated **?** scale), because a low raw score on scale **5** produces elevations on the women's profile.

5-2 See p. 105.

5-3 See also the **5-4** combination that follows.

1. If men have homosexual impulses and scales **5** and **3** are high, they tend not to have acted upon their sexual impulses but may only be thinking about them (Singer, 1970).

5-4 See also the **5-3** combination above.
the **4-5** combination, p. 149.

1. If men have homosexual impulses and scales **5** and **4** are high, they tend to be overt homosexuals (Singer, 1970).

2. Males with this combination may have a passive-aggressive personality.

3. This combination may be associated with male sexual delinquents of the more passive type.

4. The **5-4** combination is a common configuration for men who are nonconformists. They seem to delight in defying social conventions in their behavior and dress (Carson, 1969). Many male homosexuals who have this combination are proud of their unconventionality and tend to flaunt it.

5. Women who are rebelling against the female role tend to have this combination (Carson, 1969). Their behavior becomes more atypical with increasing elevation of the **4** scale (Carson, 1969).

5̄-4 (5 Scale T = 45 or Below)

5

1. Men with this combination tend to be flamboyantly masculine. In teenagers, this is often manifested in delinquent behavior (Carson, 1969).

2. Women with this combination may be hostile and angry, but they are unable to express these feelings directly. Therefore, they may provoke others to get angry at them. Then they can pity themselves, because they have been mistreated (Carson, 1969).

3. Women with this pattern may be passive-aggressive (Good & Brantner, 1974).

5-6

1. Adolescents in treatment with the 5-6/6-5 pattern (Marks et al., 1974) had more intellectual interests and valued wealth and material possessions more than other adolescents in treatment. They were irritable and acted out. They were sometimes suicidal and homocidal. The Marks, Seeman, and Haller book should be consulted for further information concerning this pattern.

5-7

1. Male college students with this profile usually were tense, indecisive, unhappy, worrying, and wanting reassurance (Drake & Oetting, 1959).

2. In another study of college clients, the men usually complained about academic problems and interpersonal difficulties, especially with their girlfriends (King & Kelley, 1977).

5-8

1. For college students with this profile, men report being confused, unhappy, and having conflicts at home (Drake & Oetting, 1959).

5-8-9

1. When the 5-8-9 pattern is present, the lack of academic motivation seen for males with the high 8-9/9-8 profile is not manifested. The 5 scale acts as a suppressor (Drake & Oetting, 1959).

5-9

1. Adolescents in treatment with the **5-9/9-5** pattern (Marks et al., 1974) were peaceable, rational, and ambitious. They had high aspirations and aesthetic interests. They also had relatively few school problems. However, emotional dependency and lack of self-assertiveness were problems for them and many were drug users. The Marks, Seeman, and Haller book should be consulted for further information concerning this pattern.

2. Male college counselees with the **5-9** pattern present problems concerning conflicts with their mothers, especially when scale **0** is low (Drake, 1956).

5-0

1. Adolescents in treatment with the **5-0/0-5** pattern (Marks et al., 1974) had intellectual interests. However, they were slow to make friends and were shy, timid, and submissive. They had conflicts about sexuality and asserting themselves. They tended to overcontrol their impulses. The Marks, Seeman, and Haller book should be consulted for further information concerning this pattern.

2. Male college counselees with the **5-0** pattern tend to show introverted behavior (Drake, 1956).

5

SUMMARY OF 5 SCALE INTERPRETATIONS
FOR MALES*

T-score	Interpretations
45 or below	A man scoring in this range may be pre-occupied with being tough and virile (the he-man syndrome).
45 thru 55	A man scoring in this range usually is interested in traditional masculine pursuits such as sports, hunting, outdoor life. Between 50 and 55 is the typical range of this scale for non-college males, engineers, and men studying agriculture.
55 thru 80	This level is typical for males with more than one year of college, particularly in the humanities and fine arts. This person usually has an interest in aesthetics. There also may be some passivity. This latter is more likely as the 5 scale gets closer to 80. For non-college educated males, a score above 70 on the 5 scale usually indicates passivity with a possible interest in aesthetics.
80 or above	At this level, the person is most likely passive and also interested in aesthetics.

Relation to Research scales

Dy scale and **St** scale—if the 5 scale is elevated above 60 T-score points, the relative heights of the **Dy** and **St** scales above 50 T-score points can indicate how much passivity (**Dy**) and/or aesthetic-achievement interests (**St**) are present.

---

*Where T-scores are listed in two categories (i.e., 45 or below and 45 through 55) and a score is obtained that is listed for two categories, use whichever interpretation seems to be most appropriate for the individual.

SUMMARY OF 5 SCALE INTERPRETATIONS
FOR FEMALES;*

T-score	Interpretations
35 or below	A woman scoring in this range may appear to be coy, seductive, and helpless (the southern belle syndrome). In this case the **Dy** scale will be above 50 T-score points. The behavior may be a manipulative device, or the woman may be truly helpless.
35 thru 50	The majority of women score in this range. A woman with a **5** scale in this range usually is interested in traditional feminine and domestic activities. However, she can also be interested in a career that is feminine in nature (teaching, being in a helping profession).
50 or above	A woman scoring in this range may see herself as being unique and not like a typical woman.

Relation to Research scales

Dy scale and **St** scale—if the **5** scale is below 45 T-score points, the relative heights of the **Dy** and **St** scales above 50 T-score points can indicate how much passivity (**Dy**) and/or aesthetic-achievement interests (**St**) are present.

*Where T-scores are listed in two categories (i.e., 35 or below and 35 through 50) and a score is obtained that is listed for two categories, use whichever interpretation seems to be most appropriate for the individual.

SCALE 6
(Pa, Paranoia Scale)

Scale **6** measures three things. First, at the lower elevations (60 through 70), the scale usually shows interpersonal sensitivity, usually of the kind "What are you thinking and feeling, and how can that affect me?" Second, when the **6** scale gets above 70, suspiciousness is usually added to the sensitivity. The motives of others are assumed to be malevolent, and therefore the client feels a need to watch out for others and what they can and will do to him/her. Very rarely is this scale elevated above 70 without the sensitivity and/or suspiciousness being seen. Thus, these people typically are difficult persons with whom to work, because the suspiciousness and sensitivity towards others can include the therapist. We have had this suspiciousness and sensitivity take the form of questioning our credentials, checking whether the client will be fairly treated, and doubting the good intentions of others. In transational analysis terms, this person exemplifies the "I'm O.K., you're not O.K." stance. If the suspiciousness is widespread the **Pr** scale will be above 50 T-score points. If the suspiciousness is confined to one or two people, usually someone close, the **Pr** scale will be below 50 T-score points.

The third element in scale **6** is much like a subtle spice and flavors the whole scale. This pervasive element is self-righteousness. A person with an elevation on this scale tends to have the feeling "I've done all this for you, and now look what you have done to me in return." Occasionally this statement actually is expressed, but more commonly this attitude is implied strongly.

Kunce and Anderson (1976, 1984) posit an underlying dimension for this scale which they call inquiring. When other factors suggest good adjustment for an individual, this scale indicates an inquisitive and investigative orientation. The individual is likely to be curious, questioning, perceptive, and discriminatory. Hovey and Lewis (1967) have found the positive characteristics connected with individuals with moderate elevations on the **6** scale to be that they are sensitive, kind, poised, and show clear thinking and initiative. These individuals are inclined to be progressive and have broad interests. When the individual is under stress, these positive characteristics become suspiciousness, hypersensitivity, and distorted perceptions.

6

This scale is rarely elevated by itself; usually other scales also are elevated. In addition, this scale rarely is the highest peak on our profiles but most likely the second or third highest point. The person may come for therapy because of some situational stress. Once this stress is alleviated successfully, the person typically will leave counseling with the paranoid behavior gone.

Scale 6 rarely goes below 40, but when it does two interpretations are possible. The first is that the person really is a high 6, sensitive and suspicious. Because the scale has somewhat obvious items, he/she has avoided marking these items in the scored direction; and instead has answered them in the typical way to such an extent that he/she has over-compensated and is unusually low on this scale. These people are fairly easy to spot in therapy because the sensitivity/suspiciousness is not always easy to hide in this kind of intimate relationship.

The second interpretation for a low 6 scale is that the person is answering honestly. He/she tends to be a gullible type of person who is taken in occasionally by some others, because he/she is not sensitive enough to perceive what others really are like.

GENERAL INFORMATION

1. The 40 items of scale 6 reflect suspiciousness, interpersonal sensitivity, and self-righteousness.

2. Harris and Lingoes (1955) have divided the 6 scale into 3 subscales: ideas of external influence, poignancy, and moral virtue.

3. This scale is made up of obvious items. Thus, the paranoid person, who is typically interpersonally sensitive and suspicious, can mark the answers so as to show only what he/she wants you to see on this scale.

   Therefore a suspicious person can score low on scale 6. In this instance, the person is too cautious, avoids obvious material, and overcompensates beyond normal limits.

4. This scale rarely produces false positives. People with elevations are suspicious and sensitive and readily show these characteristics (Carson, 1972).

5. Caldwell (1985) has hypothesized that people with this scale as one of their highest have a fear of attack. When the scale is quite elevated, a fear of physical attack is present. At lower elevations, the fear is of moral attack or judgment. This fear is frequently based upon a conditioning experience of having the person's integrity violated.

6. Trimboli and Kilgore (1983) have found that this is a character scale with the person typically using projection and externalization as defense mechanisms.

7. Hovanitz et al. (1983) have found that both the subtle and obvious items (Weiner, 1948) on this scale predict various criteria. Their study found correlations between obvious items and ideas of persecution and between subtle items and naivete. Therefore both the subtle and obvious items of this scale are useful.

8. Schenkenberg et al. (1984) have found that younger psychiatric patients score higher on this scale than older psychiatric patients.

9. Hibbs et al. (1979) also have found the **6** scale to be higher for younger people.

   They also have found that Mexican American women score higher than Mexican American men and white men and women on this scale. They suggest that this may be a cultural effect.

10. In a study of a normal population, the men's mean score was 55 and the women's 56 (Colligan et al., 1984).

11. This scale is more elevated in profiles of wives in marriage counseling than in profiles of wives from the general population (Arnold, 1970; Ollendick et al., 1983).

12. Test-retest reliabilities are fair (Carkhuff et al., 1965). Scale **6** is sensitive to changes in suspiciousness.

HIGH SCORES

Moderate Elevations (T = 60 through 70)

1. This elevation tends to characterize sensitive people (Carkhuff et al., 1965).

2. Kunce and Anderson (1976) have hypothesized that when this scale is in the moderate range (and there are no other Clinical scales above 70 T-score points except the 5 scale for men), it may measure inquisitiveness and investigative behavior.

3. College women clients with an elevation in this range tend to be sensitive specifically to physical defects in themselves (Loper, 1976).

Marked Elevations (T = 70 or Above)

The behaviors mentioned for this elevation are most clearly seen when the scale is one of the highest of the clinical scales.

1. This elevation tends to characterize suspicious people.

   a. They feel that what is said or done around them is aimed specifically at them.

   b. They often interpret criticism of their ideas as criticism of themselves. This may be seen even when the T-score is as low as 55.

   c. They usually feel that they are not getting what they deserve (Carson, 1969).

2. A person with a 6 scale score of 70 or above usually is more verbal about suspiciousness and feelings of injustice than someone with a moderate elevation on this scale.

3. People with elevations on this scale tend to have an anger that is focused on specific people (Tromboli & Kilgore, 1983).

4. The most minor rejection is remembered.

5. This elevation tends to characterize people who make mistakes costly to others (Carson, 1969). This seems to be an unconscious passive-aggressive way of coping with perceived injustice.

6. Trimboli and Kilgore (1983) have found that people with elevations on this scale tend to use the defense mechanisms of projection and externalization.

7. A relationship is difficult to establish in therapy with these people because their marked suspiciousness and sensitivity includes the therapist as well as others.

   This suspiciousness towards the therapist tends to be along the dimensions of age or sex. "No young whippersnapper (the therapist) can help me." "I cannot trust a man only a woman (therapist)."

8. In treatment, high scorers tend to be argumentative and rigid (Carson, 1969).

9. VA hospital males with this scale as a high point tend to have long standing resentment towards relatives. They are supersensitive to the opinions of others and are touchy and prone to blame others for their difficulties (Hovey & Lewis, 1967).

LOW SCORES
(T = 45 or Below)

1. A score of 45 or below on scale **6** may indicate a lack of personal sensitivity to others (Drake & Oetting, 1959).

2. Low scores on this scale also characterize people who are cheerful, conventional, and trusting.

3. A suspicious person can score low on scale **6.** In this instance, the person is too cautious, avoids the obvious paranoid questions, and over-compensates beyond normal limits.

   The person resists revealing self in any way, because he/she feels a calamity will follow such a revelation (Carson, 1969).

4. If this scale is below 45 and no other scale is below 45, the person may be really a high **6.** They also may have a little elevation on the **L** scale.

5. These scores characterize college students who have problems related to underachievement or non-achievement. The necessity to deny hostility may drain off excess energy, thus reducing the student's effectiveness (Anderson, 1956; Morgan, 1952).

   In addition, difficulty with parents often exists. This difficulty may be related to repressed or denied hostility.

COMBINATIONS

All scales in the combinations are at a T-score of 70 or above and are listed in order from the highest to the lowest peaks. These scales in the combinations must be the highest Clinical scales on the profile.

1-6 See p. 92.

4-6 See pp. 150-152.

4-6-2 See the **6-4-2** pattern.

4-6-5̄ See p. 152.

4-6-8 See p. 152.

4-6-9 See p. 153.

4-9-6 See p. 159.

5-6 See p. 172.

6-2 See the **2-6** combination, p. 105.

6-3 See the **3-6** combination, p. 129.

1. When the **6** scale is higher than the **3,** a hostile egocentric person who is struggling for power and prestige is likely. He/she tends not to recognize the hostility (Lachar, 1974).

6-4 See also the **4-6** combination, pp. 150-152.

1. Marks et al. (1974) found the **4-6/6-4** pattern in a university hospital and outpatient clinic. It was primarily a female pattern. These females were described as self-centered, hostile, tense, defensive, and irritable. They usually handled their difficulties by refusing to admit them, and frequently they used rationalization as a primary defense mechanism. The Marks, Seeman, and Haller book should be consulted for further information concerning this profile.

6-4-2

1. Marks et al. (1974) found the **4-6-2/6-4-2** pattern in a university hospital and outpatient clinic. It was primarily a female pattern. A woman with this pattern tended to be acting out, depressed, critical, and skeptical. The Marks, Seeman, and Haller book should be consulted for further information concerning this profile.

6-7

1. When **6** is elevated above the **7** scale, the person is attempting to change his/her perception of the world through the use of projection (Trimboli & Kilgore, 1983).

2. Counselors rated college men with this pattern plus no elevation of scale **5** as non-responsive and had difficulty relating to them. These clients also had problems at home and were confused and worried. College women were restless and had conflicts with their siblings (Drake & Oetting, 1959).

3. Kelley and King (1979a) found the **6-7/7-6** code type primarily for women clients in one college counseling center. Although they tended to have genito-urinary problems, crying spells, feelings of inferiority, and were described as rigid, they did not have any consistent diagnosis or pattern of pathology.

6-7-8

1. This pattern may indicate a poor prognosis for vocational success (Harmon & Weiner, 1945).

6-7-8-9

1. This pattern may suggest behavioral difficulties, especially among college freshmen women (Osborne, Sander, & Young, 1956).

   These women tend to approach problems with animation, are sensitive, and feel that they are unduly controlled, limited, and mistreated.

6-8 See also the **8-6** combination, p. 209.

1. These people could have marginal psychological adjustment (Hovey & Lewis, 1967).

2. These people tend to have intense feelings of inferiority and insecurity. They are suspicious and distrustful of others and avoid deep emotional ties (Graham, 1977).

3. Relationships with others tend to be unstable and characterized by resentment (Dahlstrom & Welsh, 1960).

4. They may present a wide variety of complaints which shift from one time to the next (Dahlstrom & Welsh, 1960).

5. They tend to be drawn towards fads and quacks (Dahlstrom et al., 1972).

6. If these people can get verbally angry with the therapist, they tend to get better rapidly (Caldwell, 1974).

7. One study (Lewandowski & Graham, 1972) has found that patients with the **6-8** pattern have spent more time in a neuropsychiatric hospital than other patients. They tended to be unfriendly with others; to have less social interests; to be more emotionally withdrawn, conceptually disorganized, and suspicious; and to have more hallucinatory behavior and unusual thought content.

8. Another study reported in two references (Altman, Gynther, Warbin, & Sletten, 1972; Gynther et al., 1973) has found patients in a mental hospital with this **6-8/8-6** pattern often seem unfriendly and angry for no apparent reason. They also have thought disorders,

hallucinations, delusions, hostility, and lack of insight. Poor judgment was typical. Of those patients labeled psychotic, schizophrenia was the most frequent diagnosis, especially paranoid schizophrenia. For the **6-8** profile, the delusions are apt to be delusions of grandeur. For the **8-6** profile, the affect is apt to be blunted.

9. Marks et al. (1974) found the **8-6/6-8** pattern in a university hospital and outpatient clinic. They found this pattern primarily for females who were having unconventional, delusional thoughts. These women were also suspicious. The Marks, Seeman, and Haller book should be consulted for further information concerning this profile.

10. Black psychiatric patients show this configuration significantly more than white psychiatric patients matched on age, sex, hospital status, socioeconomic status, and duration of illness (Costello & Tiffany, 1972).

11. VA hospital males with this pattern tended to be ruminative and thinking in unusual ways. They may have had paranoid thinking verging on the delusional. They had precarious psychological and emotional adjustment and tended to be pre-psychotic (Hovey & Lewis, 1967).

12. Adolescents in treatment with the **6-8/8-6** pattern (Marks et al., 1974) were referred because of bizarre behavior. They had violent tempers and tended to be below average intellectually. They frequently used drugs. The Marks, Seeman, and Haller book should be consulted for further information concerning this profile.

13. For college students with this pattern, men tended to be indecisive, unhappy, and confused; women were restless, depressed, and had conflicts with parents and siblings. They also lacked skills with the opposite sex (Drake & Oetting, 1959).

6-8-9

1. This pattern may indicate a poor prognosis for vocational success (Harmon & Wiener, 1945).

2. It typifies male Blacks from a rural, isolated background (Gynther et al., 1971).

6-9

⟶
1. This is not a common profile pattern; however when present, it may indicate paranoid grandiosity (Lachar, 1974).

2. These people tend to be angry, rational, and insistent about why they do things. They tend to give much moral justification for whatever they do (Caldwell, 1972).

3. They have difficulty with criticism, therefore they use projection frequently as a defense mechanism (Caldwell, 1972).

4. They are vulnerable to threat and feel anxious and tense much of the time. They may alternate between overcontrol and emotional outbursts (Graham, 1977).

5. VA hospitalized men with this pattern tended to be tense and overreact to possible danger. They seemed to be unable to express their emotions in an adaptive way (Hovey & Lewis, 1967).

6. Marks et al. (1974) found the **9-6/6-9** pattern in a university hospital and outpatient clinic. It was found primarily for females who were agitated, tense, excitable, suspiciousness, and hostile. The Marks, Seeman, and Haller book should be consulted for further information concerning this profile.

7. In another study reported in two references, Gynther et al. (1973d) and Gynther (1973) found patients with this code type **6-9/9-6** to be excited, hostile, loud, and grandiose, with little likelihood of having depressive symptoms.

8. For college students with this pattern, men tended to be aggressive or belligerent, especially if the **0** scale was low. Women were restless (Drake & Oetting, 1967).

6-0

1. Women counselees with this pattern have feelings of inferiority in regard to some physical feature and shyness (Drake & Oetting, 1959).

2. Individuals with these elevations tend to be quite paranoid and may be psychotic, although they do not show the fragmentation of thought processes typically seen with schizophrenia (Trimboli & Kilgore, 1983).

8-6 See p. 209.

8-6-4-9-F See p. 211.

8-6-7-F See p. 211.

8-6-7-2 See the **8-6** combination, point 6, p. 210.

8-7-6 See p. 212.

8-9-6-F See p. 214.

SUMMARY OF 6 SCALE INTERPRETATIONS*

T-score	Interpretations
45 or below	A person may score in this range for two reasons. First, the person may be gullible and taken in by other people because he/she is not suspicious enough of other people. Second, the person may have a low score on this scale because he/she is really very sensitive and suspicious but has been able to guess which questions would reveal this and has answered them in the opposite way, thus showing low on the scale. This latter interpretation is likely if this is the only Clinical scale below 40.
45 thru 60	The majority of people score in this range.
60 thru 70	People who score in this range tend to be interpersonally sensitive to what others think of them.
70 or above	In addition to the sensitivity observed at the 60 thru 70 level, suspiciousness is usually present when this scale goes above 70. The client may assume that other people are after him/her. Righteous indignation also is usually present.

Relationship to Research Scales

When the **6** scale is above 70, the **Pr** scale indicates how widespread the suspiciousness is. When **Pr** is 50 or below, the suspiciousness may only be directed towards one person. When the **Pr** is more elevated an entire group of individuals may be included.

---

*Where T-scores are listed in two categories (i.e., 45 or below and 45 through 60) and a score is obtained that is listed for two categories, use whichever interpretation seems to be most appropriate for the individual.

SCALE 7

(Pt, Psychasthenia Scale)

Scale **7** measures anxiety, usually of a long-term nature. The scale may be elevated during times of situational stress (state anxiety), but tends to measure situational stress plus a type of living which includes worrying a great deal (trait anxiety). The state anxiety component in the MMPI is most likely measured by scale **A** of the Research scales, while the trait anxiety is most likely measured by scale **7**. For further comments about the relationship between the two scales. See the **A** scale general information section (pp. 240-241).

Scale **7** is one of the most frequent high points on profiles of clients in college counseling centers and mental health clinics. It usually is elevated with scale **2** and/or scale **8**. A special relationship exists between scale **7** and **8**. When they are both elevated special note is to be made as to which scale is the higher. When scale **7** is higher than scale **8**, especially by ten points or more, the person usually has a better prognosis than when scale **8** is higher because the person is still fighting his/her problem and is highly anxious about it. When the **8** scale is higher, mental confusion keeps the person from focusing on solutions to his/her problems, and therefore therapy usually is not as productive as it is when scale **7** is higher than scale **8**.

At the lower elevations of scale **7** (T = 60 through 70 and no other Clinical scales are elevated above 70 T-score points except perhaps the **5** scale for men), a person generally is punctual in meeting important assignments and deadlines and does not feel anxious. However, when a fear (actual or imagined) exists of not meeting an obligation, an anxious agitation emerges until the obligation is fulfilled. People with scale **7** at this level usually feel they cannot put off until tomorrow what they should do today without some dire consequences happening. As a result of their compulsivity, these people tend to make higher grades and faster promotions than others do. Of additional interest is the fact that people with an elevation of 60 through 70 on the **7** scale tend to be great intellectualizers.

Under the pressure of over-obligation, where deadlines or tasks cannot be met, scale **7** may begin to elevate for people who originally scored in the lower elevations of scale **7**. When T = 70, the anxiety usually is evident to others but not necessarily to the person. A fear of failure or of making the wrong decisions may appear also.

As the elevation of scale 7 increases, particularly beyond a T of 80, an element of omnipotence begins to emerge in that the person tends to adopt the attitude that he/she must not fail for fear of hurting others. Also, as this elevation increases, anxiety causes a loss of productivity further raising fears of failure and thereby raising more anxiety, *ad infinitum.*

Kunce and Anderson (1976, 1984) posit an underlying dimension of organization for this scale which in the normal individual with moderate elevations is shown as the ability to organize and to be punctual and methodical. Because they are systematic and convergent thinkers these individuals make good managers and mechanics. Other occupations with moderately high scale 7 scores are chemists, carpenters, math science teachers, and bankers (Kunce & Callis, 1969). For people with 7 scale elevations, stress produces such maladaptive behavior as worry, indecision, and obsession with minutia.

Persons with a low scale 7 (T = 45 or below) generally are secure with themselves and quite stable. These people are reported to be persistent and success-oriented by other authors. However, our experience has been that they do not appear to take deadlines and work obligations as seriously as others because they are less anxious about them; and therefore, these persons may give the impresssion of not caring about what others want to have done. This attitude may make employers uneasy. We hypothesize that some people with low 7 scale scores were at one time in the 70 or above T-score range, but the anxiety was so bothersome that they decided to become nonworriers and over compensated into the low range of the scale.

GENERAL INFORMATION

1. Scale 7 consists of 48 items having to do with anxiety and dread, low self-confidence, undue sensitivity, and moodiness (Carson, 1969; Dahlstrom et al., 1972).

2. This scale shows general characterological anxiety. Variations in the anxiety depend upon what other scale is elevated along with 7.

7   190

a. For example, when scale **2** is elevated with scale **7,** depression and indecisiveness are associated with the worries and anxieties.

b. When scale **8** is the second member of the high pair, confusion and disorganized thinking appear with the anxiety.

3. Elevations on this scale may indicate magical thinking, rumination, and ritualistic behaviors (Tromboli & Kilgore, 1983).

4. Caldwell (1985) has hypothesized this scale, when it is one of the person's highest, may reflect a fear of the unexpected, the unpredictable and therefore these people do not like newness. As children they tended to be teased unmercifully and unpredictably by their siblings which led to their fears.

5. Scale **7** may be indicating high level intellectualizing as a defense rather than compulsivity (Caldwell, 1972).

6. Schenkenberg et al. (1984) have found that younger psychiatric patients score higher on this scale than older psychiatric patients.

7. Scales **7** and **8** are highly correlated (+ .78), but diagnosis and prognosis depend upon their relative heights.

a. When scale **7** is higher than scale **8,** regardless of the height of scale **8,** the person is still trying to fight his/her problem and is using defenses somewhat effectively (Carson, 1969).

b. When both scales are elevated above 75 and scale **8** is higher, the problem is likely to be more severe because the person is so confused.

8. Test-retest reliabilities are high, indicating that this scale does not fluctuate drastically over time (Dahlstrom & Welsh, 1960).

HIGH SCORES

Moderate Elevations (T = 60 through 70)

1. Kunce and Anderson (1976) have hypothesized that when this scale is in the moderate range (and there are no other Clinical scales above 70 T-score points except perhaps the 5 scale for men), scale 7 may measure the ability to organize and to be punctual, decisive, and methodical.

Marked Elevations (T = 70 or Above)

The behaviors mentioned for this elevation are most clearly seen when the scale is the highest of the clinical scales.

1. Single peaks on scale 7 are not particularly frequent; elevations for this scale tend to occur with elevations on other scales (Dahlstrom et al., 1972).

2. People with an elevation in this range on the 7 scale tend to be worried, tense, indecisive, and unable to concentrate (Carson, 1969).

3. They tend to have a low threshold for anxiety and characteristically over-react with anxiety to new situations.

4. They tend not to change much. The basic personality pattern is difficult to change, but insight and relief from general stress may lead to improved adjustment (Hathaway & McKinley, 1951). Our experience has been that even with counseling the elevation usually remains in the 60 through 70 range.

5. Individuals having marked elevations on this scale almost always exhibit extreme obsessionalism. That is, they go over the same thoughts again and again.

   However, some compulsive people have no elevation on this scale, presumably because their compulsivity is working for them and wards off any feelings of insecurity and concern about their own worth (Carson, 1969).

6. The following groups tend to score high on this scale:

   a. male mental health clients, and

   b. college students who later receive personal adjustment counseling (Cooke & Kiester, 1967).

7   192

7. VA hospital males with an elevation on this scale tend to be obsessive-compulsive and over-react to problems. They have a low threshold for anxiety (Hovey & Lewis, 1967).

8. College counselees with this elevation tend to be characterized by obsessive-compulsive ruminations and introspection (Dahlstrom et al., 1972; Mello & Guthrie, 1958).

   a. The problems with which these students are concerned are usually poor study habits and poor interpersonal relationships.

   b. These counselees tend to remain in therapy over an extended period of time.

   c. They tend to become more dependent upon the therapist the longer they see him/her, particularly when they are starting to make changes.

   d. They tend to improve slowly.

LOW SCORES
(T = 45 or Below)

1. This person tends to be non-anxious, comfortable, and stable (Carson, 1972).

2. He/she may seem to be lazy or non-motivated because he/she does not respond to situations with the usual amount of anxiety.

3. In some cases, a person with a low 7 scale score may once have been a worrier (7 greater than 70 T-score points) but decided this style of life was too painful and so became even less anxious than people in general.

COMBINATIONS

All scales in the combinations are at a T-score of 70 or above and are listed in order from the highest to the lowest peaks. The scales in the combinations must be the highest Clinical scales on the profile.

1-2-3-7 See p. 87.

1-3-7 See p. 90.

2-1-3-7 See the 2-3-1-(7) combination, p. 102.

2-3-1-7 See p. 102.

2-4-7 See p. 105.

2-7-3 See p. 108.

2-7-3-1 See pp. 108.

2-7-4 See pp. 108.

2-7-4-3 See the 2-7-4 pattern, point 2, p. 109.

2-7-4-5̄ See pp. 109.

2-7-5-4 See p. 110.

2-7-8 See p. 110.

2-7-8-0 See p. 111.

2-8-7 See p. 113.

4-5-7-9 See p. 150.

4-7-2 See p. 153.

5-7 See p. 172.

6-7-8 See p. 183.

7

194

6-7-8-9 See p. 184.

7-1 See the **1-7** combination, p. 92.

7-2 See also the **2-7** combination, p. 106.

1. With the **7-2** profile less depression but more anxiety and agitation is present than with the **2-7** profile (Guthrie, 1949).

7-3 See the **3-7** combination, p. 130.

7-4 See the **4-7** combination, p. 153.

7-6 See the **6-7** combination, p. 183.

7-8 See also the **8-7** combination, p. 211.

1. People with the **7-8** combination tend to be introverted with worry, irritability, nervousness, and apathy present.

2. These people are in a great deal of turmoil and are not hesitant to admit to problems. They have feelings of insecurity, inadequacy, and inferiority; and they tend to be indecisive. They may feel inadequate in the traditional sex role (Graham, 1977).

3. If scale **7** is 10 T-score points higher than scale **8,** the tendency is to see anxiety and indecisiveness as the predominant features. If scale **8** is higher than scale **7,** the tendency is to see mental confusion as the predominant feature.

4. Long-term counseling is usually necessary.

5. Gynther et al. (1973) have found that psychiatric inpatients with this pattern, **7-8/8-7,** may have bizarre speech. Depersonalization also is present at times.

6. Gilberstadt and Duker (1965) have found this **7-8-(2-1-3-4)** pattern in a VA hospital male population. Scales **1, 2, 3,** and **4** are elevated above 70 but are not necessarily the next highest scales after **7** and **8.** A man with this profile tended to be shy, fearful, feel inadequate, and have difficulty concentrating. The Gilberstadt and Duker book should be consulted for further information concerning this profile.

7. Adolescents in treatment with the **7-8/8-7** pattern (Marks et al., 1974) were worriers. They were shy, anxious, and inhibited. Many had deviant thoughts and behavior. The **7** scale does not seem to suppress the **8** scale behaviors as it does for adults. The Marks, Seeman, and Haller book should be consulted for further information concerning this pattern.

8. VA hospital males are excessively introspective, socially maladjusted, and have chronic feelings of anxiety (Hovey & Lewis, 1967).

9. For college clients with this profile, men tended to be introverted, self-conscious, or socially insecure. They were tense, indecisive, and confused. They also had conflicts with their mothers and siblings. Women clients lacked self-confidence, were indecisive and socially insecure. They also were exhausted and nervous (Drake & Oetting, 1959).

10. Kelley and King (1980) have found with the **7-8/8-7** profile in a college client population that males have delusions, flat affect, and an extensive family history of schizophrenia and alcoholism. They were more disturbed than the **7-8-2/8-7-2** males. (See the **7-8-2** combination, below.)

    Females, although diagnosed as schizophrenic-latent type as were the males, lacked the overt psychotic features the males showed. In addition to having flat affect and disrupted thought processes, they abused drugs.

7-8-2

1. Kelley and King (1980) found the **7-8-2/8-7-2** profile group in a college client population had different descriptors depending upon the sex of the client. Males in this group had many features in common with **7-8/8-7** males. Both code types had depression, interpersonal problems, and at least one physical complaint. They also had disrupted thought processes, ideas of reference, suicidal ideations, and obsessions. They were typically diagnosed as schizophrenic-latent type. The **7-8-2/8-7-2** males in addition had social withdrawal.

    Females were less disturbed than the males. They only had interpersonal problems and suicidal ideation. Their most likely diagnosis was adjustment reaction.

7-9

1. A person with a **7-9** combination tends to present many uncon-
nected thoughts and talks compulsively about them.

2. These people may alternate between grandiosity and self-
condemnation (Hovey & Lewis, 1967).

3. Adolescents in treatment with the **7-9/9-7** pattern (Marks et al.,
1974) were seen as worrying and vulnerable to threat—real or imagined. They were basically insecure and had strong needs for attention. At the same time, they were conflicted over emotional
dependency. The Marks, Seeman, and Haller book should be consulted for further information concerning this pattern.

4. Kelley and King (1979a) found the **7-9/9-7** code type primarily for
men in their college counseling center population. Males with this
code type had lost weight, were tense, nervous, and suspicious.
Their judgment was poor and their thoughts disrupted. They were
typically diagnosed as schizophrenic.

7-0

1. Although this pattern is uncommon, when it is present, the person
has a serious generalized social inadequacy (Lachar, 1974).

2. Adolescents in treatment with the **7-0/0-7** pattern (Marks et al.,
1974) were typically referred because of shyness and extreme
sensitivity. They tended to blame themselves excessively and were
over-controlled. The Marks, Seeman, and Haller book should be
consulted for further information concerning this pattern.

3. Social problems are found in college students with the **7** and **0** scales
as the two highest points in a profile (Drake & Oetting, 1959).

   a. These students tend to be non-verbal and lack confidence
   and social skills.

   b. College counselors rate these clients as "shy."

   c. They also are tense, confused, worry a great deal, and suffer
   from insomnia.

8-2-4-7 See the **8-2-4** combination, point 2, p. 209.

8-6-7-F See p. 211.

8-6-7-2 See the **8-6** combination, point 6, p. 210.

8-7-2 See p. 212.

SUMMARY OF 7 SCALE INTERPRETATIONS*

T-score	Interpretations
45 or below	These people are non-worriers and may be secure with themselves and quite stable emotionally. They may appear to be somewhat lazy and non-task oriented.
45 thru 60	The majority of people score in this range.
60 thru 70	If no Clinical scales are above 70 T-score points, except perhaps scale 5 for men, people in this range generally are punctual in fulfilling obligations or worry if they are not punctual. This is especially true if the A scale is below 50. They usually prefer to get things done ahead of time. They tend to be seen as conscientious workers. They usually do not see themselves as anxious.
70 or above	At this level, some agitation may develop. The person tends to become more overtly anxious and fidgety. A fear of failure may become prominent. As this scale elevates, the person may become less productive because of his/her worrying.

*Where T-scores are listed in two categories (i.e., 45 or below and 45 through 60) and a score is obtained that is listed for two categories, use whichever interpretation seems to be most appropriate for the individual.

—NOTES—

SCALE 8

(Sc, Schizophrenia Scale)

Scale **8** measures mental confusion; the higher the elevation, the more confused the person is. At the lower elevations (60 through 70), scale **8** may mean different thinking of one kind or another, especially in college counseling clients. We have found avant-garde or highly creative people sometimes scoring in this range. They tend to think differently than people usually do, and thus they have a moderately elevated **8** scale; however, they do not think so differently that they are out of touch with people.

When scale **8** is between 70 and 80, usually difficulties appear in the client's logic so that it does not hold together well over a period of time. The counselor may find that the client seemingly makes sense for short periods of time during the counseling session but does not when the total session is analyzed.

With a T above 80, the client may start using terms in an idiosyncratic manner. The person can deteriorate to a point where the meaning of words is not the same for him/her as for the rest of the world. This results in much confused communication between the client and other persons. Besides confused communication, this scale also may reflect confusion in perceiving people and situations. As a consequence, the person with a scale **8** elevated above a T of 80 usually has poor judgment and may get into difficulty because of it.

Elevations on the **8** scale may be the result of a chronic disorientation or a temporary disorientation. The prognosis obviously is better when the elevation is because of a temporary disorientation, usually the result of situational pressures. Since the person has not been confused in the past, usually with some therapy and a lessening of the stress, the person returns to a non-confused state. On the other hand, chronic disorientation is much harder to change. The person who has had it for a long period of time must learn an entirely new way of thinking in order to get rid of the confusion.

Elevations on scale **8** above 90 usually are due to situational stress rather than chronic disorientation. We have found that people with identity crises ("Who am I, what am I?") frequently score in this range. We also have found that warm, supportive, somewhat directive counseling is the best approach to use until the confusion ends. The client usually cannot take nondirective counseling very well because it is too ambiguous. As a matter of fact, for most clients with scale 8 elevations above 80, we have found the more directive and less ambiguous types of therapy to be the most helpful. They provide some direction out of the confusion the person is experiencing.

Kunce and Anderson (1976, 1984) posit imagination as the underlying dimension on scale 8. Thus, when people are functioning well, moderate elevations suggest an individual who is spontaneous, advantgarde, and creative. These individuals are good at imagining what could be. Thoughts and feelings from the preconscious which would frighten others can be molded by these individuals into novel, usable forms. Researchers working with creative persons have found that they earn elevated scores on this scale, for example, architects, (MacKinnon, 1962) and writers (Barron, 1969). High ego strength seems to be required if scale 8 characteristics are to work in a positive direction. Stress can turn these positive traits into idiosyncratic and bizarre behavior.

Persons with low scale 8 scores (45 or below) tend to see themselves as pragmatic realists with little interest in contemplation, theory, and/or philosophy. These people may have difficulty letting their minds imagine possibilities. They also tend to have difficulty with persons who are unable to perceive life as they do. They tend to like a lot of structure in their lives.

When this scale is elevated with scale 0 (social introversion), the problems with the confusion shown in the 8 scale elevation tend to become greater because of the person's isolation from others. These two scales frequently are elevated together, because the confusion the person is feeling tends to foster withdrawal from others, which increases the confusion because of a lack of contact with others, which leads to more isolation, and so forth.

GENERAL INFORMATION

1. Scale 8 consists of 78 items dealing with social alienation, peculiar perceptions, complaints of family alienation, and difficulties in concentration and impulse control (Carson, 1969; Dahlstrom et al., 1972).

2. This scale indicates a person's distortion of the world. He/she perceives things differently from others, and often reacts to things in unusual ways.

3. Harris and Lingoes (1955) have subjectively developed three subscales for the **8** scale, two of which are divided into additional scales. These subscales are social alienation, emotional alienation; lack of ego mastery-cognitive, lack of ego mastery-conative, lack of ego mastery-defect of inhibition and control; and sensory motor dissociation.

4. The higher the score is on the **8** scale, the more shared verbal symbolism is lost and the odder and more disorganized thinking becomes.

   A low **0** scale appears to have some controlling effect on this disorganized thinking.

5. This scale is related to self-identity. The higher the scale, the more the person may be having difficulty in this area (Lachar, 1974).

6. Caldwell (1985) has hypothesized that this scale, when it is one of the highest for people, is based upon a childhood conditioning experience of hostility that was inescapable and unrelenting.

7. The score may be elevated by anxiety, homosexual panic, identity crisis, or sudden personal dislocation such as divorce or culture shock.

8. Schenkenberg et al. (1984) have found that younger psychiatric patients score higher on this scale than older psychiatric patients.

9. Blacks tend to have the **8** scale elevated (Costello & Tiffany, 1972; Gynther et al., 1971).

   In a prison population, Blacks tend to score higher than whites on this scale (as well as scales **F** and **9**) (Holland, 1979).

10. Test-retest reliabilities are high. This scale tends to remain stable over time, except when people receive psychological help or when the elevations are due to situations identified in point 7 (Dahlstrom & Welsh, 1960).

11. Scales **7** and **8** are highly correlated (+ .78) (Lough & Green, 1950), but diagnosis and prognosis depend upon their relative heights.

    a. When scale **7** is higher than scale **8** regardless of the height of scale **8,** the person is still trying to fight his/her problems and is using defenses somewhat effectively (Carson, 1969).

    b. When both scales are elevated above 75 and scale **8** is higher, the problem is likely to be more severe because the person is not fighting the problem as much as when the **7** scale is higher (Carson, 1969).

HIGH SCORES

Moderate Elevations (T = 60 through 70)

1. Kunce and Anderson (1976) have hypothesized that when this scale is in the moderate range (and there are no other Clinical scales above 70 T-score points except perhaps the **5** scale for men), it may measure the ability to think divergently and act creatively.

2. Some college students with this elevation may be highly creative or avant-garde.

3. This elevation may characterize relatively well adjusted college males who have internal conflicts and are at odds with themselves (Gough et al., 1955).

4. Academic nonachievers are significantly higher than academic achievers on this scale.

5. Students on probation tend to get elevations on scale **8** (Carkhuff et al., 1965).

Marked Elevations (T = 70 or Above)

The behaviors mentioned for this elevation are most clearly seen when the scale is the highest of the Clinical scales on a profile.

1. People with a T-score above 70 on the **8** scale tend to feel alienated and remote from their general social environment (Carson, 1969).

2. They may have questions about their identity (Carson, 1969).

3. In the lower part of this range, people may appear to be in contact with reality, but others usually have difficulty following their logic (Carson, 1969).

4. They may feel they are lacking something which is fundamental to relating successfully to others (Carson, 1969).

5. Adolescents frequently score in this 70 or above range. If they are intelligent, the high **8** score may indicate creative thinking. If they have low intelligence, the high **8** score may indicate poor school performance (Good & Brantner, 1974).

6. These elevations may indicate people who are confused, vague in goals, lacking in knowledge or information, and/or lacking in academic motivation.

7. Patients who are clinically diagnosed as schizophrenic usually get T-scores in the 80 through 90 range (Carson, 1969). Above this T-score range, people do not seem to be psychotic, but rather severely neurotic or under acute stress.

8. One study (Glosz & Grant, 1981) has found that the lower the **8** scale is within the elevated range, the shorter the stay in a psychiatric hospital. Also the higher the **2** scale elevation, the shorter the stay in the hospital.

9. Chronicity of the patient's problems who were in therapy in a counseling center was predicted by combining T-scores for scales **8** + **9** + **R** + **Dy** + **Do** - **3** - **Es** - **Cn** (Anderson & Kunce, 1984). For patients with index scores above 157, 60% had bizarre ideation. For those with index scores between 136 and 150, only 10% had bizarre ideation.

10. Newmark and Hutchins (1980) have found that for young schizophrenic patients (below 39) 72% of them could be diagnosed by the following formula: (Scale **8** greater than 80 but less than 100; total raw score scale **8** no more than 35% **K** items, **F** scale greater

than 75 but less than 95, **7** scale is less than **8** scale.) For older patients this formula was not predictive.

11. VA hospital males with this scale as a high point have trouble being accepted by their peers. They may be somewhat eccentric, and interpersonally isolated. They also may be disoriented and have strange attitudes and beliefs (Hovey & Lewis, 1967).

12. For non-hospitalized patients, elevations on this scale were associated with the following (Anderson & Kunce, 1984):

    a. feeling isolated (73%).

    b. heterosexual relationship difficulties (57%).

    c. stressful home life (53%).

For this non-hospitalized group of patients, the majority did not have severe psychopathology. Instead many times the elevated scores reflected stressful identity or personal crises.

13. College counselees with scale **8** peaks present problems with peer relationships and people's acceptance of them. Sexual preoccupation is frequent along with sexual confusion and bizarre fantasies (Mello & Guthrie, 1958).

    a. They tend to persist in treatment even though their response to treatment is quite variable.

    b. They do not have the psychotic features seen in older people with high **8** scales.

14. For another group of college counselees, males were indecisive, unhappy, and confused. Women were depressed, had conflicts with parents or siblings, and lacked skills with the opposite sex (Drake & Oetting, 1959).

15. High school counselees should be aware that a male high school student with a high **8** scale could be a future dropout even if bright (Hathaway, Reynolds, & Monachesi, 1969).

LOW SCORES
(T = 45 or Below)

1. People with a score of 45 or below on the **8** scale may appear unimaginative, rigid, non-creative, or restrained (Hovey & Lewis, 1967).

COMBINATIONS

All scales in the combinations are at a T-score of 70 or above and are listed in order from the highest to the lowest peaks. The scales in the combinations must be the highest Clinical scales on the profile.

1-3-8 See pp. 90-91.

1-3-8-2 See the **1-3-8** pattern, point 4, p. 91.

2-4-8 See p. 105.

2-4-8-9 See p. 105.

2-7-8 See p. 110.

2-7-8-0 See p. 111.

2-8-1-3 See p. 113.

4-6-8 See p. 152.

4-8-F See p. 155.

4-8-2 See the **8-2-4** combination, p. 208.

4-8-9 See p. 156.

4-8-9-2 See the **4-8-9** combination, point 4, p. 156.

5-8-9 See p. 172.

8

6-7-8 See p. 183.

6-7-8-9 See p. 184.

6-8-9 See p. 185.

7-8-2 See p. 196.

8-F See the **F-8** combination, p. 56.

8-1 See the **1-8** combination, p. 92.

8-1-2-3

1. Gilberstadt and Duker (1965) found the **8-1-2-3-(7-4-6-0)** pattern in a VA hospital male population. Scales **7, 4, 6,** and **0** are elevated above 70, but they are not necessarily the next highest scales after scales **8, 1, 2,** and **3.** A man with this profile typically was inadequate in all areas of his life. He usually had confused thinking and flat affect. The Gilberstadt and Duker book should be consulted for further information concerning this profile.

8-2 See also the **2-8** combination, pp. 111-113, especially point 6.

1. Marks et al. (1974) found this **2-8/8-2** pattern in a university hospital and outpatient clinic. People with this pattern were usually anxious, depressed, and tearful. They tended to keep people at a distance and were afraid of emotional involvement. They tended to fear loss of control and reported periods of dizziness or forgetfulness. The Marks, Seeman, and Haller book should be consulted for further information concerning this profile.

8-2-1-3 See the **2-8-1-3** combination, p. 113.

8-2-4

1. Marks et al. (1974) found this **4-8-2/8-4-2/8-2-4** pattern in a university hospital and outpatient clinic. A person with this profile tended to be distrustful of others, keeping them at a distance. He/she usually was described as depressed, tense, irritable, and hostile. The Marks, Seeman, and Haller book should be consulted for further information concerning this profile.

8   208

2. Gilberstadt and Duker (1965) also found an **8-2-4-(7)** pattern in a VA hospital male population. Scale **7** is elevated, but it is not necessarily the next highest scale after **8, 2,** and **4.** They found that a person with this profile was immature and had confused and hostile thinking. He tended to be irritable, tense, and restless. The Gilberstadt and Duker book should be consulted for further information concerning this pattern.

8-2-4-7 See the **8-2-4** combination, point 2, above.

8-2-7 See the **2-8-7** combination, p. 113.

8-3 See also the **3-8** combination, p. 130.

1. This pattern combines a moderate amount of distress, plus some somatic complaints, especially headaches and insomnia (Lachar, 1974).

2. Marks et al. (1974) found the **8-3/3-8** pattern in a university and out-patient clinic. The pattern usually was for a woman who was having difficulties thinking and concentrating. She usually was seen by others as apathetic, immature, and dependent. The Marks, Seeman, and Haller book should be consulted for further information concerning this profile.

8-4 See also the **4-8** combination, p. 154.

1. These people tend to be high school dropouts (Hathaway et al., 1969).

8-4-2 See the **8-2-4** combination, point 1, p. 208.

8-5

1. The inhibition suggested by the **5** scale and the fragmentation suggested by the **8** scale may lead to an isolated, destructive act by an individual who is typically overcontrolled (Trimboli & Kilgore, 1983).

8-6 See also the **6-8** combination, pp. 184-185.

1. A person with this pattern is usually in a panic and has diffused thinking. The person tends to break down when supports are gone (Caldwell, 1972).

2. Often these people do not marry, but if they do marry, they tend to show poor judgment in mate selection (Caldwell, 1972).

3. Women often have a little girl quality about them and look younger than they really are (Caldwell, 1972).

4. In a psychiatric hospital, this may be the profile of an assaultive person (Caldwell, 1972).

5. Marks et al. (1974) found this **8-6/6-8** pattern in a university hospital and outpatient clinic. They found this pattern primarily for females who were having unconventional, delusional thoughts. These women also were suspicious. The Marks, Seeman, and Haller book should be consulted for further information concerning this profile.

6. Gilberstadt and Duker (1965) found the **8-6-(7-2)** pattern in a VA hospital male population. Scales **7** and **2** are elevated but are not necessarily the next highest scales after scales after **8** and **6**. A man with this pattern tended to have thinking disturbances, such as confusion and poor concentration. He tended to be shy and withdrawn. The Gilberstadt and Duker book should be consulted for further information concerning this profile.

7. Megargee and Bohn (1979) found a group of incarcerated criminals with the **6-8/8-6** profile (Group Charlie). (Others in the groups had an **8-4** profile.)

   These men tended to be antisocial, bitter, hostile, aggressive, and sensitive to perceived insults. They had extensive criminal records and ranked high in substance abuse. However, because they were socially isolated they did not have a number of disciplinary write-ups.

8. Anderson et al. (1979) have found this pattern as one of three profiles in a group of sex offenders. (The other two profiles were **4-9** and **2-4**.) These people often had sex offenses that blatantly degraded the victim. They showed long term socially maladaptive behavior. They tended to act out in self-defeating ways and showed chronic bad judgment. The **F** scale was also elevated for this profile.

9. In one study (Kurlychek & Jordan, 1980) of criminals judged responsible or not responsible for their crimes due to mental illness, those judged not responsible had the **8-6** code as the modal code type (30% of the cases). However, this study had a small number of subjects.

8-6-4-9-F

1. In a Mexican prison, thirty women were found with this profile pattern. All were convicted of homicide, nine of them were self-made widows (Palau, 1972).

8-6-7-F

1. Anderson and Holcomb (1983) found two of their five MMPI code types of murderers to have this configuration.

    a. Murderers with the most elevated **8-6-7-F** code type came from the most disturbed background. They were confused, immature, and perhaps mentally deficient. They tended to have killed strangers.

    b. Murderers with the lower **8-6-7-F** profile were more likely (88%) to be considered to have no mental disorder despite their profile elevation. However, 47% had had previous psychiatric evaluations or treatment. They were most likely on drugs or drinking at the time of their crimes. They also tended to kill strangers. They fit Megargee and Bohn's (1979) Group Charlie.

8-6-7-2 See the **8-6** combination, point 6, p. 210.

8-7 See the **7-8** combination, p. 195.

1. Panic plus withdrawal may be present for a person with the **8-7** pattern (Caldwell, 1972).

2. The **8-7** pattern may indicate long-standing feelings of inadequacy, inferiority, and insecurity (Halbower, 1955). Very frequently the person feels himself/herself to be the inferior member of the family (Caldwell, 1972).

3. These people tend to be passive-dependent. If they are the **Dy** scale will be above 50 T-score points.

4. A clear cut psychosis with great turmoil is likely (Lachar, 1974).

5. Prognosis for therapy is poor, because these people do not form stable, mature, or warm relationships easily. They usually do not integrate what they learn or profit from their own experiences (Halbower, 1955).

6. This profile indicates more serious problems than a **7-8** profile does. There may have been mental hospitalization and/or therapy.

7. With a high **F** scale and an **8-7** pattern, the person may feel unreal (Caldwell, 1972).

8. With a high **0** scale and an **8-7** pattern, social withdrawal may exist (Caldwell, 1972).

9. With a low **0** scale and an **8-7** pattern, inappropriate behavior may exist (Caldwell, 1972).

10. In one study (Kurlychek & Jordan, 1980) of criminals judged responsible or non-responsible for their crimes due to mental illness, those judged responsible for their crimes had the **8-7** code as the modal code type (20% of the cases). However this study had a small number of subjects.

8-7-2

1. Marks et al. (1974) found this **2-7-8/8-7-2** pattern in a university hospital and outpatient clinic. A person with this pattern typically was described as tense, anxious, and depressed with confused thinking and much self-doubt. The Marks, Seeman, and Haller book should be consulted for further information concerning this pattern.

8-7-6

1. This pattern was found in a group of male alcoholics. Also found were the **2-1-3**, **2-4-7**, and **4-9** combinations (Conley, 1981).

8-9 See also the **9-8** combination, p. 225.

1. This is usually a serious pattern, indicating severe psychological disturbances (Carson, 1969).

2. The person may be confused, disoriented, overly verbal, and under tremendous pressure (Caldwell, 1972).

3. People with this pattern are hyperactive and emotionally labile. They may have a high need to achieve but perform poorly. They tend to be uncomfortable in heterosexual relationships and poor sexual adjustment is common (Graham, 1977).

4. These people's problems may center around lack of achievement or impending failure (Caldwell, 1972).

5. This pattern may indicate an identity crisis in which the person does not know who or what he/she is (Caldwell, 1972).

    a. Onset of the crisis is usually sudden.

    b. The crisis does not usually last long when the person receives counseling.

6. Other scales usually are elevated with this pattern.

7. Therapy is difficult with these people, because they have a hard time settling down to anything long enough to deal with it (Carson, 1969).

8. Psychiatric inpatients with **8-9/9-8** pattern are more likely to have hostile-paranoid excitement than patients in general. They also have frequent ratings for flight of ideas, loud voice, labile mood, and unrealistic hostility. They may be quite erratic and have considerable confusion and perplexity. Onset of this behavior frequently is rapid, however there may have been behavior problems in school. For the **8-9** profile increased speech and activity typically are found. With the **9-8** profile, the patient may not know why he/she is hospitalized (Altman et al., 1973).

9. Marks et al. (1974) found this **8-9/9-8** pattern in a university hospital and outpatient clinic. They found the pattern usually for females who were characterized by delusional thinking, rumination, anxiety,

and agitation. The Marks, Seeman, and Haller book should be consulted for further information concerning this profile.

10. Gilberstadt and Duker (1965) found this **8-9** pattern in a VA hospital male population. A person with this profile tended to be hyperactive and to have confused thinking. He also tended to be tense and suspicious. The Gilberstadt and Duker book should be consulted for further information concerning this profile.

11. VA hospital males with this profile are hyperactive and over-ideational. They are likely to have persecutory hallucinations and delusions and react to them aggressively (Hovey & Lewis, 1967).

12. Adolescents in treatment with the **8-9/9-8** pattern (Marks et al., 1974) tended to act out and resent authority figures. Those with the **8-9** pattern were tearful and cried openly. Those with the **9-8** pattern were more demanding. Both groups had rapid talking and movement. The Marks, Seeman, and Haller book should be consulted for further information concerning this pattern.

13. Megargee and Bohn (1979) found a relatively small group (Group Jupiter) of incarcerated criminals with the **8-9/9-8** profile combination. These men tended to do better than one would expect from their backgrounds which were poor. A larger percentage of Blacks were in this group (60%) than in the other groups and perhaps some of the scale elevations came from that fact. They had a high incidence of drug abuse but low violence and generally did well in prison. However, when they did get into trouble, they had a higher percentage of assaults than the other groups. They had one of the lowest recidivism rates.

14. College male counselees with this pattern are unhappy, confused, and worrying. Females were restless, depressed, confused, lacking in skills with the opposite sex, and in conflict with parents and siblings (Drake & Oetting, 1959).

8-9-6-F

1. This pattern was found in a group of rural, isolated, Black males (Gynther, Fowler, & Erdberg, 1971).

8-0 See also the **0-8** combination, p. 232.

1. Marked withdrawal and people avoidance is most likely with this pattern (Lachar, 1974).

2. VA hospital males with this combination are worried, confused, and indecisive (Hovey & Lewis, 1967).

3. College counselees with this pattern tend to be nervous and nonverbal as well as introverted and shy. They tend to be poor communicators in counseling sessions (Drake & Oetting, 1959).

SUMMARY OF 8 SCALE INTERPRETATIONS*

T-score	Interpretations
45 or below	These people tend to see themselves as realists and usually are not interested in contemplation, theory, or philosophy. They may be unimaginative and like structure and routine in their lives.
45 thru 60	The majority of people score in this range.
60 thru 70	Persons with scores in this range may think somewhat differently than other people. These may be avant-garde or highly creative individuals.
70 thru 80	At this level, difficulties in logical thinking may develop. To follow the person's train of thought over a period of time may be difficult.
80 thru 90	People start seeming very confused. Communication usually becomes quite difficult. The person also may have trouble perceiving people and situations accurately and thus may have poor judgment.
90 or above	People at this level usually are suffering from some kind of identity crisis, not knowing who or what they are. This elevation is usually the result of situational stress.

*Where T-scores are listed in two categories (i.e., 45 or below and 45 through 60) and a score is obtained that is listed for two categories, use whichever interpretation seems to be most appropriate for the individual.

SCALE 9

(Ma, Hypomania Scale)

Scale **9** measures psychic energy; that is, the higher the elevation, the more energetic a person is, and the more he/she feels compelled to act using that energy. Another element which seems to occur with an elevation on this scale is an increase in diversity and multiplicity of thoughts. As with some of the other scales, elevations must be interpreted in light of the population involved.

In college populations, particularly with graduate school students, elevations of 60 thru 70 are typical and indicate mental activity, probably with accompanying physical energy. As the scale increases to over 70, a concomitant increase in psychic energy often presents difficulties. The person may begin to "spin his wheels," become over involved and over committed, and get fewer things completed. A good phrase for a person with a score over 80 is "running around like a chicken with its head cut off."

Scale **9** is one of the most common elevations on the MMPI, especially with college populations. This scale and scale **5** for men are the most frequent peaks on college profiles.

Kunce and Anderson (1976, 1984) posit zest as the underlying dimension for scale **9.** In the cases where a person is well adjusted, the appropriate descriptors for the individual with a moderately high elevation would be: enthusiastic, eager, talkative, and versatile. He/she has a drive to be involved and to get others involved in activities. Hovey and Lewis (1967) find that while these people may be expansive and hyperactive, they also may be quite friendly and happy.

The members of a large number of occupations have moderately high scores on scale **9.** For example, social scientists, physicians, writers, and radio announcers have characteristics consistent with those outlined above. When placed under stress, the maladaptive behavior of these individuals will be superficiality, unreliability, and noncompletion of tasks.

9

Low scale **9** scores with a college population are unusual, especially with graduate students. When this occurs, several interpretations might be made.

1. If these people are succeeding in college with little difficulty and scale **2** is not elevated, they may be directing all their available energy into academic pursuits. In other words, they are succeeding in college even with low energy because they have directed what energy they have into academic activities.

2. If these people are succeeding in college with little difficulty and scale **2** is near 60, they could have been tired when they took the inventory, or they could be at the bottom of a mood swing (such as a post-exam letdown). In this instance, these people's usual scale scores are a **9** scale near 60 and a **2** scale near 45.

3. If these people are not succeeding in college, they probably have limited energy available which they are either channeling into a single non-academic pursuit such as a job, emotional concerns, or social activities, or they are dissipating their limited energy into too many areas.

The typical level on scale **9** for non-college educated people is near 50, which is adequate for usual occupational and recreational pursuits. As the scale increases to 60, a need for activity is manifested. If this need for activity is not fulfilled (particularly on the job), an agitation may set in with a mild dissatisfaction about life in general. Where opportunities for the release of this energy occur, no difficulty usually is noted. As the elevation increases over 70, usually not enough opportunity exists to release all of the energy. As a result, fantasy may become a part of the person's life, while the activity also increases (usually not directed too wisely). If people with scale **9** scores over 70 also have scale **2** scores below 45, they may report becoming depressed if they cannot be highly active.

A low scale **9** score (45 or below) in a non-college population usually evidences itself in lethargy. The person tends to feel chronically tired, has difficulty getting out of bed, and may have poor job performance.

For both college and non-college populations, an elevation on the **9** scale tends to energize the behavior or problems seen in elevations on the

9   218

other Clinical scales. For example, if scale **4** also is elevated with scale **9**, the fighting out of scale **4** usually is accentuated and tends to become overt behavior rather than covert thinking about fighting out.

GENERAL INFORMATION

1. The 49 items on this scale measure self-centeredness, grandiosity, and irritability (Carson, 1969).

2. Scale **9** also seems to measure sensation seeking, high activity level, self-confidence, competitiveness, impatience, personal invulnerability, and a contemptuousness of timidity and weakness (Lachar, 1974).

3. Harris and Lingoes (1955) have subjectively divided the **9** scale into four subscales. These are amorality, psycho-motor acceleration, imperturbability, and ego inflation.

4. This is a psychic energy scale. When other scales are elevated, they tell the direction in which the energy will be expended. For example, a high **4-9** combination may mean the person is overtly fighting someone or something, whereas a high **2-9** combination may mean the person is an agitated depressive.

5. Up to T-score of 70, the person is probably active, energetic, and exuberant.

6. Above a T of 70, the person may be overactive, have maladaptive hyperactivity, be irritable, and/or have insufficient restraints on his/her behavior.

7. High scores on scale **9** probably do not indicate classic textbook hypomaniacs, because classic hypomaniacs will not sit still long enough to take MMPI (Carson, 1972).

8. Trimboli and Kilgore (1983) in their research consider this a character scale.

9. Caldwell (1985) has hypothesized that this scale when it is one of the highest, measures a fear of future frustration of wants. People with

9

this scale elevated cannot relax because they believe their future depends upon their activity level.

10. Hovanitz and Gynther (1980) have found that the **9** scale subtle and obvious items (Weiner, 1948) are equally useful in predicting manic behavior, however the subtle items predict certain criteria that are not predicted by the obvious scales.

    Snyder and Graham (1984) have also found this to be true.

11. Scores on scale **9** are lower for older people in a nonpsychiatric population, perhaps as an indication of lower energy levels (Colligan et al., 1984).

12. Schenkenberg et al. (1984) also have found that younger psychiatric patients score higher on this scale than older psychiatric patients.

13. Hibbs et al. (1979) have found that men have significantly higher **9** scores than women (as well as higher **1** scale scores). They suggest that this may be due to a sex-role sanctioning of acting-out behavior.

14. In a study of a normal population, the average men's score on this scale was 55 (Colligan et al., 1984).

15. Education is positively correlated with scale **9.**

16. For a prison population, Blacks tend to score higher than whites on this scale (as well as scales **F** and **8**) (Holland, 1979).

17. Test-retest reliabilities are rather low (Dahlstrom & Welsh, 1960).

HIGH SCORES

Moderate Elevations (T = 60 through 70)

1. A person with a moderate elevation tends to be gregarious (Carson, 1969).

2. Kunce and Anderson (1976) have hypothesized that when this scale is in the moderate range (and no other Clinical scales are above 70 T-score points except perhaps the 5 scale for men), it may measure zestfulness and enthusiasm.

3. If the person with a 9 scale at this level is on a boring job (such as an assembly line), he/she may fantasize a lot.

4. Scale 9 tends to be one of the two most frequent high points for college students. The other is scale 5 for college males.

5. A moderate elevation on the 9 scale (T = 60 through 70) usually is desirable for college students, particularly graduate students, indicating energy enough to carry projects through.

6. Under ideal-self instruction ("take this test trying to look as good as possible"), scale 9 tends to be the high point on the MMPI clinical profile and to be at a moderate elevation (Gloye & Zimmerman, 1967; Hiner et al., 1969; Lanyon, 1967).

Marked Elevations (T = 70 or Above)

The behaviors mentioned for this elevation are most clearly seen when the scale is one of the highest of the Clinical scales in the profile.

1. As scale 9 goes up, people tend to become increasingly involved in activities but less efficient in what they are doing. They may start "spinning their wheels."

2. Three features characterize a high scorer on this scale—over-activity, emotional excitement, and flight of ideas.

3. The mood of the person with a marked elevation on this scale may be good-humored euphoria, but on occasion he/she can become irritable with outbursts of temper (Dahlstrom et al., 1972).

4. Elevations on this scale may reflect the use of the defense mechanisms of denial and acting-out. The latter defense mechanism is especially seen when the 4 scale is also elevated (Trimboli & Kilgore, 1983).

9

5. The following groups of people tend to have marked elevations on scale **9**:

    a. Juvenile delinquents (in conjunction with a high **4** scale).

    b. Highly aggressive boys (not necessarily labeled as delinquent).

    c. College underachievers.

6. A high **9** and low **0** (45 or below) combination is called the "socializer" pattern, whereas a high **0** and low **9** combination is called the "nonsocializer" pattern (Good & Brantner, 1974).

7. Gilberstadt and Duker (1965) found this pattern, a spike **9**, in a VA hospital male population. The men with only scale **9** elevated were hyperactive and talkative people who were involved in many projects. They may have had previous attacks of depression. The Gilberstadt and Duker book should be consulted for further information concerning this profile.

8. VA hospital males with this scale elevated were expansive, hyperactive, grandiose, and talkative (Hovey & Lewis, 1967).

9. When scale **9** is the peak score in college counselees, other traits the person has are expressed in a more energetic fashion than when the **9** scale is low (Drake, 1956).

10. In a college population, some females with the spike **9** profile were considered normal but other women with the profile had a past history of criminal activity and barbituate abuse. They were also anti-social. Males were also anti-social, impulsive, irritable, and tended to use drugs (Kelley & King, 1979a).

LOW SCORES
(T = 45 or Below)

1. People with low scale **9** scores tend to have low energy and a low activity level. They can be difficult to motivate and may be apathetic.

2. This level of **9** may indicate a severe mood disturbance that includes apathy and feelings of emptiness. This can be true even if the **2** scale is not elevated (Tromboli & Kilgore, 1983).

3. Some individuals have learned to channel their limited energy into their most important projects and therefore get them done without unduly taxing themselves.

4. When this scale is near a T of 45, it may indicate that the person is tired or temporarily ill (for example, has a cold).

5. At the lowest levels of this scale, people may be depressed, even if the scale **2** is not elevated (Carson, 1969).

6. Male college counselees with scale **9** at a low level are perceived as dependent and wanting reassurance. Women counselees are perceived as shy especially if the **0** scale is elevated above 55 (Drake & Oetting, 1959).

COMBINATIONS

All scales in these combinations are at a T-score of 70 or above and are listed in order from the highest to the lowest peaks. The scale in the combinations must be the highest Clinical scales on the profile.

1-3-9 See p. 91.

2-4-8-9 See p. 105.

4-5-7-9 See p. 150.

4-5-9 See p. 150.

4-6-9 See p. 153.

4-8-9 See p. 156.

4-8-9-2 See the **4-8-9** combination, point 4, p. 156.

4-9-6 See p. 159.

9

5-8-9 See p. 172.

6-7-8-9 See p. 184.

6-8-9 See p. 185.

8-6-4-9-F See p. 211.

8-9-6-F See p. 214.

9-F See the **F-9** combination, p. 56.

9-K See the **K-9** combination, p. 67.

9-1 See also the **1-9** combination, p. 93.

1. Medical patients with the **9-1** combination who were seen by a physician were all in acute distress. They seldom were hypomaniac; but they were tense, restless, and ambitious. They were frustrated by their failure to reach their high levels of aspiration. Physical complaints for men centered around the gastrointestinal tract and headaches (Guthrie, 1949).

9-2 See also the **2-9** combination, p. 114.

1. The **9-2** combination tends to typify people for whom activity is no longer effective in warding off their depression. These people may be seen as agitated depressives (Dahlstrom et al., 1972).

2. Activity may alternate with fatigue (Caldwell, 1972).

3. These people may set it up so they will fail when they feel they cannot succeed (Caldwell, 1972).

9-3 See the **3-9** combination, p. 130.

9-4 See also the **4-9** combination, pp. 157-159.

1. People with this combination may use acting out as a defense mechanism (Tromboli & Kilgore, 1983).

9   224

2. Patients seen by a physician with the **9-4** pattern showed the general effects of tension and fatigue. These effects followed periods of great overactivity (Guthrie, 1949).

    a. These patients showed poor family adjustment and had problems centering around their sexual adjustments.

    b. They did not stay in treatment long; therefore, they could only be treated superficially.

3. The **9-4** combination is the most common one found in entering college freshmen (9 percent of the men's profiles and 8 percent of the women's) (Fowler & Coyle, 1969).

9-5 See the **5-9** combination, p. 173.

9-6 See the **6-9** combination, p. 186.

1. Marks et al. (1974) found the **9-6/6-9** pattern in a university hospital and outpatient clinic. The profile primarily was found for females who were agitated, tense, excitable, suspicious, and hostile. The Marks, Seeman, and Haller book should be consulted for further information concerning this profile.

9-7 See the **7-9** combination, p. 197.

9-8 See also the **8-9** combination, p. 213.

1. The **9-8** pattern is more likely found in mental hospital populations than in non-hospitalized populations. It indicates more serious problems than the **9-4** combination (Dahlstrom et al., 1972).

The **F** scale elevation tends to vary with the severity of these people's condition. The higher the **F** scale with the **9-8** pattern the more serious the condition tends to be.

2. Marks et al. (1974) found the **8-9/9-8** pattern in a university hospital and outpatient clinic. The pattern occurred mostly with women characterized by delusional thinking, ruminations, anxiety, and agitation. The Marks, Seeman, and Haller book should be consulted for further information concerning this profile.

9

9-0

1. In college counselees, when the **9-0** pattern occurred the behavior shown by the **0** scale seemed to dominate in that the people were socially shy and withdrawn even though agitated (Drake & Oetting, 1959).

SUMMARY OF 9 SCALE INTERPRETATIONS*

T-score	Interpretations
45 or below	Persons may have scores in this range of scale **9** for two reasons. One, they may have been tired when they took the test; or two, they may have a limited amount of energy.
45 thru 60	This range of scores is typical and indicates an average amount of energy. College students tend to score in the upper range of these scores from 55 to 60.
60 thru 70	Persons with these scores tend to be quite active and have many projects which they usually complete. This range is typical for graduate students.
70 or above	People in this range seem to have an excess of energy. They may take on more projects than they can complete. They may fantasize a lot if they cannot keep busy. With a low **2** scale, people may report that if they cannot keep busy, they tend to become depressed.

*Where T-scores are listed in two categories (i.e., 45 or below and 45 through 60) and a score is obtained that is listed for two categories, use whichever interpretation seems to be most appropriate for the individual.

SCALE 0

(Si or Sie, Social Introversion Scale)

Scale **0** measures a person's preference for being alone (high **0**) or being with others (low **0**). The difficulty in working with this scale is in avoiding the value judgments implied in the scale's title (social introversion). We have found it best not to use the scale name when interpreting the MMPI to clients because the tendency in our culture is to think that extroversion is good, whereas introversion is bad. This is not true, of course. Each type of social adjustment has its advantages and disadvantages, depending upon the context in which it is operating.

Persons with scale **0** elevated between 60 and 70 prefer to be by themselves or with a few select friends. This fact usually does not mean that they cannot interact with others; it only means that this is not their preference. One advantage of this preference in college is that these people are able to isolate themselves from others so that assignments, studying, and reading can be done. One disadvantage of **0** scores between 60 and 70 for college students is that people with these scores may not be socially adept. Because they prefer to be by themselves, they tend not to be at ease with many people and may not know current music or slang. One procedure I have found helpful in working with people having scale **0** in this range is to have them join one activity of their choice, so they can keep social ties, while not overwhelming them with people. The **0** scale may elevate to between 60 and 70 as a person becomes older.

Persons with scale **0** scores above 70 tend to be people who are withdrawing from others, not because of an inherently introverted nature, but because they either have been hurt in some way or the problems indicated by other Clinical scale elevations are overwhelming them and consequently they are isolating themselves. In these situations, the **0** scale accentuates the problems seen in other Clinical elevations because the person withdraws from people who might be helpful. People with **0** scale scores above 70 usually do not enter counseling because of their aversion to being with others. If they do become clients, the reason is because their problems are overwhelming them.

A real difficulty with an elevated scale **0** in conjunction with an elevated scale **8** is that these two scales tend to accentuate each other. As people become confused (high **8**), they also tend to isolate themselves.

0

And, as they become more isolated, they tend to become more confused because they lack contact with others.

People with low scale **0** scores (45 or below) prefer to be with people as opposed to being alone. They tend to be socially adept and involved with people. An advantage of the low **0** score for these people is that they remain in touch with the world when there is psychological difficulty. This level of the **0** scale particularly is helpful when people have an elevated scale **8** and are confused. The primary disadvantage for person with this level of the **0** scale is that they may have difficulty being alone. Thus, in college, they usually would rather go to a party than study by themselves. These people also tend to have difficulty in occupations where they are not involved with people.

Kunce and Anderson (1976, 1984) posit autonomy as the underlying dimension of this scale. Well functioning individuals with moderate elevations will be independent and resourceful. When stressed this may turn into a withdrawal from social interactions.

We find most college students (non-clients) scoring in the low range on the **0** scale, with the average for this group being near 45.

An interesting use of the **0** scale is to note its location for each of the persons in marital counseling. Good and Brantner (1974) have suggested that the behavior shown on the **0** scale can be an important factor in marital conflict if the couple are 20 or more T-scores apart on the scale. When the **0** scale scores are that much apart, one of the couple is more of a socializer than the other; and this may be one cause of their marital difficulty.

GENERAL INFORMATION

1. Scale **0** consists of 70 items concerning uneasiness in social situations, insecurities, worries, and lack of social participation (Dahlstrom et al., 1972).

2. The higher the scale, the more the person prefers being by himself/herself; the lower the scale the more the person seeks social contacts.

3. The normal range for this scale is 30 through 70 T-score points (Carson, 1972); however, college students are in the 40 through 45 range.

4. Tromboli and Kilgore (1983) in their research see this as a character scale.

5. As a high point, scale **0** is most frequently paired with scales **2, 7,** and **8.**

6. In one study done on a normal population, the women's mean score was 56 for this scale (Colligan et al., 1984).

7. This scale is negatively correlated to education (Colligan et al., 1984).

8. Reliability studies show stability over time for this scale (Dahlstrom et al., 1972).

9. In a study comparing males who had committed incest with males who were non-incestuous child sexual molesters, the profiles were relatively similar except that the **0** scale was much higher for the incestuous males (67 vs. 53) (Panton, 1979).

10. Husband and wife profile pairs in which at least 15 T-score points difference on this scale exists are found more often for couples in marriage counseling than for couples from the general population (Arnold, 1970; Ollendick et al., 1983).

HIGH SCORES

Moderate Elevations (T = 60 through 70)

1. A moderate elevation on this scale indicates that an individual feels more comfortable alone or in a small group whose members are well known (Cottle, 1953).

2. Kunce and Anderson (1976) have hypothesized that when this scale is in the moderate range (and there are no other Clinical scales above 70 T-score points except the **5** scale for men), it may measure personal autonomy, self-direction, and perhaps self-actualization.

3. It indicates less participation in activities (Gough, 1949a).

4. College people with this elevation tend to be more introverted than the typical college student, because the median score for college students is near a T of 45.

Marked Elevations (T = 70 or Above)

The behaviors mentioned for this elevation are most clearly seen when the scale is one of the highest of the Clinical scales on the profile.

1. People with marked elevations tend to be withdrawn and anxious around people (Carson, 1969). They are also shy and socially insecure. A person with a 0 scale at this level may have an attachment deficit (cannot connect with others).

2. Elevations on this scale may reflect the use of avoidance and withdrawal which may be accompanied by suspiciousness (Tromboli & Kilgore, 1983).

3. Kelley and King (1979a) have found a spike 0 profile (the only scale above 70) in a college counseling center population. These clients typically came in for religious problems and/or marital difficulties. They were not withdrawn but did date infrequently. They were typically diagnosed as adjustment reaction (most often marital adjustment).

4. Other scales when combined with scale 0 often give an indication of the type and seriousness of the social adjustment problems.

   An elevation on this scale tends to suppress the acting out behavior typically seen with high 4 and 9 scale elevations; however, it may enhance the ruminating behavior seen with the high 2 and 7 scales, and especially may enhance the ruminating behavior seen with the high 8 scale.

5. A high 0 and low 9 scale combination is called the "non-socializer" pattern, while the high 9 and low 0 combination is called the "socializer" pattern (Good & Brantner, 1974).

LOW SCORES
(T = 45 or Below)

1. Low scores indicate socially extroverted persons who are poised and confident in social and group situations (Carkhuff et al., 1965; Drasgow & Barnette, 1957).

2. Caldwell (1977) has hypothesized that a low score on this scale may show a liking to be in front of people or a certain amount of exhibitionism.

3. Carson (1985) believes people with very low **0** scores may have an excessive dependency upon being attractive to others.

4. Scores of 45 or below seem to be indicative of an adequate social adjustment even when other Clinical scales are high, particularly scales **2, 7,** and **8,** which usually are associated with serious problems (Graham, Schroeder, & Lilly, 1971).

5. With women, low scale **0** scores seem to be associated with good social adjustment including parental relationships. With men however the social adjustment does not necessarily mean freedom from parental conflicts (Drake & Oetting, 1959).

6. This elevation seems to be related to social aggressiveness in some men (Drake & Oetting, 1959).

7. These scores tend to be typical of college students.

   Gulas (1974) found the **0** scale to be the most frequent (39%) low point for a group of college males, N = 60.

8. Low scale **0** scores typify college students who underachieve because of their tendency to be involved in many social activities (Cottle, 1953).

9. Below a T of 30, persons may show a certain flightiness and superficiality in their relationships. These individuals have well-developed social techniques and many social contacts, but they do not tend to establish relationships of real intimacy.

0

COMBINATIONS

All scales in these combinations are at a T-score of 70 or above and are listed in order from the highest to the lowest peaks. These scales in the combinations must be the highest Clinical scales on the profile.

2-7-8-0 See p. 111.

0-2 See also the **2-0** combination, p. 115.

1. In college counselees, men with a **0-2** combination typically appear unhappy and tense, worry a great deal, and lack effective social skills, particularly with members of the opposite sex (Drake & Oetting, 1959).

2. College women also show the same presenting picture as college men, with the addition of depression, lack of self-confidence, and (when scale **1** is the low point) feelings of physical inferiority (Drake & Oetting, 1959).

0-4 See the **4-0** combination, p. 159.

0-5 See the **5-0** combination, p. 173.

0-6 See the **6-0** combination, p. 186.

0-7 See the **7-0** combination, p. 197.

0-8 See also the **8-0** combination, p. 214.

1. Counselees with a high **0-8** combination tend to be shy and have problems communicating with the counselor (Drake & Oetting, 1959).

2. Women counselees with a high **0-8** combination may vacillate between conflicts with mother and conflicts with father (Drake & Oetting, 1959).

3. Women counselees tend to be nonrelaters and have serious problems, especially when scale **5** is the low point of the pattern (Drake & Oetting, 1959).

0   232

0-9 See the **9-0** combination, p. 226.

SUMMARY OF 0 SCALE INTERPRETATIONS*

T-score	Interpretations
45 or below	A person with a score in this range prefers to be with others and not by himself/herself. The typical range for college students for this scale is between 40 and 45.
45 thru 60	The majority of people score in this range.
60 thru 70	At this level, the person prefers to be alone or with one or two good friends.
70 or above	A score in this range may indicate that the person's problems are causing active withdrawal from others.

*Where T-scores are listed in two categories (i.e., 45 or below and 45 through 60) and a score is obtained that is listed for two categories, use whichever interpretation seems to be most appropriate for the individual.

—NOTES—

CHAPTER **VI**

RESEARCH SCALES

The MMPI originally was developed to include only the Validity and Clinical scales. However, over a period of time, more than 550 experimental scales have been constructed by researchers. Of the more than 550 experimental scales, 11 were selected by National Computer System to be scored as part of their regular profile printouts. While using this computer scoring system, we became acquainted with the 11 scales which we have used in this section for the first and second editions. Currently, however, only **A, R,** and **Es** are scored by National Computer System. The rest of the scales must be scored either by using scoring keys available from Psychological Assessment Resources or making scoring keys from the items listed for each scale in Appendices A and B. The Research scales which we have used in the previous editions and are continuing to use in this edition are as follows:

A First Factor or Conscious Anxiety
R Second Factor or Conscious Repression
Es Ego Strength

235

Lb Low Back Pain
Ca Caudality
Dy Dependency
Do Dominance
Re Social Responsibility
Pr Prejudice
St Social Status
Cn Control

In addition to these 11 scales, in this third edition we are including the MacAndrew Addiction Scale, **Mac,** which has proven to be extremely useful in diagnosing alcoholism and drug addiction. We find these Research scales to be tremendously helpful in interpreting the MMPI; however, little information about them has appeared in the research literature. Consequently, this chapter is based primarily upon our work in various counseling and clinical settings (four university counseling centers, a community mental health center, a psychiatric clinic, and a drug treatment center).

In contrast to the Clinical scales, elevations on these Research scales do not necessarily have negative connotations. In some instances, they have positive interpretations. To interpret most accurately these scales, each one must be dealt with individually, then in combination with other scales, and finally in light of the context in which it occurs. This last factor especially is important. For example, an elevation on scale **A** (which indicates conscious anxiety) may or may not have negative implications. Such an elevation is appropriate if the person is awaiting sentencing for a crime or if his/her mate has just died. Such an elevation may have a negative connotation if the person does not have an outside reason for worry, but instead has much free-floating anxiety. Conversely, a low scale **A** may be positive if the person is well balanced psychologically and is taking the MMPI as part of experiment; but such a score generally would not be considered appropriate for a person in difficulty with the law. In general, then, these scales are most accurately interpreted when all the factors noted above are taken into consideration.

We use some of these scale in combination with each other such as scales **A** and **R, Dy** and **Do, Re** and **Pr,** and **Do,** and **St.** These combinations will be dealt with specifically in the various scale sections.

We are now beginning to work on developing profile configurations for the New scales. The first profile configurations were easy to develop.

236

These were extensions of the traditional all-true, all-false, all-X, all-O and random response set profiles found in the *MMPI Handbook* (Dahlstrom et al., 1972). These profiles, including both the Clinical and Research scales (but excluding the **Mac** scale), are found in the Validity scale section.

We believe we also have isolated two additional profiles for the Research scales, one indicating good mental health and the other indicating poor mental health. Good mental health seems to be indicated primarily by elevations (T = 55 or above) on **Es**, **Do**, and **St**, and low scores (T = 45 or below) on **A**, **Dy**, and **Pr**. The poor mental health profile is indicated primarily by low scores (T = 45 or below) on **Es** and **Do**, and high scores (T = 55 or above) on **A**, **R**, **Dy**, and **Pr**.

In Appendix C are shown the intercorrelations among the Validity, Clinical, and Research scales, excluding the **Mac** scale, for two groups of non-psychiatric subjects. The figures reported in the light type are scale intercorrelations for over 50,000 medical out-patients at the Mayo Clinic (Swenson, Pearson, & Osborne, 1973). Psychiatric patients were excluded from this sample.

The second set of figures, reported in bold type, are intercorrelations for 847 profiles from people in the Muncie, Indiana, area. Many of these profiles came from students in graduate level courses in Counseling Psychology at Ball State University and their friends who took the test to help these students fulfill requirements for a testing course. As far as could be determined, none of the people in this sample was being counseled for psychological problems.

Pertinent intercorrelations for each of the Research scales is reported in the chapters on the individual scales. Our hope is that these correlations will help clarify the relationships between the various Research scales and the more familiar Validity and Clinical scales.

As a final note, these Research scales are not always considered moderately elevated at 60 or markedly elevated at 70 as are the Clinical scales. What is called high for each scale differs from these conventional classifications. Each scale section must be consulted to find out what is considered elevated for that scale.

We are hoping that our presentations in this chapter will encourage others to start using these scales in their work, particularly with non-hospitalized populations. We feel much more research needs to be done with them before a truly comprehensive understanding of them can be achieved.

A SCALE

(First Factor or Conscious Anxiety Scale)

The **A** scale seems to measure the amount of overt anxiety present when the test was taken. Scores on this scale frequently are elevated on profiles of clients seeking help for personal problems in college counseling centers and in mental health agencies. The higher the **A** score, the more anxiety the person is reporting. A low scale score (T = 45 or below) indicates relative freedom from conscious anxiety. The **A** scale correlates highly with measures of anxiety for medical out-patients, (.90 with scale 7, .85 with the **Ca** scale Appendix C) (Swenson et al., 1973).

An individual with a high **A** score is likely to have the following characteristics:

1. self-doubt,
2. difficulty in concentrating,
3. a tendency to worry and brood,
4. lack of energy, and
5. a negative outlook on life generally.

The high **A** scale score with high Clinical scale scores is an indication that the person is hurting enough to be a good therapy risk, unless the situation that provoked the high **A** has changed dramatically since the test taking, thereby lessening the pressure on the client. Clients with low **A** scale scores (45 or below), but with many problems indicated on the Clinical scales, are usually poor therapy risks because they are not highly anxious about their problems and/or have learned to live with them even though these problems have not been solved.

People with high **A** scores and high Clinical scores may be good therapy risks. First, high **A** scorers tend to be very ready to admit to having psychological problems, and therefore, the Clinical scales may be elevated because of this tendency and not because of having serious problems. Second, because high **A** scorers have much self-doubt, they may be more aware of a need to change their behavior and may be willing to work at doing so. Third, high **A** scorers may be cautious about showing unusual feeling and behavior. Such individuals do not want to be viewed as abnormal, and they may be in less trouble because of their cautious behavior.

A

In summation, a client who is highly anxious (high Scale **A**) and who generally feels maladjusted (high Clinical scales) is more likely to seek help and work on changing than a client whose answers on the test indicate pathology (high Clinicals) but who does not seem to be overtly anxious about his/her psychological adjustment (low **A** scale).

Scale **A** seems to represent short-term, situational anxiety, whereas scale **7** (the other anxiety scale on the MMPI) seems to represent long-term characterological anxiety, a way of dealing with life by ruminating and worrying a great deal. This rumination and worrying may go on all or most of the time, even when a specific situation about which to worry is not present. High scale **7** people, in general then, tend to be chronic worriers, even when the worry is not immediately necessary.

Scale **A** usually shows anxiety in response to a particular situation and may be high when scale **7** is in the typical range (45 through 60). A person with this combination (high **A** scale, average **7** scale) is usually worrying about a specific problem but does not have the chronic worrying shown by a high scale **7**. We have found that a typical reason for a person having this combination is because he/she is anxious about taking the test but is not an anxious person or worried about a large number of things.

In some cases, the **7** scale may be elevated without the **A** scale being above 60. In this instance, the person tends to be a chronic worrier, but at the time of taking the test he/she was not overtly worried about a specific situation.

An examination of the items that make up the **A** scale in comparison with those which make up the **7** scale is useful in pointing out some of the differences between the two scales. One group of items on both scales has to do with self-doubt. The **7** scale self-doubts seem to involve the total person more than those on the **A** scale. For example, "I certainly feel useless at times," is an item on scale **7**. The self-doubt of the individual with a high **A** scale score is more in regard to interactions with people such as, "I feel unable to tell anyone all about myself."

A second group of items that sets the **A** scale apart from the **7** scale is those that have to do with phobias which are on the **7** scale but not on the **A** scale. A third set of items indicates that a high **7** scale individual is likely to have fits of excitement and anxiety; whereas, the high **A** scale individual is more likely to report the presence of steady anxiety.

A   240

Despite these differences, scales **7** and **A** have much overlap and usually are seen as elevated together rather than one elevated and the other not. When these two scales are elevated, the anxiety is both chronic and situational.

Scales **A** and **R** have a unique relationship to each other. In addition to looking at them separately, they also should be looked at together and interpreted in light of each other. In your work with the **A** scale as well as the individual **A** scale interpretations, we would suggest that you look at the **A** and **R** combinations, pp. 251-252.

GENERAL INFORMATION

1. The 39 items of the **A** scale reflect general, conscious emotional upset by asking questions concerning thinking and thought processes, negative emotional tone, lack of energy, pessimism, and personal sensitivity.

2. Welsh (1956) factor analyzed the MMPI items, and from this analysis he derived the **A** scale as a measure of one of the two main MMPI factors. (Scale **R** measures the other factor.) This first factor has high positive loadings on scales **7** (.90) and **8** (.79) and a high negative loading on scale **K** (-.71) (Swenson et al., 1973).

3. The **A** scale is strongly related to indices of overt anxiety and seems to measure tension, nervousness, and distress.

4. The **A** scale measures general conscious anxiety of a situational nature, as contrasted to scale **7**, which measures a more characterological, long-term anxiety.

5. Welsh's **A** scale (1956) appears to be the most satisfactory single measure of conscious anxiety on the MMPI.

6. High and low scores can be "good" or "bad," appropriate or inappropriate, helpful or a hindrance, depending upon the specific situation of the person.

For example, if a person is facing a situational trauma and he/she is not very anxious about it (low to average **A** score), this lack of anxiety could be a hindrance to working through the trauma.

7. Heppner and Anderson (1985) have found that ineffective problem-solvers tend to be significantly higher on this scale than effective problem solvers.

8. In addition to interpreting the **A** scale alone, in certain instances the **A** scale should be considered in relationship to the **R** scale. See the **A** and **R** combination table, pp. 251-252.

9. In one test-retest study, over a period of 11 days, the **A** scale was unstable (Jurjevich, 1966). This fact implies that the scale is quite mobile, hopefully in response to differing levels of anxiety.

10. Items of the **A** scale tend to be of uniformly low social desirability (Wiggins & Rumrill, 1959).

11. Under ideal-self instructions ("Take this test trying to look as good as possible") the one scale with the largest shift was the **A** scale; it became significantly lower (Parsons et al., 1968).

12. An excellent reference for the **A** scale is "Factor Dimensions **A** and **R**" by Welsh in *Basic Readings on the MMPI in Psychology and Medicine* (Welsh & Dahlstrom, 1956).

HIGH SCORES
(T = 60 or Above)

See also the **A** and **R** combinations, pp. 251-252.

1. High **A** scores indicate that the person is overtly anxious. The higher the score, the more anxious the person is.

2. Men with high **A** scores have been described as lacking confidence in their own abilities and unable to make decisions without hesitation, vacillation, or delay (Block & Bailey, 1955).

a. They tend to be suggestible and respond more to evaluations made of them by others than they do to their own self-evaluations. However, they may not act on others' evaluations but just worry about them.

b. These men tend to lack social poise and are upset easily in social situations.

c. They usually are pessimistic about their own professional future and advancement.

3. Gough (Welsh & Dahlstrom, 1956) reported people with high **A** scores have slow personal tempo and are pessimistic, hesitant, and inhibited.

LOW SCORES
(T = 45 or Below)

See also the **A** and **R** combinations, pp. 251-252.

1. Clients with low scores tend not to be consciously anxious.

2. This non-anxiety may be "good" (when nothing exists about which to be anxious) or "bad" (when the Clinical scales indicate problems exist which should concern the person).

COMBINATIONS

A-R

1. Nine combinations of **A** and **R** are discussed by Welsh (1965) and are found in the 1972 Dahlstrom, Welsh, and Dahlstrom *MMPI Handbook*. These interpretations have not been very accurate for our populations, except for the high **A** and high **R** interpretation, which follows:

High **A** (55 or above) and high **R** (55 or above): Depression often is encountered with accompanying tenseness and nervousness as well as complaints of anxiety, insomnia, and undue sensitivity. Generalized neurasthenic features of fatigue, chronic tiredness, or exhaustion may be seen. These subjects are perceived as rigid by others and are chronic worriers. They suffer from feelings of inadequacy and a brooding preoccupation with their personal difficulties (Welsh, 1965).

2. For a summary of selected **A** and **R** scale combinations, see the chart on pp. 251-252.

SUMMARY OF A SCALE INTERPRETATIONS*

T-score	Interpretations
45 or below	This person is not consciously anxious. The average score for well functioning individuals is 45.
45 thru 60	This person has minimal (T = 45 to 50) to mild (T = 50 to 60) conscious anxiety. The majority of people score below 50 T-score points.
60 or above	This person has a high level of conscious anxiety, which may cause debilitation as the scale is elevated. The person may lack poise, be easily upset, pessimistic, and not trusting of himself/herself. Such a person tends to be influenced by others' evaluations of him/her, although he/she may not always act overtly on these evaluations.

*Where T-scores are listed in two categories (i.e., 45 or below and 45 through 60) and a score is obtained that is listed for two categories, use whichever interpretation seems to be most appropriate for the individual.

R SCALE

(Second Factor or Conscious Repression Scale)

We feel the **R** scale is a conscious repression scale (or suppression scale to be more accurate). A person with a high score on this scale seems to be saying, "Some areas of my life are none of your business." Determining what areas are off limits is impossible until the client is asked. For example, in one recent situation, a client with a high **R,** but with an otherwise average profile, stated that he did not want to talk about his recent departure from the ministry of his church. He felt fairly comfortable about his decision, as was indicated by the MMPI profile in general, but was still not ready to talk with others about his change in vocation.

While the high **A** scale seems to have some relationship to seeking help at a university counseling center, the **R** scale does not. Clients coming for help with personal problems tend to score above 55 T-score points on the **A** scale whereas they average around 50 for the **R** scale. Normal college students tend to score below 45 T-score points on the **A** scale whereas they average around 50 for the **R** scale (Anderson & Duckworth, 1969). Thus the **R** scale seems to average around 50 T-score points regardless of personal adjustment.

Another unusual feature of the **R** scale is that it does not correlate above .50 with any of the other scales on the MMPI. (See Appendix C.) This is in spite of the fact that it is supposed to be a scale that accounts for the second largest amount of variance in the MMPI. [The **A** scale measures the largest amount (Welsh, 1956).]

The items in the scale are quite varied. A high score on the **R** scale suggests that the person

1. has health concerns,
2. denies feelings of anger,
3. is socially introverted,
4. denies being stimulated by people, and
5. is not aggressive and lacks social dominance.

As has been mentioned previously, the **R** scale is not frequently elevated in clients seeking help at a college counseling center. Some clinical impressions however based on a sample of 32 MMPI's from a college counseling center population are as follows.

1. When the **R** scale is elevated 60 T-score points or higher and the **A** scale is 5 T-score points or more lower than the **R** scale, the client is likely to be seen as shy and guarded in his/her behavior or in his/her reactions to the interviewer. In some cases, these clients may even be resistive to being in therapy or to having a psychological evaluation. In spite of the client's resistance to this particular situation, a history of dependency is likely. Physical complaints are common and are of an unshakable nature. No comments are in the case notes of these people to indicate that they have any insight into their problems. People working with them find them quite unresponsive to psychological explanations for their problems.

2. On the other hand, when the **R** scale is elevated above 60 T-score points and the **A** scale is at least 5 T-score points or more *higher,* a much more pathological picture of the client is represented. The person not only is shy and guarded, but also is typically complaining of being isolated, depressed, and having suicidal thoughts. In a disproportionate number of these cases, some attempt at suicide has been made, although some of these attempts will have been attention seeking. These people complain of difficulty in concentrating and have periods of confusion. Usually also a negative family history is present, but this could be the result of a phenomenon which Chance (1957) reported in her investigation of individuals who had pleasant memories as opposed to those who had unpleasant memories. Those individuals with pleasant memories had **R** scores higher than their **A** scores. Those with unpleasant memories had **A** scores higher than their **R** scores.

3. When both the **R** and the **A** scales are above 60 T-score points and approximately equal to one another (within 5 T-score points), the person tends to be shy and guarded with feelings of isolation, depression, and some history of dependency upon others for support.

This analysis of college student profiles would suggest that the interpretation of an elevated **R** scale is highly dependent upon its relationship with the **A** scale. A summation of the relationship between these two scales is found on pp. 251-252.

The low **R** score indicates a lack of conscious repression and perhaps a willingness to be open and self-disclosing to others. The **R** scale, as a conscious repression scale, contrasts with the **3** scale, which we see as an unconscious repression scale. In general, when a person has an **R** scale score above 55, scale **3** also is elevated. One scale may be elevated however without the other one being so. In the previous example of the ex-minister's non-willingness to talk about his departure from his church, the **R** scale was elevated (above 60) whereas the **3** scale was not. He recognized the problem area (average level **3** scale) but did not want to talk about it (high **R**). We have seen many situations where the opposite also was true: the clients used unconscious repression and denial a great deal (scale **3** high), but they were not consciously saying some areas were off limits (**R** scale average or below). These people are willing to talk about their problems if they recognize them, which they may not (high **3**).

Scale **R** also has points in common with the **K** and **Cn** scales. An elevated **K** scale indicates that the person feels everything is all right with his/her life. A person with this scale elevation may not be able to look at things that are not going well. An elevated **Cn** scale indicates that the person controls to whom his/her behavior is shown. Some profiles have all four of these points (**K, 3, R,** and **Cn**) above 65. When this pattern occurs, these people may be saying in many ways and on many scales that they tend to restrict themselves to talking about some subjects (**R**) that usually are positive (**K** and **3**), and that they will not expose themselves or their behavior to all people (**Cn**). The overall impression is that of a highly constricted person.

GENERAL INFORMATION

1. The **R** scale consists of 40 items measuring health and physical symptoms; emotionality, violence, and activity; reactions to other people in social situations; social dominance, feelings of personal adequacy and personal appearance; and personal and vocational interests.

2. From his factor analyses of the MMPI, Welsh (1956) developed the **R** scale as a measure of the second factor in the MMPI. (The first factor is measured by scale **A**.)

3. This scale appears to measure the use of denial and rationalization as coping behaviors and a lack of effective self-insight.

4. The **R** scale measures conscious repression and denial, as contrasted with scale **3**, which tends to measure unconscious denial.

5. High or low scores can be "good" or "bad," appropriate or inappropriate, helpful or a hindrance, depending upon the specific situation of the person.

   For example, if a person has lost a loved one, a high **R** score may indicate a situation that is therapeutic for a while, thus helping the person to keep going in daily life without collapsing.

6. Scale **R** items are more heterogenous and neutral in social desirability value as compared to scale **A** items, which are homogeneous and of low social desirability (Wiggins & Rumrill, 1959).

7. Because all the items on the **R** scale are keyed false, one study has proposed that the **R** scale seems to be a measure of acquiescence, with low **R** scores indicating more acquiescence than high **R** scores (Edwards & Abbott, 1969).

8. In addition to interpreting the **R** scale alone, the **R** scale should be considered in relationship to the **A** scale. in certain instances shown in the **A** and **R** combination table, pp. 251-252.

9. An excellent reference for the **R** scale is "Factor Dimensions **A** and **R**" by Welsh in *Basic Readings on the MMPI in Psychology and Medicine* (Welsh & Dahlstrom, 1956).

HIGH SCORES
(T = 60 or Above)

See also the **A** and **R** combinations, pp. 251-252.

1. Clients scoring high on **R** seem to be saying that some areas of their lives exist which they do not want to talk about with others.

2. Graham (1977) reported that high **R** scale scorers may be plodders and unimaginative people.

3. In one study, high **R** males were seen as people who readily made concessions and sidestepped trouble or disagreeable situations rather than face unpleasantness of any sort (Block & Bailey, 1955).

   a. They appeared highly civilized, formal, and conventional.

   b. They seemed clear-thinking, but they were rated slow, painstaking, and thorough.

LOW SCORES
(T = 45 or Below)

See also the **A** and **R** combinations, pp. 251-252.

1. People with low **R** scores are not trying to repress consciously any topics covered on the MMPI.

2. They probably are willing to discuss with someone problem areas covered by the MMPI insofar as they recognize these problems.

3. Their willingness to discuss these areas with a counselor may depend upon whether they see the counselor as one in whom they can confide and whether they feel the subject matter is appropriate to their counseling goals.

COMBINATIONS

A-R

1. For a summary of selected **A** and **R** scale combinations, see the summary on pp. 251-252.

SUMMARY OF R SCALE INTERPRETATIONS*

T-score	Interpretations
45 or below	A person with a score in this range is not consciously repressing feelings or attitudes. The person is usually willing to discuss recognized problems that are perceived as relating to his/her counseling goals.
45 thru 60	This person has minimal (T = 45 to 50) to mild (T = 50 to 60) conscious repression of feelings. The person may feel reluctant to discuss some topics with the counselor.
60 or above	A person with a score in this range has a strong need to consciously repress feelings. The higher the T-score, the greater the need to repress. This person usually prefers to avoid unpleasant topics and situations. He/she may be seen as formal, logical, and cautious.

*Where T-scores are listed in two categories (i.e., 45 or below and 45 through 60) and a score is obtained that is listed for two categories, use whichever interpretation seems to be most appropriate for the individual.

SUMMARY OF A AND R COMBINATION
INTERPRETATIONS

If the A Scale Score Is	If the R Scale Score Is	Interpretations

45 or
below
	45 or
	below
		This person is neither consciously anxious or consciously repressing feelings. Three types of persons are in this category:
		
		    1. Persons taking the MMPI as part of an experiment or class assignment.
		    2. Persons seeking counseling for vocational guidance.
		    3. Clients who are unconcerned about their behavior, such as alcoholics, hoboes, sociopathic persons, and so forth. These people may have a poor prognosis for change in therapy.

60 or above	45 or below	This person appears to be both anxious and open. This score combination usually is helpful for the counseling situation; the anxiety serves as motivation to work on problems, and the openness allows flexibility in both depth and breadth of subject areas. This combination is more common for people voluntarily seeking counseling for problems.
45 or below	60 or above	This person is not consciously anxious, but he/she is consciously repressing information. This person is difficult to work with in therapy, because he/she is limiting the areas of discussion and is not sufficiently anxious to work on his/her problems. This combination is common for two groups of people: 1. Persons seeking vocational counseling. The person feels that exploring certain areas of his/her life is not relevant to the task.

2. Job applicants who hold back certain data from the prospective employer and who wish to present themselves in a good light.

60 or above	60 or above	This person is both consciously anxious and consciously repressing talking about areas on the test; however, if the **R** scale is higher than the **A** scale, the person could be denying he/she is anxious. This combination frequently occurs with an elevated **3** scale. This person is very difficult to work with in therapy. The prognosis for successful therapy is indicated by the relative heights of the two scales. If the **A** scale is 5 or more T-score points higher than **R**, the person may overcome his/her repressive tendencies because of the greater anxiety. If the **R** scale is 5 or more T-score points higher than **A**, the person might terminate counseling rather than look at his/her problems realistically.

For an additional interpretation of this combination, see Welsh's (1965) interpretation on p. 243.

Es SCALE

(Ego-Strength Scale)

The ego-strength scale seems to be one of the best indicators of psychological health on the MMPI. The higher the **Es** scale, the more likely the person is to be able to bounce back from problems without becoming debilitated by them. The lower the **Es** scale, the more likely the person is to have difficulty coping with his/her problems. This scale, then, seems to be a measure of ego-resiliency.

The lower the **Es** scale, the more worthless the person usually feels. When the score is below a T of 30, the person may be having some problems connected with employment. He/she may be unable to hold a job at this time because of feelings of worthlessness.

Besides measuring the actual ability to bounce back from problems, the **Es** scale may occasionally measure how much a person *feels* he/she can recover from problems without measuring the actual ability to do so. Obviously, determining whether or not this second interpretation rather than the first one is true for a client is important in order to treat him/her most adequately.

Some other characteristics also may exist with an elevated **Es** scale which usually would not be interpreted as positive. In another study, Barron (1956) found that high scorers sometimes had higher than average aggression and hostility. Further investigation showed that this was related to how pathological their early childhood was. Those who had the most difficulty as children were the most likely to be hostile as adults. That is, a high score on **Es** may show poor control over hostility along with general ego strength if the individual has had childhood experiences characterized by friction in the home, poor relations with his parents, or a mother lacking in emotional warmth. Low scores on the **Es** scale did not always present a consistent picture in the way people handled hostility; but, in general, they were submissive, rigid, and unadaptive.

Crumpton, Cantor, and Batiste (1960) did a factor analysis of the ego strength scale. The five most important factors would suggest that a reconsideration of the label might be needed. Factors 1, 4, and 5 seem to be related to absence of symptoms or denial of symptoms. Factor 1 was associated with the absence of physical symptomatology and phobic behavior. Factor 4 was the absence of symptoms related to anxiety, rumination, and distractability; and factor 5 seemed to be the denial of weakness in the face of distress. Factor 2 was related to moderate religious interests, such as attending church but the avoidance of more fundamentalist beliefs or behaviors. Factor 3 was correlated with lack of rebelliousness.

The authors feel on the basis of this factor analysis that what is being measured is the absence of specific ego weaknesses and not the presence of ego strength.

Dahlstrom and Welsh (1960) seem to feel on the other hand that ego strength is probably the best measure of personality control that we have on the test and it probably should be used in this vein.

GENERAL INFORMATION

1. The **Es** scale of 68 items measures physiological stability and good health, a strong sense of reality, feelings of personal adequacy and vitality, and spontaneity and intelligence (Barron, 1953).

2. Barron (1953) developed the **Es** scale to differentiate those individuals who showed a greater degree of improvement after psychotherapy from individuals with similar problems who did not improve.

   Some studies (Fowler, Teel, & Coyle, 1967; Getter & Sundland, 1962) have found that the **Es** scores are unrelated to changes in treatment progress. These studies used change after hospitalization to measure the **Es** predictability however instead of the change after psychotherapy that Barron (1953) used.

3. The **Es** scale elevation may show the length of time therapy will be needed by the client. The lower the **Es** the longer the client/patient will need therapy.

   One study of nonschizophrenic inpatients (Young et al., 1980) has found that the higher the **Es** scale the shorter the hospital stay.

4. The **Es** scale seems to be a measure of ego-resiliency; that is, the ability to recover from environmental pressures and problems.

5. Crumpton et al. (1960) have suggested in one study that what is measured by the **Es** scale is the absence of specific ego weaknesses and not the presence of ego strength.

6. While the **Es** score originally was developed as an index of prognosis in therapy, it also can be used as a criterion of improvement in therapy. That is, people in therapy originally may have low **Es** scores, but with psychological improvement the **Es** scores tend to rise.

   Abnormally low **Es** scores may result from a large number of unanswered items (see the **?** scale score) giving the impression erroneously of greater "ego weakness" than may be present (Dahlstrom et al., 1972).

7. The **Es** scale has high negative correlations with scales **2** (-.51), **0** (-.51), **A** (-.68), **Ca** (-.61), **Dy** (-.64), and **Pr** (-.53) for a group of normal people (See Appendix C.). The **Es** scale has high positive correlations with **Do** (.60) and **St** (.54) for the same group.

8. Among normals, the **Es** scale seems to measure an underlying belief in self-adequacy along with a tolerant, balanced attitude (Harmon, 1980).

9. Arnold (1970) has found that marital conflict is more likely to occur if the Ego-Strength scores for the couple are below 50 or if a difference exists of more than 15 points between the two T-scores.

10. Heppner and Anderson (1985) have found that self-appraised ineffective problem solvers tend to be significantly lower than effective problem solvers on this scale.

11. A shortened form (50 items) of the **Es** scale has been proposed (Canter, 1965). It was found essentially equivalent to the longer form (68 items) in a separate study (Gravitz, 1970a).

12. Women tend to score lower than men on **Es**. This difference may be because of sex related items (MMPI booklet No. 140, 153, 174, 187, 261, 488, 510, 548). When these items were removed in one study

(Holmes, 1967), male and female differences on **Es** were cancelled out, but the predictive effect of **Es** in regard to psychotherapy was not affected.

13. The **Es** scale is positively related to intelligence and to education (Tamkin & Klett, 1957).

14. Some studies (Tamkin & Klett, 1957) have found no correlation between age and **Es** score, but others (Getter & Sundland, 1962) have found that older people tend to have lower **Es** scores.

15. The **Es** scores for college students average between 55 and 65 (Anderson & Duckworth, 1969).

16. For individuals in a weight reductions program, **Es** was positively correlated, .43, with weight loss (Wadden, 1980).

17. Barron's original article proposing this scale is in the *Basic Readings on the MMPI in Psychology and Medicine* (Welsh & Dahlstom, 1956).

HIGH SCORES
(T = 55 or Above)

1. High scores usually indicate an ability to deal with environmental pressures.

2. Occasionally, high scores are indications that people feel they can deal adequately with pressures when they really cannot.

   Dahlstrom et al. (1975) have suggested that when a person has a high **Es** score and is having problems shown by Clinical scale elevations above 70 but is denying them, the high **Es** score may *not* be indicating a favorable response to treatment. If the person, however, has a high **Es** score *and* admits to having difficulties, the **Es** score probably indicates a favorable response to treatment.

3. A person with a high score generally can profit from psychotherapy.

4. People with **Es** scores in this range can be confronted in therapy without falling apart psychologically.

5. The high score indicates that the person may be able to work within the cultural, social, and personal limits of his/her society.

6. A high score may indicate that a person can deal effectively with others, gain their acceptance, and create favorable impressions on them.

7. Anderson and Kunce (1984) have found that for clients who have markedly elevated **8** scale scores, elevations on **Es** and **Cn** scales may indicate those who are aware of pathological feelings and their potential for acting out impulsively, but their conscious awareness (**Cn**) and adequate level of ego strength (**Es**) may enable them to better control their behavior.

8. High scores tend to be typical of college students. The usual score for such students is near 60 (Anderson & Duckworth, 1969).

LOW SCORES
(T = 45 or Below)

1. Low scores may indicate less self-restraint and environmental mastery than average scores do.

2. The person with a score in this range frequently perceives situations as stressful when others do not. Therefore, he/she is chronically under more stress than the person with a high **Es** score.

3. Occasionally, low scores are indications that people feel they cannot deal adequately with problems when they really can.

4. Low scores may occur when the person is feeling he/she needs help in therapy (the "cry for help" syndrome). A person who feels this way typically has a high **F** score as well as the low **Es** score.

5. Extraordinarily low scores (T = 30 or below) usually indicate real or imagined poor work records and an inability to cope with every-day occurrences.

6. Cernovsky (1984) has found in one study that alcohol use was related to the average profile elevation of the Clinical scales more clearly for people with low **Es** scores than for those with high **Es** scores. In other words, those people with high average profiles *and* low **Es** were more likely to have alcohol abuse than those people with high average profiles and high **Es** scores.

7. In one study, self-appraised ineffective problem solvers were significantly lower on **Es** (Heppner & Anderson, 1985).

COMBINATIONS

Es-Do-St (T = 55 or Above)

1. This combination tends to be typical of college students and well adjusted individuals.

E̅s̅-D̅o̅-S̅t̅ (T = 45 or Below) plus Dy (T = 55 or Above)

1. These people feel they are not worth much and do not expect much out of life. They also feel they must rely on others to make decisions for them.

SUMMARY OF Es SCALE INTERPRETATIONS*

T-score	Interpretations
30 or below	A person with this score tends to have a very poor self-concept and usually feels helpless to act in bettering his/her situation. This person often frustrates the counselor by having good intentions but not acting on them. The person usually has a poor work record. Prognosis for successful employment at this time is poor.
30 thru 45	This person tends to have a poor self-concept, is unable to face challenges at this time, and usually is devastated by even minor setbacks. The person needs ego building before he/she is able to deal with problems.
45 thru 60	This person usually has enough ego strength to deal with life's stresses and minor setbacks. For a college student, an **Es** score in the lower part of this range (45 through 50) may indicate that he/she is not as confident of his/her abilities as other college students are.
60 or above	This person is or feels that he/she is resilient and able to recover from most setbacks. If a client has emotional difficulties indicated by elevated Clinical scales and recognizes this, he/she usually will make a good response to treatment. If he/she has emotional problems and does not recognize this, the client may not have a favorable response to treatment and indeed may be resistive to suggestions of the necessity of treatment. The person with high **Es** usually is able to tolerate confrontation in counseling regardless of his/her response to therapy. This level is typical for college students. Usually, scales **9, Do,** and **St** also are elevated.

*Where T-scores are listed in two categories (i.e., 30 or below and 30 through 45) and a score is obtained that is listed for two categories, use whichever interpretation seems to be most appropriate for the individual.

Es

—NOTES—

Lb SCALE

(Low Back Pain—Functional Scale)

In the first edition of this book (1975), the suggestion was made not to use the **Lb** scale because we (Duckworth & Duckworth) had not been able to discover any useful interpretation of it for college counseling centers or mental health clinic populations. In the process of analyzing the scale according to the content of the items since that printing, we (Duckworth & Anderson) feel we have some leads on the possible interpretation of high scores (above 60 T-score points) for this scale.

In the original study by Hanvik (1951) this scale was developed to differentiate between those people with organic low back pain and those with functional low back pain (no organic reason for the pain). The scale has 25 items, twelve of which are claims to being unflappable, seldom angry, and always in control of feelings; for example, answering false to "It makes me angry to have people try to hurry me."

These items alone however would not make any major elevation on the scale. The addition of items which indicate that all is not what it seems to be in this person's professed Eden is what raises the score to interpretable levels (above 60 T-score points): "I wish I could be as happy as others seem to be (true);" "I have periods of restlessness when I cannot sit long in a chair (true)." An additional four items indicate the presence of physical complaints, and several items which deny religious beliefs also are included.

The message that the individual seems to be giving is that "I'm a wonderful person. I love people, and they never annoy me, but for some reason I am uncomfortable and not as happy as I should be."

Dynamically, we have a picture of an individual who at one level of awareness feels comfortable with the demands that others place on him/her but who at another more unconscious level is saying "get off my back." Considerable psychic energy maybe going into maintaining a friendly facade.

These personality characteristics are true even if no back complaints are present. While this seems similar to a conversion reaction which is shown by an elevated **3** scale, an elevation on the **Lb** scale represents a more specific reaction to stress than a conversion reaction. Basically, **Lb** is only a denial of anger/irritation without any physical conversion, while the **3** scale involves denial in many areas, plus a physiological conversion. When the stress is gone, we hypothesize that the **Lb** score will come down below 60 T-score points whereas the **3** scale will not become lower.

We predict that if **Lb** is elevated and the **3** scale is not, the possibility of an isolated conversion reaction exists. If both the **Lb** scale and scale **3** are up, a more general conversion syndrome exists.

In summary, the **Lb** scale seems to be measuring a person's ability to maintain a friendly, calm facade while feeling frustration and discontent/anger at a preconscious level. We hypothesize that this "conversion" is less entrenched as a characterological trait than the conversion reaction shown by the **3** scale; and therefore we believe the **Lb** scale will be more mobile, rising and falling more readily than the **3** scale, while showing many of the same characteristics.

GENERAL INFORMATION

1. In Hanvik's (1951) original study, this scale of 25 items differentiated between two groups, each of 30 patients, one group with diagnosed organic low back pain (low **Lb**) and the other group with back pain but no clearcut organic reason for the pain (high **Lb**).

2. The correlation of **Lb** with other scales is minimal.

    a. Hanvik (1951) found the **Lb** scale to correlate highly with scales **1** and **3**; however, we have found **Lb** to have a correlation only of .32 with scale **1** and .39 with scale **3** in a group of 847 normals (Appendix C). Swenson et al. (1973) for a group of 50,000 medical patients found a .21 correlation between **Lb** and scale **1** and a .26 correlation for **Lb** and scale **3** (Appendix C).

    b. The scale does correlate .45 with an anxiety score, .45 with a neurotic score, and .41 with a subtle hysteria scale in Swanson, Pearson, and Osborne's medical population (1973). The correlations with other scales however are minimal.

c. In our population of 847 normals (Appendix C) the **Lb** scale does not correlate above .40 with any other scale on the MMPI.

3. Swenson et al. (1973) found that the **Lb** scale varied little according to age.

4. The mean T-score on this scale was 54 for a medical population (Swenson et al., 1973). This also is the mean T-score found in a group of counseling center clients (N = 406) (Anderson and Duckworth, 1970) who had no Clinical scales above 70 T-score points with the possible exception of the **5** scale.

5. The original article proposing this scale is in *Basic Readings on the MMPI in Psychology and Medicine* (Welsh & Dahlstrom, 1956).

HIGH SCORES
(T = 60 or Above)

1. A person with a **Lb** score in this range may be feeling anger/irritation but not want to acknowledge it or perhaps the amount of feeling.

2. If these people are aware of the anger/irritation, they may feel that they should not have it.

   a. The person may think his/her needs are not that important.

   b. The person may think he/she is selfish to have the anger/irritation.

3. One study of college students has found that clients with psychosomatic disorders scored higher on **Lb** than clients without psychosomatic disorders (Klein & Cross, 1984).

4. In this same study, women who reported problems with their mothers were more likely to have psychomatic disorders.

5. Klein and Cross suggested that psychotherapists ask college female clients who have **Lb** above 60 about their relationships with their mothers. In their study, almost one-half of the women who reported

frequent problems with their mothers had psychomatic disorders, whereas only 12% of the women who did not report these problems had psychosomatic disorders.

SUMMARY OF Lb SCALE INTERPRETATIONS*

T-score	Interpretations
60 or below	The interpretation is unknown at the present time.
60 or above	People with scores in this range may see themselves as not angry and in control of their feelings. Underneath they may be irritated and unhappy with what is happening. They may recognize that they are uncomfortable but not the depth of their unhappiness or anger.
	They like to see themselves as "nice" and they believe that anger is not nice.
	They may have this elevation because they feel they cannot do anything about the situation which makes them angry.
	They may feel they "should" not be angry, their needs are not that important, or it seems selfish to have them.

*Where T-scores are listed in two categories (i.e., 60 or below and 60 or above) and a score is obtained that is listed for two categories, use whichever interpretation seems to be most appropriate for individual.

Ca SCALE

(Caudality Scale)

In the 1975 edition of this book, we (Duckworth & Duckworth) suggested not using this scale because we were not sure of its meaning for our populations.

The **Ca** scale originally was developed to differentiate patients with focal cerebral damage in the parietal area from patients with focal lesions in the temporal areas. Because this judgment is better made medically, the scale would seem to have little relevance for the populations with which we are mainly concerned. In a normal college population the scores on this scale tend to be lower than in the original norm group since the mean for the college population is 45 (Anderson & Duckworth, 1969).

As we have worked with the **Ca** scale, we (Anderson & Duckworth) have found that when it is elevated it seems to be measuring the same thing as the **A** scale; that is, a general conscious anxiety. The **Ca** scale correlated .88 with the **A** scale for a large population of medical out-patients (Appendix C). These high correlations are found even though little item overlap between the two scales exists. Only eight of the 36 items of the **Ca** scale are on the **A** scale.

The **Ca** scale however does not always correlate so highly with the **7** scale, another measure of anxiety. In a group of normals (Appendix C), the **Ca** scale correlated only .57 with the **7** scale. This would seem to indicate that the anxiety shown by this scale may be more a conscious reaction to some stressful situation that is shown also by the **A** scale and is less likely the ruminative, obsessive thinking more characteristic of the **7** scale.

The **Ca** scale has the greatest number of high correlations with other MMPI scales of any of the 24 MMPI scales. For a group of normals (Appendix C), the **Ca** scale correlates in the positive direction with the following scales: **F** (.53), **2** (.62), **7** (.57), **0** (.63), **A** (.84), **Dy** (.80), **Pr** (.61); and in the negative direction with the following scales: **K** (-.65), **Es** (-.61), **Do** (-.57), **St** (-.51). Approximately the same number of high correlations are found in an out-patient population (Appendix C).

An investigation of the items in the **Ca** scale suggests why the scale correlates so highly with the previous scales. The item groups are as follows:

1. Ten items which suggest a fear of loss of control or decrease in mental ability. ("I am afraid of losing my mind.")

2. Nine items which have to do with nervousness and brooding. ("Most of the time I feel blue.")

3. Six items dealing with physical concerns, especially tiring easily. ("I feel tired a good deal of the time.")

4. Four items indicative of social introversion. ("I find it hard to make talk when I meet new people.")

5. Seven miscellaneous items. ("I dislike to take a bath.")

Eight of the 36 items overlap with the **A** scale, seven of which suggest an inability to make and stay with decisions. Nine of the items overlap with scale **7** and convey a feeling of unhappiness and discomfort. Nine of the items overlap with scale **2**; five of which also overlap with scale **7** and indicate general unhappiness and dissatisfaction with life.

In summary, an elevated score (60 T-score points or more) on the **Ca** scale would indicate an individual who has a great deal of overt, conscious anxiety. He/she has a poor attitude towards self, fears loss of control, and lacks enthusiasm for becoming involved in activities. On the other hand, low scorers (45 T-score points or below) would tend to feel in control of their own actions, have little anxiety, and feel comfortable in social situations.

GENERAL INFORMATION

1. This scale consists of 37 items selected by Williams (1952) to discriminate those patients with frontal brain lesions (low scores on the scale) from those with posterior brain lesions (high scores on the scale).

2. In Williams' (1952) original study, high scorers tended to show anxiety, depression, guilt, introversion, feelings of inadequacy, worry about the future, and somatic concern.

   Low scorers tended to deny anxiety and worry; to have attitudes of acceptance, affability, and self-confidence; and to have rather low levels of aspiration.

3. The original article by Williams in which this scale was proposed in *Basic Readings on the MMPI in Psychology and Medicine* (Welsh & Dahlstrom, 1956).

SUMMARY OF Ca SCALE INTERPRETATIONS*

T-score	Interpretations
45 or below	A person with a score in this range feels in control of his/her own actions, has little anxiety, and feels comfortable in social situations. This is the range in which most college students usually score.
45 thru 60	This person has a score similar to that of the general, non-college population.
60 or above	A person with a score in this range is reporting a great deal of overt, conscious anxiety. Check the **A** and **7** scales to see if they also are elevated as additional confirmation of this anxiety.

*Where T-scores are listed in two categories (i.e., 45 or below and 45 through 60) and a score is obtained that is listed for two categories, use whichever interpretation seems to be most appropriate for the individual.

—NOTES—

Dy SCALE

(Dependency Scale)

The dependency scale is a fairly easy one to interpret. The higher the scale score, the more the person would like to or actually is psychologically leaning on others. The lower the scale, the more independent the person usually is.

Most mentally healthy persons will have their **Dy** scales below a T-score of 50, whereas the typical client's profile has the **Dy** scale above a T-score of 55. As the client becomes better able to cope with his/her problems, the **Dy** scale typically will be reduced below 50, thus becoming like the **Dy** scales in the healthy profiles.

Benefits can be obtained by interpreting the **Dy** scale in conjunction with the **Do** (Dominance) scale; therefore, we have included a summary table of **Dy-Do** combinations, pp. 277-278.

In general, when dependency is high, dominance is low and vice versa, but occasionally both scales will be elevated above a T-score of 50. When this happens, an important procedure is to note which of the two scales is the highest. When **Do** is higher than **Dy,** while both are above 50, persons will seem independent and liking to take charge of their lives but will frequently remain in bad relationships because their dependency needs are being met that way.

If the **Dy** is higher than the **Do,** people seem to be ambivalent about whether or not they want to take charge of their own lives. This ambivalence tends to come out as passive-aggressive or passive-demanding behavior. These people may ask others to help them by making decisions for them (dependency), but then they become aggressive about or critical of the decision that is made (dominance). Persons with this **Dy-Do** combination are especially difficult to deal with in therapy because the therapist usually is one of the people the client is passive-aggressive or passive-demanding toward. The prognosis for these clients is not as good as it is for other clients (even those with high **Dy** and low **Do**) because the ambivalence usually gets in the way of therapy, unless it is handled adroitly by the therapist.

GENERAL INFORMATION

1. Navran (1954) developed the **Dy** scale of 57 items to identify people who are highly dependent upon others.

2. Navran developed the scale by asking 16 judges to specify, independently, MMPI items they felt reflected dependency. The resulting 157 items were tested and cross-validated on neuro-psychiatric patients and a scale of 57 items was derived.

3. One study (Birtchnell & Kennard, 1983) has found that the **Dy** scale

   a. is related to the sex of the individual. Women chose more **Dy** items than men, 25 versus 19 on the average.

   b. is not related to age. More **Dy** items are not chosen as one gets older.

   c. is related to psychiatric pathology, the more severe the symptoms, the higher the **Dy** score.

   d. is related to depression. A .60 correlation exists between **Dy** and scale **2**. (For normal subjects the correlation is .54. See Appendix C.)

   e. is related to anxiety. A .72 correlation exists between **Dy** and scale **7** even though only 11 items are shared out of 57. (For normal subjects the correlation is .56. See Appendix C.)

   f. is positively correlated to poor quality marriages.

   g. is negatively correlated to the **Do** scale even though only 5 items are shared. (For normal subjects the correlation is -.63. See Appendix C.)

   h. is higher for women with dominant husbands.

4. Another study (Nacev, 1980) found the **Dy** score to be negatively correlated with the **Es** scale (-.62). In this same study, elevation of the **Dy** scale was not found to be a predictor of patient's attendance in psychotherapy for an adult, nonpsychiatric outpatient population.

5. Heppner and Anderson (1985) have found that self-appraised ineffective problem solvers tend to be significantly higher on this scale than effective problem solvers.

6. The mean for this scale is low (44 T-score points) for college students (Anderson & Duckworth, 1969).

7. In addition to interpreting the **Dy** scale alone, the **Dy** scale can be considered in relationship to the **Do** (dominance) scale, in certain instances shown in the **Dy** and **Do** combination summary, pp. 277-278.

HIGH SCORES
(T = 55 or Above)

See also the **Dy** and **Do** combinations, pp. 277-278.

1. High scores tend to indicate that the person is dependent and somewhat passive.

2. Graham (1977) felt that this scale might be a good measure of self-reported dependency, however other people might not judge the person as dependent.

3. Birtchnell and Kennard (1983) have found that high **Dy** scores are related to being female, having high depression (**2** scale), anxiety (**7** scale) scores, having early loss or separation experiences, and having a poor quality marriage and a dominant marital partner.

LOW SCORES
(T = 50 or Below)

See also the **Dy** and **Do** combinations, pp. 277-278.

1. Persons with low scores tend to be independent of others.

2. This level tends to be typical for college students, with the mean score being 44 T-score points (Anderson & Duckworth, 1969).

COMBINATIONS

Dy-Do

1. For a summary of selected **Dy-Do** scale combinations, see pp. 277-278.

SUMMARY OF Dy SCALE INTERPRETATIONS*

T-score	Interpretations
50 or below	This person tends to be independent of others; this can be either from choice or necessity. The mean score for college students is 44.
50 thru 55	A person at this level feels a need to be somewhat dependent.
55 or above	This person has a strong need to be dependent at this time; the higher the elevation, the more dependent the person feels. Such a score may be either characterological or situational. These persons also may be somewhat passive. This is the typical range of scores for clients coming in voluntarily with serious problems for which they want some help.

See pp. 277-278 for **Dy-Do** combinations.

---

*Where T-scores are listed in two categories (i.e., 50 or below and 50 through 55) and a score is obtained that is listed for two categories, use whichever interpretation seems to be most appropriate for the individual.

Do SCALE

(Dominance Scale)

The **Do** scale is a fairly simple measure of a person's ability to take charge of his/her own life. The higher this scale, the more the person is saying that he/she is able to take charge of his/her own life. The **Do** scale may show domineering behavior when the scale is very high (above 70) and the **4** scale is above 70 T-score points. Even then, the person may not always show domineering behavior. The presence of the behavior seems to depend upon certain other scales being elevated with the **Do**, if the **5** scale is elevated 5 or more T-score points above the **4** scale for men or is below 40 T-score points for women, it may temper the domineering behavior.

The lower the **Do** scale, the more the person is saying he/she does not want to take charge of his/her life. The lower **Do** score usually is accompanied by an elevation on the **Dy** scale. When this happens, the person usually wants other people to take over his/her life and wants to be dependent upon them.

In addition to interpreting this scale alone, its relationship with the **Dy** scale should be considered. We have found an elevation on the **Do** scale (when **Dy** is below 50) to be a good sign of progress in therapy. Also, elevations above a T-score of 60 on **Es, Do,** and **St** usually are signs of a healthy profile. The **Dy-Do** relationships are summarized on p. 277.

GENERAL INFORMATION

1. The **Do** scale of 60 items was developed by Gough, McClosky and Meehl (1951) and measures poise, self-assurance, resourcefulness, efficiency, and perseverance.

2. The scale was developed by the "peer group nomination technique." One hundred college and 124 high school students were asked to nominate the members of their group whom they considered to be the most and least dominant. Those items on the MMPI that differentiated between the two groups were used for the **Do** scale.

3. This scale seems to measure a person's ability to take charge of his/her own life.

4. The **Do** scale has been shown to be successful in predicting staff ratings and peer nominations for dominance and in identifying outstanding leaders in high school programs (Dahlstrom & Welsh, 1960).

5. In one study (Birtchnell & Kennard, 1983) no significant relationship was found between elevation on **Do** and age or sex.

6. Heppner and Anderson (1981, 1985) have found that ineffective problem solvers tend to be significantly lower on this scale than effective problem solvers.

7. College students tend to score high on this scale with a mean of 60 T-score points (Anderson & Duckworth, 1969).

8. A group of college achievers scored higher than non-achievers on this scale (Morgan, 1952).

9. An elevated score on the **Do** scale has been found to be significantly related to middle management success (Miles, 1968).

10. In addition to interpreting this scale alone, in certain instances shown in the **Dy** and **Do** combination summary and discussed in the opening paragraphs of **Dy** scale, the **Do** scale is to be considered in relationship to the **Dy** scale.

11. The article originally proposing this scale is in the *Basic Readings of the MMPI in Psychology and Medicine* (Welsh & Dahlstrom, 1956).

HIGH SCORES
(T = 60 or Above)

See also the **Dy** and **Do** combinations, pp. 277-278.

1. High scorers tend to be people who take charge of their lives.

2. When the person has a **Do** score above T of 75, he/she may be seen as a leader and/or domineering.

LOW SCORES
(T = 50 or Below)

See also the **Dy** and **Do** combinations, pp. 277-278.

1. A person with a low **Do** score usually would like others to take charge of his/her life.

COMBINATIONS

Es-Do-St (T = 55 or Above) See p. 258.

$\overline{\textbf{Es}}\textbf{-}\overline{\textbf{Do}}\textbf{-}\overline{\textbf{St}}$ (T = 45 or Below) See p. 258.

Dy-Do

1. For a summary of selected **Dy-Do** scale combinations, see pp. 277-278.

SUMMARY OF Do SCALE INTERPRETATIONS*

T-score	Interpretations
50 or below	A person with a score in this range prefers to have others take charge of his/her life at this time. This level is typical for clients in therapy.
50 thru 60	A person with a score at this level is able to control much of his/her life and at the same time is able to be dependent upon others periodically. This range is typical for people who do not have a college education.
60 or above	This person tends to take charge of his/her own life. He/she is able to meet deadlines, plan, and organize his/her life. At higher levels (T = 70 or above), a person may be seen by others as imposing or domineering if his/her 4 scale score is also above 70 T-score points. The mean for college students is a T-score of 60,

See **Dy-Do** combinations, pp. 277-278.

---

*Where T-scores are listed in two categories (i.e., 50 or below and 50 through 60) and a score is obtained that is listed for two categories, use whichever interpretation seems to be most appropriate for the individual.

SUMMARY OF Dy AND Do COMBINATION
INTERPRETATIONS

If the Dy Scale Score Is	If the Do Scale Score Is	Interpretations
50 or below	45 or below	This combination is found rarely. In a group of over 500 profiles, only 12 had this combination. Ten of these persons were previously long-term dependent persons (**Dy** = 60 or above, **Do** = 45 or below) who were no longer dependent but who had not yet learned to control their own lives. The other two persons were hostile males who were successful in business and who insisted that the significant women in their lives (mothers or wives) maintain a quiet, isolated, womb-like home.
50 or below	50 or above	This person likes to control his/her life and feels comfortable doing it.
45 or below	60 or above	This person may be a leader since leaders usually fall in this category. This combination is usual for well adjusted college students.
60 or above	45 or below	This person feels unable to take charge of his/her life and feels that others must be relied upon at this time. The individual may feel more comfortable being a follower or in a semi-dependent position and may be unable to make major decisions. When the ego strength (**Es**) and status (**St**) scales also are low, the person may feel worthless. Most likely, the person feels the need to lean on someone and will use either the therapist or another person for this purpose. These clients rarely miss appointments and usually try hard to please the therapist.
50 or above	50 or above	People with this combination may seem ambivalent about whether to be dependent or dominant. This is especially true if the two scales are close together in elevation.

Dy-Do

When the **Do** is 5 points or more above the **Dy,** the person appears more dominant than dependent but may stay in bad relationships because of the dependency needs.

When the **Dy** is 5 points or more above the **Do,** the person may be passive-aggressive, that is the person controls through weakness. The person appears to be dependent, but is actually in charge of the situation. This person usually manipulates others (including the counselor) by appearing to be dependent, when in fact the person is determining the course of his/her own behavior and the counseling sessions.

Re SCALE

(Social Responsibility Scale)

The **Re** scale originally was developed to determine the social responsibility of a person. That is, persons receiving high scores on this scale were seen as socially responsible, willing to accept the consequences of their behavior, trustworthy, and dependable, while persons receiving low scores were seen as socially irresponsible. We have noted however that persons receiving low scores could be equally as socially responsible as persons receiving elevated scores. Instead of social responsibility then, we feel this scale measures the acceptance (high score) or rejection (low score) of a previously held value system.

For persons under age 25, an elevation on this scale (T = 50 through 65) indicates that they accept in general the value system of their parents. A score in the 40 through 50 range usually indicates that the person is questioning the parental value system (a typical procedure for college students and for those mental health clients going through a traumatic life change). Scores below 40 usually indicate that the person is not just questioning but actually is rejecting the parental value system.

One caution must be noted. Many people tend to presume that a person is showing acceptance or rejection of white middle class values by his/her score on the **Re** scale. What this scale seems to be showing for this below 25 age group is acceptance or rejection of the *parental* values which may or may not be those of the white, middle class. For example, Black ghetto-reared college students may receive low scores on this scale because they are rejecting the ghetto values with which they were reared and now are accepting white middle class values. Thus, to tell accurately what values are being accepted or rejected, one must know the person's background.

For persons above the age of 25, interpretation of this scale is based upon the person's present value system which may or may not be similar to the parents. Persons with elevations on the **Re** scale (T = 50 through 65) tend to accept their present value system and intend to continue using it. Persons with scores of 40 through 50 are questioning their present value system and those below 40 are rejecting their most recently held value system. An illustration of this is a 40 year old male with a **Re** score of 35. He had been reared with one value system (his parents') which he had rejected in his early 20s. Now at age 40, he was re-evaluating his own value system and felt that the values of his parents (those rejected 20 years previously) now were more valid for him than those he had held more recently.

For people of all ages, the higher a score above 65 on the **Re** scale, the more rigid a person seems to be in his/her acceptance of values and the less willing to explore other values.

As one examines the items and the intercorrelations of this scale with other scales, a consistent picture of a person with a high score emerges.

High scorers report that they had little trouble with authorities as they were growing up. They answer false to such items as "In school I was sometimes sent to the principal for cutting up" and "My parents have objected to the kind of people I went around with." This self-report receives some support from **Re**'s -.48 correlation with the obvious Psychopathic Deviate Scale (Swenson et al., 1973).

Part of their comfort with authorities may be based on the fact that they seldom admit to taking risks. Seven of the 32 items on this scale indicate a lack of interest in creating excitement. They answer true to "I have never done anything dangerous for the thrill of it" and false to "I enjoy a race or game better when I bet on it."

This conservative approach to life does not appear to be related to fear but rather to a lack of interest in this kind of stimulating situation because they report that they feel comfortable with a variety of other situations that could produce anxiety. They answer true to "I do not dread seeing a doctor about a sickness or injury" and "I usually work things out for myself rather than get someone to show me how."

The items concerning not taking risks seem to support the presence of a control factor in high **Re** people's behavior. This also is supported by a correlation of -.53 with Impulsivity and -.50 with Neurotic Undercontrol scales (Swenson et al., 1973).

High scorers on **Re** also report that they expect others to be positive in their behavior. They answer false to "A large number of people are guilty of bad sexual conduct" and "I have often found people jealous of my good ideas, just because they had not thought of them first." This also is supported by **Re**'s correlation of -.49 with the **Pr** scale and .52 with the **K** scale (Appendix C).

This would seem to be one scale on which a certain type of good student would get high scores. This would be the student who reports liking school since **Re** correlates .61 with academic achievement, .51 with intellectual efficiency, .51 with intellectual quotient, and .51 with teaching potential (Swenson et al., 1973).

All of these factors together indicate someone who is confident, even-tempered, non-pretentious, comfortable with authority, and competent in academic areas, with little need to pursue adventure.

While high scorers have many strong points, several defects are possible. They may be unimaginative and non-creative. This is particularly likely to be true if scales **7** and **8** are below 45 T-score points. Their lives may be controlled by a considerable number of "ought to's" with which they are comfortable but which could annoy other people who have to work with them. That is, they may expect others to live up to their standards and be as comfortable with them as they are. Consequently they may have difficulty understanding why others cannot or will not perform as they do.

In addition to interpreting the **Re** scale alone, in certain instances shown in the **Re** and **Pr** combination summary, pp. 292-293, considering the **Re** scale in relationship to the **Pr** (prejudice or rigid thinking) scale is helpful. At first glance the **Re** and **Pr** scales would appear to be positively correlated; that is, those who question their previous values (low **Re**) also would be open to alternate viewpoints (low **Pr**). Similarly, those who wholeheartedly accept their previous values (high **Re**) would not be open to alternate viewpoints (high **Pr**). Certainly these combinations do appear; however, other combinations also appear. Specifically, at least one segment of people who are questioning their previous values (low **Re**) (they usually consider themselves to be "liberal" thinkers) are not tolerant of others (high **Pr**), particularly others who accept the more traditional American value system. Apparently, these people are not as liberal as they believe themselves to be, at least about others who believe differently than they do.

Conversely, some people who accept their middle-class background with all its implications (high **Re**) also are able to listen to alternative beliefs held by others (low **Pr**). These people appear to have taken a position for themselves, but they are able to allow others to have their own positions.

If, however, the **Re** scale is above 65 T-score points and the **Pr** is low, the person's tolerance may be a willingness to let others express their beliefs as long as the others are responsible with these beliefs.

Interestingly, the **Re** scale tends to be correlated with age; the older the person, the higher the **Re** scale tends to be. We usually find the **Re** scale low for college students as they question how they were reared and some of the values of their parents.

GENERAL INFORMATION

1. The **Re** 32-item scale was developed by Gough (1952) to measure social responsibility.

2. Social responsibility was defined by Gough as the willingness to accept the consequences of one's own behavior, dependability, trustworthiness, and sense of obligation to the group.

3. Gough used the "peer nomination" method with this scale, asking college and high school students to choose the most and least responsible members of their groups. The MMPI items that differentiated between these two groups were the basis for the scale.

4. Instead of measuring social responsibility, the **Re** scale seems to measure how much the person accepts the values with which he/she was reared. Persons below age 25 who score high on this scale tend to accept their parents' values. When people question or reject the values of their parents, they usually score low on the **Re** scale.

   Persons above age 25 who score low on this scale may be rejecting their most recently held value systems which may or may not be the same as their parents.

5. Heppner and Anderson (1985) have found that ineffective problem solvers were significantly lower on this scale than effective problem solvers.

6. In addition to interpreting this scale alone, consideration of the **Re** scale in relationship to the **Pr** scale is helpful. See the **Re** and **Pr** combination summary, pp. 292-293.

7. The **Re** scale has differentiated "responsible" from "irresponsible" people (school disciplinary problems, people nominated for responsibility, and good school citizenship) (Dahlstrom & Welsh, 1960).

8. A group of college achievers scored higher than non-achievers on this scale (Morgan, 1952).

HIGH SCORES

See also the **Re** and **Pr** combinations, pp. 292-293.

1. People under the age of 25 who score high on the **Re** scale tend to accept their parents' values.

   Persons over the age of 25 accept their present value system, which may or may not be the same as their parents'.

2. Persons with high **Re** scores tend to have positions of leadership and responsibility (Knapp, 1960; Olmstead & Monachesi, 1956).

LOW SCORES
(T = 40 or Below)

See also the **Re** and **Pr** combinations, pp. 292-293.

1. When people under the age of 25 reject their parents' values, they tend to score low on the **Re** scale.
   Persons over the age of 25, scoring in this range, tend to reject their present value system, which may or may not be the same as their parents'.

2. Low scorers may have substituted a new religion, philosophy, or political outlook for their old values.

COMBINATIONS

Re-Pr

1. For a summary of selected **Re** and **Pr** scale combinations, see pp. 292-293.

SUMMARY OF Re SCALE INTERPRETATIONS*

Interpretations

T-score	Below Age 25	Over Age 25
40 or below	This person tends to deny the value system of his/her parents. Such a person may have substituted another value system for the paternal one.	This person tends to deny his/her most recently held value system (which may be different from the parents'.)
40 thru 50	People in this range tend to question their parent's values. They may be exploring alternative viewpoints. Their values seem to be in flux.	People in this range tend to be questioning their most recently held value system and are usually exploring different values.
50 thru 65	People with scores in this range tend to accept their parents' values. The higher the score in this range, the more the person has accepted these values.	A person with a score in this range tends to accept his/her present value system. The higher the score, the more the person has accepted these values.
65 or above	The higher a score is above 65, the more rigid a person seems to be in his/her acceptance of values and the less willing to explore other values.	

Relationship to Clinical scales: If the **4** scale is above 70 T-score points and the **Re** scale is below 50, the person may be rebellious.

*Where T-scores are listed in two categories (i.e., 40 or below and 40 through 50) and a score is obtained that is listed for two categories, use whichever interpretation seems to be most appropriate for the individual.

—NOTES—

Pr SCALE

(Prejudice Scale)

The **Pr** scale was designed originally to measure anti-Semitic prejudice. While the scale does measure prejudice, it appears to be concerned with the much broader concept of rigidity in thinking. That is, elevations on this scale seem to indicate that a person is able to accept only concepts and values similar to his/her own and rejects alternative ways of thinking. Elevations on this scale also may identify persons who are not secure with their present value systems and therefore must shut out alternative viewpoints.

People with low **Pr** scores usually are able to tolerate opinions different from their own. These lower scores also can indicate a person who is secure with his/her values and thus is able to allow others to have theirs. Thus, the **Pr** scale seems to indicate a person's willingness to accept or to look at alternate viewpoints.

The **Pr** scale consists of 32 items. The largest number (12 items) reflects negative, cynical, and contemptuous attitudes toward the motivations of others. "I can't blame anyone for trying to grab everything he can get in this world." Nine items of foreboding or unreasonable fears are included. "Sometimes I feel as if I must injure either myself or someone else."

Seven items indicate uncertainty of self and social skills. "I refuse to play some games because I am not good at them." The remaining four items are miscellaneous types, e.g., "I feel there is only one true religion."

Split half reliability coefficients are .79 and .81 and test-retest reliability is .56 (Jensen, 1957). The scale is thus subject to change or at least is somewhat unstable over a period of time.

Evidence exists that prejudice may be a general response tendency which influences the individual's reactions to a variety of situations and persons. English (1971) has pointed out that a sizable majority of studies seems to confirm the belief that prejudice is a general pervasive attitudinal characteristic of some individuals. These people tend to reject any group they consider significantly different from their own, particularly those with ethnic, racial, or religious differences.

Some interesting correlations were found by Gough (1951a) in his original study. Low scorers had an average I.Q. of 111, whereas high scorers had an average of 98. A later correlation was found (1951b) between **Pr** and Intellectual Quotient of -.70 and **Pr** and Intellectual Efficiency of -.63. Further support for this negative relationship between intellectual ability and prejudice comes from college students who have a mean score of 40 on **Pr** (Anderson & Duckworth, 1969).

Social class also is related to prejudice. Again, in Gough's original study (1951a), the socioeconomic status (SES) scale he used correlated -.60 with **Pr** with higher SES students scoring lower on the **Pr** scale. Thus an elevated score is not unusual for an individual of lower social status or for one of more limited intellectual potential; but an elevated score for someone of better than average intelligence, such as a college student, needs to be looked at in another way.

Therapists should explore the possibility that their more intelligent clients with high **Pr** scores may be in a period of poor expectations, that is, these clients may have some doubts as to whether or not they can cope with the problems that are bothering them. They may have a pervasive sour grapes attitude which could be temporary and subject to therapeutic intervention. The possibility exists that some resistance to therapy may occur because these clients tend to be blaming others for what has gone wrong in their lives. They also may be very resistive to accepting new ideas during the counseling session.

In addition to interpreting this scale by itself, it should be interpreted in combination with the **Re** scale. The summary of the various combinations of **Re** and **Pr** is found on pp. 292-293.

GENERAL INFORMATION

1. The **Pr** 32-item scale was devised by Gough (1951a) to differentiate those high school students who score high on an anti-Semitism test (were most prejudiced) from those who scored low.

2. The scale seems to measure the much broader area of rigidity in thinking, with people who are more rigid scoring high on the scale.

3. Heppner and Anderson (1985) have found that self-appraised ineffective problem solvers tended to be significantly higher on this scale than effective problem solvers.

4. In addition to interpreting this scale alone, considering the **Pr** scale's relationship to the **Re** scale is helpful in certain instances shown in the **Re** and **Pr** combination summary, pp. 292-293.

5. The **Pr** scale correlates positively with the California **F** Scale (Jensen, 1957).

6. College students tend to score in the low range on this scale with a mean of 40 T-score points (Anderson & Duckworth, 1969).

7. Gough's original article proposing this scale is in the *Basic Readings on the MMPI in Psychology and Medicine* (Welsh & Dahlstrom, 1956).

HIGH SCORES
(T = 55 or Above)

See also the **Re** and **Pr** combinations, pp. 292-293.

1. High scorers on this scale tend to be rigid and not willing to look at others' points of view.

2. They may not be willing to question their own value systems.

3. The higher the score, the more rigid and adamant these people usually are about their beliefs.

4. This rigidity can either be a permanent attitude ("I am always correct") or the result of situational stress ("I need to maintain my present position so that I don't become disoriented"),

5. High scorers in college may have poor academic achievement.

6. High scorers are more likely to come from the lower social classes (Gough, 1951b).

7. They also are likely to have lower IQ scores (Jensen, 1957).

LOW SCORES
(T = 45 or Below)

See also the **Re** and **Pr** combinations, pp. 292-293.

1. Low scorers tend to be open to alternative points of view.

2. The person usually has a positive view of the world and tends to be effective in coping with his/her life.

3. A score in the 45 or below range is helpful in counseling, because the client is receptive to opinions different from his/her own.

COMBINATIONS

Re-Pr

1. For a summary of selected **Re** and **Pr** scale combinations, see pp. 292-293.

SUMMARY OF Pr SCALE INTERPRETATIONS*

T-score	Interpretations
45 or below	Persons in this range usually are seen as open-minded and willing to entertain opinions contrary to their own. They are likely to have a positive outlook on life. College students tend to score in this range.
45 thru 55	The majority of people score in this range.
55 or above	Persons with elevations on this scale usually are rigid in their beliefs. That is, they are not open to considering alternative points of view or questioning their own value systems. As the score increases, the person becomes more rigid and restricted in his/her thinking. He/she also tends to be cynical and distrustful of other people and of the world in general.

Relationship to Clinical Scales: If a person has an elevated score on scale **6** (Paranoia), the higher the **Pr** scale is above 50 the more encompassing the suspiciousness. For example, a recently divorced woman client with a **6** scale at 70 and a **Pr** of 50 may be only suspicious of her ex-husband, whereas a recently divorced woman client with a **6** scale of 70 and a **Pr** of 65 may be suspicious of all men.

---

*Where T-scores are listed in two categories (i.e., 45 or below and 45 thru 55) and a score is obtained that is listed for two categories, use whichever interpretation seems to be most appropriate for the individual.

Pr

SUMMARY OF Re AND Pr SCALE
COMBINATION INTERPRETATIONS*

If **Re** is	and **Pr** is	Interpretations
40 or below	50 or below	A person with this combination usually has rejected a previously held value system and has adopted a new one. He/she is willing to let others express their beliefs however and can tolerate being around people with different opinions.
	50 or above	People with this combination usually have rejected a previously held value system and have adopted a new one. They also tend to be rigid about their new beliefs and cannot tolerate others who have beliefs different from theirs.
40 thru 50	50 or below	People with this combination usually are questioning their value system and are open to exploring other people's ideas and values.
	50 or above	People with this combination are usually questioning their own beliefs and may not be able to tolerate others around them who are not also in the process of questioning their beliefs.
50 thru 65	50 or below	A person with this combination tends to accept the value system with which he/she was reared but is still able to associate with people who have different value systems.
	50 or above	People with this combination usually are accepting of the value system with which they were reared but have a difficult time

accepting other people who believe differently than they do.

65 or above	50 or below	A person with this combination may be rigid in his/her beliefs and value system but is willing to let others express different beliefs as long as they are seen as "good" people and carry out their responsibilities.
	50 or above	A person with this combination may be rigid in his/her beliefs and value system. He/she also is intolerant of others who have different beliefs. He/she is likely to reject things that are "different."

*Where T-scores are listed in two categories (i.e., 40 or below and 40 through 50) and a score is obtained that is listed for two categories, use whichever interpretation seems to be most appropriate for the individual.

—NOTES—

St SCALE

(Status Scale)

The **St** scale was developed originally to distinguish those people who had high socioeconomic status from those who had low socioeconomic status. Instead of measuring the socioeconomic status the person has, we feel this scale is measuring the socioeconomic status the person desires. It also may be measuring a liking for some of the finer things of life (books, art, music, clothes, and nice surroundings) which go along with higher socioeconomic status. This last interpretation of a high status score is especially true when the **5** scale is elevated above 60 for males and is below 45 for females. In many respects, the **5** and **St** scales are measuring some of the same aspects of a person's life.

When the **5** scale is low for males or high for females, a high **St** score then may be measuring the strivings of a person to better himself/herself, to achieve recognition, and to improve his/her way of life. It also may be measuring an emphasis which the person has on acquiring some of the materialistic trappings of a better life, i.e., a nicer home, better car, or more material goods. In other words, when the **5** scale indicates that a person has aesthetic interests, the **St** scale also seems to be measuring this. When the **5** scale indicates that a person does not have many aesthetic interests, then the elevated **St** scale seems to be measuring a desire for upward mobility and recognition.

Many times an MMPI profile has problem areas indicated on it, and the **St** scale is elevated. This elevation may be a good sign, because the client is saying he/she desires some of the better things of life and may be willing to improve in order to achieve them. An elevation on the **St** scale may be showing why a person is striving to remain in college or in a good job when everything is collapsing around him/her.

We also find this scale a very useful one to look at in marriage counseling. If the **St** scale is at approximately the same level for both people, usually no problem exists in this area. If one of the couple's **St** scores is high while the other's is low or average, then this may be an indication of a problem area. One of the couple desires a high status while the other one does not and indeed may see no reason for striving in this way. A frequent occurrence with married couples coming in for counseling is to have a wife scoring high on **St** and the husband not. She wants to better their life (usually by him getting better job) while he is content where he is. A compounding factor may be that the wife feels unable to specify her ambitions because "a wife should not criticize her husband's work if he's happy with it." Frequently, we have been able to persuade the wife to find a job herself or to go back to school for further education to satisfy her status needs, without necessarily disturbing the husband with his lesser status needs.

The **St** scale frequently is elevated above 60 T-score points with the **Es** and **Do** scales. This shows a very normal pattern for college students and people with good psychological functioning.

People with low **St** scores tend to fall into three groups. The first is composed of those people who work in low status jobs, are from a low socioeconomic status background, and are reasonably content with their lot in life. In fact, these people may become uncomfortable in high status situations. The second group of people with low **St** scores is made up of those who have achieved middle status positions but who feel that their upward mobility is ended. The third group of people with low **St** scores is made up of those who also have low **Es** and **Do** scores and high **Dy** scores. These people usually feel that they are not worth much and therefore should not expect much from life including high status. When counseling persons in this third group, we have found that it is usually necessary to build their self-concept before other counseling can be done.

To explore further the implications of the low **St** score, we took a group of college counseling center clients (N = 16) with a low **St** score and examined the case notes for these clients. Some marked consistencies were found among the clients. Almost all of them had disturbed profiles, that is, three or more of the Clinical scales were above 70 T-score points. All these clients reported dissatisfaction with themselves and how they were adjusting to their environment. Often the dissatisfaction centered around an inability to make decisions or to deal in a comfortable fashion with people.

All of the case notes for these people reported inappropriate social behavior. The clients did not always interpret it as such, but the case notes indicated that the behavior was unusual for the situations in which the clients found themselves. For example, "The client came in and kept his finger in a page of a book he was reading. He would go back to reading after finishing a sentence." And again, "She appeared to come on very strongly as one who desired much closeness and friendship.

Whenever anyone came close to her however she would turn her back to them psychologically and refuse to acknowledge them. At this point she would react with surprise and anger when they because upset with her."

Another common behavior for these clients was resistance to counseling, that is, they found it difficult to talk, avoided subjects, and frequently missed sessions. A close corollary to this was the large number of these clients who terminated counseling either by becoming no-shows or by quitting before the counselor felt that they had reached maximum benefit. As a result, these clients generally had poor outcomes although several of them made great gains in terms of changing their behavior. To a lesser extent, some of them seemed to be easily influenced by others.

In summation, this group of individuals in a college counseling center with low social status scores were people who generally had disturbed profiles, were dissatisfied with themselves, and were engaged in some inappropriate social behavior. In spite of their stated desire to change some of the above, they generally were resistive to counseling and were likely to terminate counseling before the counselor felt that any real progress had been made.

These generally unfavorable implications of the *low* status score are borne out in the favorable implications found for the high status scores for a group of normal persons not coming in for counseling (Appendix C). The status scale correlates highly with the following MMPI scales: **0** (-.61), **Es** (.54), **Ca** (-.51), **Dy** (-.53), and **Do** (.61).

GENERAL INFORMATION

1. The **St** scale of 34 items was developed by Gough (1948) to distinguish between two groups of high school students, those with high socioeconomic status and those with low socioeconomic status.

2. These 34 items can be grouped as follows: literacy and aesthetic interests; social poise, security, and confidence in self and others; denial of fear and anxiety; broadminded attitudes toward moral, religious, and sexual matters; and positive, dogmatic and self-righteous opinions (Gough, 1948).

3. A significant positive correlation exists between this scale and the **K** scale.

4. Gough (1949b) has found an interesting relationship when objective status measures (such as amount of money earned) are compared to the **St** scale score. Persons of low objective status, but upwardly mobile, tend to score relatively higher on the **St** scale than on the objective status measures. The reverse is true of people tending toward downward mobility.

5. Heppner and Anderson (1985) have found that ineffective problem solvers were significantly lower on this scale than effective problem solvers.

6. Gough's original article proposing this scale is in the *Basic Readings on the MMPI in Psychology and Medicine* (Welsh & Dahlstrom, 1956).

HIGH SCORES
(T = 55 or Above)

1. High scores tend to indicate a desire for the better things of life which are associated with education and/or upper socioeconomic status.

2. A person with a high **St** score, as compared to a person with a low **St** score, seems to have greater reserve in connection with personal affairs and problems, fewer somatic complaints, more satisfactory overall adjustment, greater intelligence, high scholastic aptitude, and less social introversion (Gough, 1949b).

3. College students typically score high on the **St** scale, with the mean being between 55 and 60 (Anderson & Duckworth, 1969).

4. A person with **St** scores in this range may be dissatisfied if his/her job is not of high status.

5. If a wife has an **St** score in the high range but her husband does not, she may be dissatisfied because he does not want or strive for higher status.

6. If a person has an **St** score in this range and is coming in for help for serious problems, the elevated **St** score can indicate good motivation for counseling. The client may be willing to work very diligently on these problems in order to achieve higher status.

LOW SCORES
(T = 40 or Below)

1. People with scores of 40 or below tend to have status desires similar to people from the lower socioeconomic levels.

2. Three groups of people tend to have low **St** scores.

   a. Those who work in low status jobs, are from a low socio-economic background, and are reasonably content with their status.

   b. Those who are in middle status positions and feel they have gone as high as they can.

   c. Those who also have low **Es** and **Do** scores and high **Dy** scores. These people usually have low self-esteem and low self-confidence and feel they do not deserve any higher status.

   These people may be unmarried, may stay in a bad marriage, or may have been in a series of bad marriages.

3. If a person with a score in this range is in college, the motivation to remain in college may be lacking unless family pressure helps to keep him/her there.

COMBINATIONS

Es-Do-St (T = 55 or Above) See p. 258.

E̅s-D̅o-S̅t̅ (T = 45 or Below) See p. 258.

SUMMARY OF St SCALE INTERPRETATIONS*

T-score	Interpretations
40 or below	These people have status desires similar to people from the lower socio-economic levels. They usually have low achievement needs and do not expect or strive for a higher status. If these people are from a lower socio-economic group, they tend to be reasonably content with their lives. If they are from a middle socio-economic group, they may feel their upward mobility is ended and not be so contented with their lives. When this scale is low and the **Es** and **Do** scores are also low, people may have extremely poor self-esteem and no self-confidence. They may feel they do not deserve a better life. These people may be unmarried, may stay in a bad marriage, or may have contracted sequential bad marriages. If people with these scores are in college, they may not really want to be there but may remain in college through family pressure.
40 thru 55	These people have status desires similar to the general, non-college population.
55 thru 60	People at this level have status desires similar to those of the general college graduate. They tend to like having some of the nicer things in life, such as good books and a nice home. They may be dissatisfied if their jobs lack status or the financial rewards are insufficient to provide the material that goes with status.
60 or above	People at this level have status desires similar to those of a graduate student or someone from a high socio-economic level. They usually have high achievement needs and especially like to be recognized for doing a good job at work or school. They may be dissatisfied if they do not have some of the nicer things in life, such as good books or nice homes. They may complain of job dissatisfaction if their status needs are not met by their jobs.

St   300

*Where T-scores are listed in two categories (i.e., 40 or below and 40 through 55) and a score is obtained that is listed for two categories, use whichever interpretation seems to be most appropriate for the individual.

—NOTES—

Cn SCALE

(Control Scale)

The control scale is an especially useful one on the MMPI. An elevated **Cn** scale can be a clue as to how much of the behavior indicated by elevations on the Clinical scales will be exhibited in the presence of other people. If the **Cn** scale is elevated with other Clinical scale elevations indicating some problems, the client has some ability to control his/her problem behavior and to show only what he/she wishes others to observe. While these others may not always be the people the counselor wishes would or would not see the client's behavior, the elevation on **Cn** does indicate a strength, because the client has the ability to control problem behavior to some extent. A problem occasionally occurs when the client chooses to hide certain or all problem behavior from the counselor as well as from others.

When the **Cn** scale is above the typical range (55 or above) with no elevations above 70 on the Clinical scales, the client may appear somewhat reserved and non-emotional. This behavior is especially true the higher the **Cn** scale. Many people with this combination have grown up in an environment where emotions were not readily expressed or encouraged. Some of these people may express the wish that they could be freer with other people or at least more expressive of their emotions. In these instances, a sign of therapeutic progress may be a lowering of the **Cn** scale. Elevations on the **Cn** scale can thus indicate client strength (when the Clinical scales are high) or potential problems (when the Clinical scales are low).

A low **Cn** score means that the person tends to show the behavior indicated by his/her Clinical scale score elevations. If the Clinical scores are low (below 70), the person has no behavior that needs to be controlled. This does not mean however that the person cannot control his/her behavior if the Clinical scales should become elevated. The **Cn** scale in this latter instance might also become elevated. However if a person has Clinical scale elevations of 70 or above, a low **Cn** score does mean that the behavior indicated by the elevated Clinical scale scores is not being controlled by the person, and the Clinical scale behavior is exhibited in the presence of others.

Elevations on the **Cn** scale, especially when accompanied by elevations on the **K, 3,** and **R** scales may indicate a type of person who is constricted in many ways. For further discussion of these scales, see the **R** scale commentary, p. 247.

The important thing to remember in interpreting the **Cn** scale is to look at the accompanying Clinical scales and to use their elevations in combination with **Cn** scale placement to get the most accurate interpretation of the **Cn** scale.

A rather wide combination of items make up the **Cn** scale. The items can be divided into seven major categories:

1. The first group of items appears to be an awareness of and an admission to base impulses and behavior. "I sometimes feel like swearing." "I gossip a little at times." This may lead to an openness in counseling interviews which interviewers like.

2. A second group of items indicates that the individual is uncomfortable at the conscious level. "I sometimes feel that I am about to go to pieces." "I wish I could be as happy as others seem to be." In a college population, people with elevated Clinical scales and high **Cn** scores report uncomfortable feelings but seem to see their cause as being situational, that is, a bad marriage situation, lack of vocational choice, or inability to set appropriate goals because of the university structure.

3. A group of manic items is the third major category. "When I get bored I like to stir up some excitement." "At times my thoughts have raced ahead faster than I could speak them." This suggests that a rather high activity level exists for the person with a high **Cn** Scale score.

4. Some religious items are included as a fourth group. They appear to be a rejection of some of the more fundamentalistic beliefs such as miracles and the accuracy of prophets.

5. A fifth group of items concerns the denial of certain symptoms such as the use of alcohol and fainting spells.

6. Some items referring to family relations compose a sixth group. People with a high **Cn** scale report their relations are

poor. They answer false to "I love my mother" and to "Members of my family and my close relatives get along quite well."

7. A final group of items deals with the expectations of others. In this area, some would say that people with high **Cn** scores simply are being realistic because they agree with an item such as "People generally demand more respect for their own rights than they are willing to allow for others."

In looking at these groups of items, people with high **Cn** scores appear to have a tendency to be very aware of their feelings, especially their feelings of discomfort and impulsivity. A hypothesis we would like to suggest is that persons with a high control scale may have a set to admit that these impulses exist and this may raise the pathological scales unduly high. The **Cn** scale then may be picking up a response bias. People with a high control scale and high Clinical scales may overemphasize the pathological feelings they do have and therefore may not truly be as disturbed as individuals with high Clinical scales but lower control scales.

GENERAL INFORMATION

1. Cuadra (1953) developed the 50 item **Cn** scale as a measure of personality control.

2. After identifying 30 pairs of similar MMPI Clinical scale profiles, where one person of the pair was hospitalized and the other was not, Cuadra isolated the MMPI items that differentiated these two groups and developed the **Cn** scale.

3. Cuadra's original article proposing this scale is in the *Basic Readings on the MMPI in Psychology and Medicine* (Welsh & Dahlstrom, 1956).

HIGH SCORES
(T = 60 or Above)

1. A person with a high **Cn** score may have a measure of personal control that can prevent problem behavior (as shown by elevations on the Clinical scales) from being exhibited in the presence of others.

2. People who have high **Cn** scores without elevations on the Clinical scales may appear to be over-controlled and somewhat unemotional. Their lack of Clinical scale elevations would seem to indicate that no need exists for the amount of personal control shown by the elevations on the **Cn** scale.

3. Anderson and Kunce (1984) have found that for clients who have markedly elevated **8** scale scores, elevations on **Es** and **Cn** scales may indicate clients who are aware of pathological feelings and their potential for acting out impulsively, but their conscious awareness (**Cn**) and adequate level of ego strength (**Es**) may enable them to better control their behavior.

LOW SCORES
(T = 50 or Below)

1. A person with a low **Cn** score, but with elevated Clinical scale scores (T = 70 or above), readily shows the behavior indicated by the Clinical scale elevations.

2. A person with a low **Cn** score and no elevated Clinical scale scores (T = 70 or below) has no behavior which needs to be controlled and the **Cn** score reflects this.

These combinations do not mean that the person is unable to control his/her behavior should the Clinical scales go above 70. If the Clinical scales do go above 70, the **Cn** scale also may rise.

SUMMARY OF Cn SCALE INTERPRETATIONS*

If the Highest Clinical Scale is	and **Cn** is	Interpretations
70 or below	50 or below	This combination of scores is usual for persons with minor or no psychological problems.
	50 thru 60	This person may appear to be somewhat unemotional. He/she may tend to mask feelings. The person is usually aware of keeping some emotions hidden and may have good reasons for doing so.
	60 or above	The person tends to be over-controlled, objective, and detached. He/she tends to suppress outward expression of inner feelings and impulses and probably has difficulty expressing warmth.
70 or above	50 or below	The person cannot keep the impulses and/or behavior shown by the Clinical scale elevations from being observed by others.
70 or above	50 thru 60	The person has some control over the amount of behavior that is shown but not as much as when **Cn** is above 60.
70 or above	60 or above	The person is able to conceal and control the impulses and behavior indicated by the Clinical scale elevation, although, if the person chooses to do so, the impulses

and behavior may be revealed. If the person chooses not to show the behavior indicated by the Clinical scales, he/she may fantasize about them.

---

*Where T-scores are listed in two categories (i.e., 50 or below and 50 through 60) and a score is obtained that is listed for two categories, use whichever interpretation seems to be most appropriate for the individual.

Mac SCALE
(MacAndrew Addiction Scale)

The **MacAndrew Addiction** scale (**Mac**) was developed by Craig MacAndrew (1965) originally to differentiate male psychiatric outpatients who were in treatment for alcohol abuse from male nonsubstance-abusing psychiatric outpatients. Fifty-one MMPI items were identified that made such a differentiation. Two of the 51 items were excluded from the scale (booklet items No. 215 and No. 460) since they were too obvious in asking about alcohol symptoms, leaving 49 items. A cut-off score of 24 and above was used by MacAndrew to identify alcoholics and this score correctly classified 81.5% of his population.

Since 1965, this 49 item scale has been cross validated many times and with many different populations; VA hospital inpatients (Burke & Marcus, 1977), general hospital inpatients (de Groot & Adamson, 1973), and nonpsychiatric outpatients (Lachar et al., 1976; Rhodes, 1969). In these studies and others, again approximately 85% of the alcoholics were correctly identified, whereas 15% of them were classified falsely as non-alcoholic. MacAndrew (1981) has hypothesized that these 15% false negatives are not primary alcoholics but really "reactive" or secondary alcoholics. He described these people as "neurotics who also happen to drink too much" and believed that they do so to remove themselves from the pain of their daily living.

This is in contrast to the primary alcoholic who is reward-seeking rather than punishment-avoidant as the secondary alcoholic is. Primary alcoholics are described by Finney, Smith, Skeeter, and Suvenshine (1971) as "bold, uninhibited, self-confident, sociable people who mix well with others. They show rebellious urges and resentment of authorities. They tell of carousing, gambling, playing hookey, and generally 'cutting up.' Yet their answers show that they are drawn to religion" (p. 1058). Burke (1983) also saw the **Mac** scale as a measure of the impulsivity, the pressure for action, and the acting-out potential that lead to alcoholism and probably also to the misuse of other substances.

Female alcoholics also have been studied but much less frequently than male alcoholics. In general, their MacAndrew scores are lower than the males'. Authors of one study (Svanum et al., 1982) have found 23 and above as the most accurate cut-off score for their population of female alcoholics. In work that Duckworth has done with non-psychiatric clients, she also has found that women in general score lower than men on the **Mac** scale. The females' average score was 19 whereas the males' average score was 21 (Duckworth, 1983).

After the **Mac** scale was used with alcoholics for a period of time, drug abusers were tested (Burke & Marcus, 1977; Kranitz, 1972; Lachar et al., 1976; Sutker et al., 1979) and the scale was found to differentiate them from non-drug abusers with approximately the same degree of accuracy as was found in the differentiation of alcoholics from non-alcoholics. The scale accurately classified heroin and poly-drug abusers in these studies; however, Caldwell (1985) has reported that the scale does not pick up cocaine abuse in the populations he had tested (medical center inpatients and outpatients) nor has it differentiated recreational marijuana users in the population with whom the authors work (college students).

In college and mental health settings, the scale may need to be used somewhat differently than it is in a psychiatric population. If people are having trouble with alcohol or drug use, we find the cut-off scores that MacAndrew and others have used, 24 and above for men, and 23 and above for women, to be useful. However, if people are not having trouble with drinking or drug abuse, we have felt safer in labeling men addictive only when their scores are 27 or above and women when their scores are 25 or above. When men and women score his high, most of them recognize the "pull" of alcohol or drugs, but they have not been having problems with addiction because they have worked very hard at controlling themselves. Many of these people seem to be motivated by the "horrible example" of an alcoholic parent or parents, and they use this example to limit their drinking or drug use.

People in college and mental health settings who have scores of 24, 25, or 26 on this scale may also report some of this "pull" of alcohol or drugs, but much less frequently than the people with scores of 27 or more. We also have found many people in this range who have never tried alcohol or drugs because of religious beliefs. Possibly if they did not have those beliefs and had tried drinking and/or drugs, they might indeed be alcoholic or drug abusers.

What a low score, below 15 raw score points, means on the MacAndrew scale is currently unknown. However, Caldwell has hypothesized (1985) that people scoring 10 raw score points or below cannot tolerate alcohol. People in general score from 15 through 22 raw score points on this scale.

We have found that the score on this scale does not tend to change over time. Duckworth has found that on retesting people after a six month period, the MacAndrew score typically changed 2 raw score points or less. Indeed, so stable is this scale, that a score has been found not to change with successful treatment for alcoholism (Huber & Danahy, 1975; Rohan et al., 1969; Rohan, 1972; Lanyon et al., 1972). MacAndrew also has noted (1981) that the **Mac** scores of alcoholics do not change with treatment or even after prolonged substance abuse. He also found that the **Mac** scores are not related to age or race. What the scale does seem to measure is a fundamental character dimension. He endorses Finney's (1971) description of the primary alcoholic noted earlier as the personality characteristics measured by elevations on the **Mac** scale.

GENERAL INFORMATION

1. This 49 item scale measures the potential for addiction to alcohol and/or drugs.

2. Schwartz and Graham (1979) factor analyzed the scale and found it measures impulsivity, high energy level, interpersonal shallowness, and general psychological maladjustment.

3. Test-retest reliability is high.

    a. Scores do not change significantly with successful treatment for addiction.

    b. Over a 6 month period, **Mac** scores for subjects did not change significantly (Duckworth, 1983).

4. Schwartz and Graham (1979) have found the scale correlates .55 with scale **9** (impulsivity and energy) and -.62 with scale **R** (repression). In another study of therapy clients (Duckworth, 1983) the scale correlated with **K**, -.34; **9**, .39; **R**, -.38; **Re**, -50; and **Pr**, .36.

5. It has not correlated with race in some studies (Lachar et al., 1976; Page & Bozler, 1982; Uecker et al., 1980), however Walters et al. (1983) found that this scale did not discriminate between Black alcoholics and Black non-alcoholics in an active duty military sample.

6. The scale does not correlate with age (Appledorf & Hunley, 1975; Friedrich & Loftsgard, 1978; MacAndrew, 1965; Uecker et al., 1980; Duckworth, 1983).

7. The average range of scores for a group of non-addictive normals (N = 433) was from 15 through 23 (Duckworth, 1983):

    The mean score for women was 19
    The mean score for men was 21

8. The scale seems to show discrimination between substance abusers and nonabusers as early as late adolesence (MacAndrew, 1979b).

9. The scale may be predictive of future alcoholism as early as entrance to college. Hoffman, Loper, and Kammeier (1974) found the mean **Mac** scale scores of 25 hospitalized alcoholics was not significantly different than their average score at the time of their entrance to college, some 13 years earlier.

10. Suicide prone alcoholics are likely to be those who are using alcohol but *not* scoring in the addictive range on the scale (MacAndrew, 1981).

11. Craig (1984b) has found that drug addicts with a co-existing alcohol problem have higher **Mac** scores than addicts without a current alcohol problem.

12. Researchers have found that the scale can be administered as a separate test of 49 items with no significant difference in the **Mac** score than the score obtained when the scale is administered embedded in the total MMPI (MacAndrew, 1979a; Duckworth, 1983).

13. If the shortened version of Form R has been given (399 or 400 items), the **Mac** scale can be scored and multiplied by 1.34. This approximates the **Mac** score which would be obtained if all of the items were answered (Streiner & Miller, 1981).

14. The items making up the **Mac** scale are located in Appendices A and B.

15. Four items of the scale [Booklet No. 61(T), 156(T), 251(T), and 378(F)] plus two additional items [No. 215(T) and 460(T)] may show

how willing the person is to admit to alcoholism since these are very obvious items. Conley and Kammeier (1980) suggest these might be used as a measure of willingness to admit to alcoholism.

16. T-score conversion tables for the **Mac** scale for men and women are available in the book by Greene (1980).

HIGH SCORES
(24 and Above for Males)
(23 and Above for Females)

1. The cut off scores of 24 and above for men and 23 and above for women work best for people self-referred or brought in by others for substance abuse problems.

2. For people who are having psychological difficulties, but substances abuse is not one of them, scores of 24, 25, and 26 raw score points for men and 23, 24, and 25 raw score points for women may not indicate current substance abuse but a potential for it if psychological pressure should be increased.

   a. Some people in this range may recognize the "pull" of substance abuse but work hard at controlling it because of the example of an addicted parent.

   b. Others may have religious beliefs that keep them from using alcohol or drugs.

3. With a raw score of 27 and above for men, and 25 and above for women, most people recognize that they have an addictive potential. The higher the score and the more psychological pressure the person is under, the greater the likelihood that there will be substance abuse.

4. Clopton and Weiner (1980) found 27 and above to be the best cut off score for their sample of psychiatric inpatients.

5. Alcoholics who score in the addictive range on this scale (primary alcoholics) report four times as many symptoms of "brain dysfunction" in childhood as do alcoholics who do not score in the addictive range on the **Mac** (secondary alcoholics) (MacAndrew, 1981).

LOW SCORES
(Below 15 Raw Score Points)

1. Caldwell (1985) has hypothesized that people who score 10 raw score points or below cannot tolerate alcohol.

SUMMARY OF Mac SCALE INTERPRETATIONS*

Raw Score	Interpretations
0 thru 10	A person scoring in this range may not be able to tolerate alcohol.
16 thru 22 (Women) 16 thru 23 (Men)	This is the average range of scores for people in general. If people are substance abusers and score in this range, they may be secondary alcoholics, that is, their alcoholism is secondary to their personal problems and it is used to avoid the pain they feel. Suicide prone alcoholics come from this group. Approximately 15% of diagnosed alcoholics are secondary alcoholics.
23 thru 24 (Women) 24 thru 26 (Men)	If the person is self or other referred because of substance abuse problems, the **Mac** score confirms the diagnosis. If the person has psychological problems but substance abuse is not one of them, he/she may not be abusing alcohol 1. because of the ''horrible'' example of an alcoholic parent. 2. because of religious beliefs.
25 or above (Women) 27 or above (Men)	For people without any psychological problems of addictions, this score may be a false positive (labeling people addictive when they are not). Scores in this range indicate addictive potential that may be acted upon (in alcoholics and drug abusers) or not (for those who recognize the addictive potential but control it, perhaps through abstinence). The higher the **Mac** scale and the more psychological pressure the person is under, the greater the likelihood of substance abuse.

Mac

CHAPTER **VII**

SAMPLE MMPI
INTERPRETATIONS

This chapter presents two different methods of interpreting MMPI profiles using the Research scales as well as the Validity and Clinical scales. The first section of the chapter was written by Jane Duckworth and the second section was written by Wayne Anderson. In interpreting the MMPI many similarities occur for the two methods as well as many differences. Both approaches are presented to show different ways of doing MMPI interpretations.

317

MMPI INTERPRETATIONS

by

Jane Duckworth

When I interpret a MMPI, I usually am focusing my attention on two things: (1) what are the current *behaviors* and *feelings* of the individual who took the test, and (2) what are the *underlying reasons* for these behaviors and feelings. If the person is coming in for counseling and/or therapy, I also am interested in *what type of treatment* might prove most effective for the individual.

Some limitations of the applicability of the way I do MMPI interpretations may exist. I have worked mainly with bright people both young (students) and old (faculty) at a university counseling center. If a choice of interpretations for the MMPI is possible, I tend to err on the side of the optimistic one. I have found that the high points of a profile for these two groups do not always have the dire implications that are attached to them in the MMPI interpretations derived from clinical populations. True, the behavior and feelings of these counseling center clients may be maladaptive, but because of the client's intelligence and residence in an environment geared to trying new things, the manifestations of the maladaptive behavior and feelings usually are milder and the likelihood of positive change is much greater than with clients in clinical populations. If the profile being interpreted is from a different population than that found in a counseling center, checking to see if the optimistic approach I use is applicable may be necessary.

Another difference between the way I do interpretations and the way some others do them is that I operate from a philosophy that emphasizes looking for the strengths within a client and building on those while minimizing maladaptive behavior. I tend to ignore maladaptive behavior if it is not causing the client or the people around him/her a great deal of trouble, and I reinforce or try to build upon the adaptive behavior the client is exhibiting. A further difference in the way I do interpretations is that while I am aware of the underlying dynamics of the client's behavior as shown in the MMPI, my main focus in the interpretation is on the client's behavior and the way his/her feelings affect that behavior.

My impression is that this interpretative approach emphasizing client strengths rather than weaknesses, focusing on behavior and feelings rather than underlying dynamics is becoming more applicable to the mental health centers and private clinics populations than it used to be. As state outpatient mental health systems become prevalent and therapy is more available and less stigmatized, my feeling is that more "normal" people (non-neurotic, non-psychotic) are coming for help with everyday problems such as dealing with their children or marriage or divorce concerns. Clients in these agencies resemble the ones seen in college counseling centers more than they resemble patients in mental institutions, and the approaches stressed in this chapter may be very applicable to them.

For a more clinical approach to MMPI interpretation, I suggest the books by Graham (1977) and Greene (1980) on the MMPI in which their general interpretive strategies are discussed. These books and the two approaches presented in this chapter provide a broad overview of MMPI interpretation.

When working with the MMPI, I divide the interpretation into three parts, those concerning the Validity, Clinical, and Research scales. I deal with each section separately at first and then look at them together. In general, I do not pay attention to scales appearing between 45 and 60 T-score points, except for certain research scales (**Dy, Do, Re, Pr,** and **St**) because scales in this middle range do not tend to indicate unique behavior. I start by individually interpreting the very highest scales in each section and then work down to the scales closest to 60 T-score points. After this, I look at the scales that are the farthest below 45 T-score points. In most profiles many more high points occur than low points.

I start an MMPI interpretation by looking at the *Validity scales* and use them as an indication of the general test-taking attitude of the individual: for example, is the client saying he/she is feeling good (high **K**) or bad (high **F**) about life on the day he/she took the test. The higher these Validity scales are above 60 T-score points, the more likely the person is to be emphasizing that particular feeling and maybe even exaggerating it: "I feel like I'm overwhelmed with problems" (high **F**); "Life is absolutely beautiful, nothing is the slightest bit wrong with what's happening" (high **K**). In the Validity scale section of this book are some typical combinations of Validity scales and their interpretations.

After getting a general idea about the mood of the person taking the test, I then proceed to the *Clinical scales* and interpret them individually from the highest scale above 60 down to the one closest to 60 T-score points. I look then at the lowest scales below 45 and interpret them and then move up to the scales closest to 45 T-score points. If several scales are above 70 T-score points, I tend to down play the scales between 60 and 70 T-score points, because these may be elevated due to the heightened emotional state of the client.

If no scales are above 760, except perhaps the **5** scale for men, then the scales within the 60-70 T-score range can be very useful for indicating behavior that is present but not necessarily a problem as it might be if the scale were above 70. Instead the behavior may be a way of dealing with life that is adaptive rather than maladaptive. The summary at the end of each Clinical scale section indicates the wealth of information that can be obtained from scale scores in this usually ignored 60-70 T-score range.

After looking at the various high and low points of the Clinical scales, I move to the *Research scales* and follow the same procedure used with the Clinical scales. I start interpreting the highest scales and work down to those scales closest to 60 T-score points. I then interpret the lowest scales and work up to the scales closest to 45 T-score points. I do not ignore the scales between 60 and 70 T-score points within this Research scale group even if a number of scales are above 70. I find that all elevations on these scales are useful regardless of their relative height.

After noting the high and low scales for the Clinical and Research scale sections, I then start the much more difficult process of considering the scales in combinations and balancing the information from one scale against the information from another. I do not ignore inconsistencies in the individual scale interpretations but rather try to determine under what conditions these two behaviors could exist in the same person at the same time. This situation is where the Research scales are of greatest use. They can help refine the information presented in the Clinical scale elevations so that the most accurate interpretation of the Clinical scales can be given. A high **2** scale may not indicate self-deprecation, for example, if the Ego Strength scale (**Es**) is above 50 T-score points. Summaries showing refinements of the Clinical scales by the Research scales are at the end of the appropriate Clinical scales.

In addition to the refinements already mentioned, the Research scales indicate strengths that a client may have that temper predictions made from the Clinical scales. The control scale (**Cn**), if elevated above 60 T-score points, indicates ability of the client to control the outward manifestation of his/her maladaptive behavior shown on the elevated Clinical scales. A client may have a 2-7-8 profile, but if he/she also has a **Cn** scale above 60 that person probably has some control over who sees the depression, anxiety, and confusion indicated by the Clinical scales. He/she also may be able to temper the amount of these behaviors shown. These Research scale refinements provide important information for the most accurate interpretation of the Clinical scales.

In addition to examining these refinements of the Clinical scale information, the practitioner should consider the Clinical scales in their various combinations. I have found two point combinations to be the most useful. Occasionally three point combinations are helpful; but, in general, they do not add more information than what is found in the two point combinations.

I believe that Graham's (1977) work with two point combinations and the work of Gynther et al. (various references in the Reference section), reported in the Clinical section of this book, are some of the best sources of information on the two point codes. Graham's book and Gynther's articles should be consulted for more thorough descriptions of these combinations.

When all this information on a profile has been gathered, the interpretations can be made. When I do an interpretation, I try to say something first about the *test-taking attitude* of the person so that the rest of the information given in the report can be interpreted in light of how the client was feeling at the time. I proceed then with the body of the report and start by mentioning those *behaviors and feelings* most likely to be overtly shown and expressed by the client, using the two or three highest Clinical scale elevations as my clues. In reference to the 2-7-8 profile mentioned previously, for example, I might say, "Mr. R. is most likely to be reporting severe depression and would appear to be highly anxious and confused."

Next I bring in the *refinements* to the Clinical scales that I may have learned from the Research scales, or from the Clinical scale combinations. If the 2-7-8 profile has an **Es** scale above 45, I would say "The depression shown by Mr. R. does not however include the self-deprecation typically seen in these cases."

After describing as accurately as I can the behavior and feelings shown by the client, I then proceed to hypotheses, if I have any, concerning why these behaviors and feelings may be present. An interpretation for a woman with a high **2-4-6** in the midst of a divorce might be "The depression, anger, and confusion shown by this woman seem most likely to be her reaction to the pending divorce. It would be helpful to verify this reaction by seeing if her anger is directed specifically toward her husband and the situation she is in or whether it is generalized to many other people and situations."

Following these hypotheses, I then go to *strengths* I may see in the profile. These strengths may be revealed by the Research scales or sometimes by lower Clinical scales elevations.

The report is closed with some predictions concerning *prognosis* and *implications for therapy*. For a **2-8** profile, statements such as the following might be made. "Miss R. should be amenable to therapy because of the amount of psychological pain she is feeling. However, I recommend that therapy progress slowly and with as many simple, specific suggestions as possible because of the amount of psychological confusion the client is experiencing."

When my students are working on an interpretation, I advise them to make a work sheet for the profile in the following manner. They are to divide a sheet of paper by drawing a vertical line two inches from the left side; then place the scale number they are interpreting on the left side of the line and the interpretation of it on the right. They do this for all the Validity, Clinical, and Research scales above 60 and below 45 T-score points starting with the highest scales and working down to 60 and then interpreting the lowest scales up to those closest to 45. After doing all the scales individually, they are to next look at pertinent combinations of scales. When all of this has been done, they can look at what they have written and try to fit the various bits of information together as a whole, emphasizing the highest Clinical scales the most and taking into consideration the refinements indicated by the test-taking attitude of the client, the Research scales, and the lower Clinical scales. After this preparation is done they are to write a summary for the profile, making sure to cover the client's behavior and feelings, strengths, and weaknesses.

With these points in mind, let's look at Figure 17, a profile of Mr. J.R. The following is a typical interpretation for a person with such a profile.

The client, Mr. R., is a thirty-four year-old white male with a masters degree in art. He is on the faculty of a small, midwestern college.

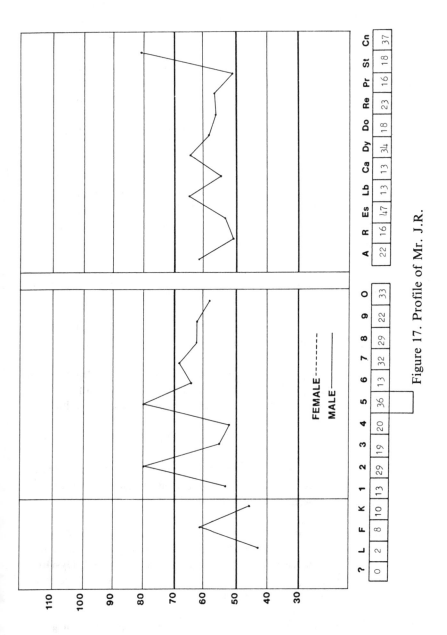

Figure 17. Profile of Mr. J.R.

323

Mr. R. is coming for therapy because he is upset about his marriage and also because his family doctor has suggested that some of the tenseness he has been experiencing may be because of psychological problems.

The man is doing well as an art professor at the college, but he reports not feeling really good about what is happening in his life. He has the feeling, he says, that something must be better somewhere. He has focused on his wife as the cause of much of his unhappiness because she is "too placid" and, he feels, not interested in discussing anything other than everyday events.

The following is an example of a work sheet and summary (interpretation) as they might be for Mr. R. When the MMPI interpretation is sent to someone, the work sheet material about the individual scales is not sent. Only the summary, without the scale identifications (material in parentheses in the summary), is sent as the interpretation.

	Validity Scales
F = 62	Slight elevation; perhaps is feeling a small amount of psychological pain.
L = 43	A typical score for a person with his educational level. He is willing to admit to some common human faults. Not of much significance unless the **L** score is high.
	Clinical Scales
2 = 80	Depression may include self-deprecation. Check **Es** score in Research scale section for clues as to whether self-deprecation is involved.
5 = 80	Aesthetic interests and possible passivity. Very likely this scale is at least partially elevated because this man is an artist and highly educated. Need to check **Dy-Do** in the Research scale section to see if passivity also is involved in this elevation.
7 = 69	Anxiety, but at a minimum level (below 70). This anxiety will most likely be seen as occasional tenseness rather than overt anxiety.

6 = 67	Some interpersonal sensitivity without the general suspiciousness seen when the scale is above 70.
8 = 64	At this level the scale may show creativity or belonging to an atypical group. Because this person is an artist, the creativity interpretation is the most likely.
9 = 63	An abundance of psychological energy. This is a typical level for a productive person.
0 = 60	Borderline for interpretation. This scale may indicate preferences for being by himself, but it does not indicate problems with being around others.

Research Scales

Control **Cn = 81**	Great ability to control who sees the behavior shown on the elevated Clinical scales. Because **Cn** is very high and Clinical scores are not greatly elevated, this person may be too controlled at times.
Low back pain **Lb = 66**	Maybe saying, "I'm a wonderful person. I love people, and they never annoy me, but for some reason I am uncomfortable and not as happy as I should be."
Dependency **Dy = 66**	Psychological dependency. He would like to lean on others at times and have them take care of him.
Anxiety **A = 62**	Some situational anxiety. This score is at about the level to be expected when the 7 scale is between 60 and 70 T-score points.
Dy-Do combination **Dy = 66** **Do = 59**	This is sometimes looked at when a small point spread exists (less than 10 T-score points) or both scales are above 50 T-score points.

For this person, it indicates the psychological dependency already mentioned, combined with a strong underlying desire to take charge of his own life. This ambivalence can create problems for this man and those close to him because he may act one way one time and the opposite way very shortly afterwards. Another way this combination may be shown is by passive-aggressive behavior. This man may subtly ask others to take care of him and then subvert that helping by complaining about the results or subverting the effectiveness of them in some way.

Refinements

F elevation compared to Clinical scales

When the **F** scale elevation is only between 60 and 70 T-score points, but the Clinicals (excluding scales **5** and **9**) are above 70 T-score points, the person is not complaining as much on the **F** scale as he is on the Clinicals. This may be because he is used to feeling the depression shown by the elevated **2** scale. He reports being definitely depressed (the elevation on **2**), but he is not greatly worried about it (lower **F** scale).

2 scale compared to Es scale

Mr. R. is feeling depressed but is not self-deprecating. He feels life is somewhat unpleasant (high **2**) but does not necessarily see himself as the cause or as unworthy of a better existence. (**Es** above 50).

5 scale compared to Dy and Do

While showing aesthetic interests, this scale (**5**) also may be showing some passivity (**Dy** = 66). However this passivity is tempered by some feelings of dominance and/or passive aggressiveness (**Do** = 59 and **Dy - Do** spread).

Summary
(Scale identifications
are added for clarity.
In a report they would
not be included.)

This profile depicts a person who was feeling somewhat bad at the time he took the test (**F** scale). He most likely was complaining about feeling depressed (**2**) and perhaps some tenseness (**7**). He is liable to have some passive-aggressive tendencies (**5** and **Dy-Do**) that could be directed at those closest to him, because he has a tendency to be quite sensitive to how others feel about him (**6**).

He has much control (**Cn**) over his behavior, and he can keep people from seeing his depression and tenseness if he wishes. However, this control is at such a high level that he may use it in the therapy situation to keep important feelings and behavior from the therapist as well as from others in the outside world.

Another problem in working with this client could be that he may not have some of the necessary insight into why he is so unhappy (**Lb**). He may feel that he tries hard and loves people, but things still do not feel right nor is he happy.

These feelings of unhappiness and depression probably have been around for a long time, so that the client is not as worried about them as others with similar feelings might be (difference between **F** elevation and the Clinical elevations). The prognosis for therapy is mixed. On the one hand, this client does report depression and tenseness and a general feeling of malaise; but, on the other hand, he is not exceptionally worried about these feelings and has such control over the expression of them that he may not be willing or able to show them in their full ramifications to the therapist. Add to this the possibility of some passive-aggressive behavior as the therapist gets closer and the interpersonal sensitivity of the client, and it can be seen that some potential problems are at hand.

This type of client tends to work well with a therapist who goes slowly and helps deal with the overt signs of discomfort before starting to delve into the underlying dynamics. Frequently a client of this type does well with a woman or a very empathetic man because of the perceived help this type of counselor/therapist can give. This client wants someone to lean on and usually will respond quickly to therapist warmth. What the client does not see and what may take longer to deal with are his underlying aggressiveness and sensitivity. The possibility exists that the client will terminate therapy once the pain is gone but before the more hidden dynamics are dealt with.

MMPI INTERPRETATIONS

by

Wayne Anderson

Interpreting MMPI profiles often takes a considerable amount of time in the beginning because of the need to think through the many possibilities and to check sourcebooks for ideas. With practice, an interpretation can be done quite quickly. As the standard characteristics associated with a certain profile become known, spotting inconsistencies and outstanding characteristics is possible. Even with experience however, it does pay to review occasionally the information given in this book, because even an experienced clinician will not always recall all possible interpretations.

A general procedure for developing an interpretation would be as follows:

1. Check the Validity scores to find out what the attitude of the client was toward taking the test; that is, was the client being open, defensive, or admitting to thoughts and behavior of an unusual nature? A frequent profile in a client population is a high **F** (70) and a low **K** (below 45). This would influence me to develop a different interpretation about the profile than if there were an **F** of 45 and a **K** of 70. In the first case, I would suspect that the client might be exaggerating symptoms and thus creating an undue elevation of the Clinical scale scores. In the second case, the client might be striving to present a normal picture and would be much less likely to be open about personal defects.

   I also pay attention to **L** scale scores over 55 although certain features may be present in the profile such as a high **Re** scale score that will allow me to interpret the profile even with a **L** scale score around 65. I would recommend special attention to the patterns of **L, F, K** which are discussed on pp. 69-71.

2. Next I establish the basic characteristics of the high Clinical scales both by themselves and in combination with each

other. For example, if a high **4** scale (70 T-score points or higher) occurs with the next highest Clinical scale half a standard deviation or more below, I use the interpretation for the marked elevation of the **4** scale. If the profile has both the **4** and **9** scales elevated with the two being within two or three points of each other, I use the **4-9** two point code interpretation.

3. Having established the interpretations of the most elevated Clinical scales, I am now in a position to consider how they are being modified. First, I check those scales which also are elevated but at a somewhat lower level than the very highest ones. If the **4** scales is at 80 T-score point and the **8** scale is at 70, for example, the **8** scale adds a bad judgment element to the usual high **4** scale interpretation. The person with a **4-8** profile may engage in bizarre actions or interpret incorrectly what another person is expecting or asking of him (**8** scale) as well as be acting out in some way (**4** scale). The **8** scale indicates more negative behavior than just the **4** scale by itself.

On the other hand, some scales may be positive modifiers of highly elevated scales, that is, elevations on them would allow the tester to interpret the higher scales more positively than usual. An example would be a profile where the **5** scale is elevated (above 60) with the **4** scale (above 70). The **5** scale may act as a supressor of the acting out usually associated with a high **4** scale. Sometimes the positive interpretation is relative; for example, a **7-8** profile with an **A** scale above 60 T-score points indicates a disturbed person. He/she usually is very uncomfortable and characteristics of maladjustment typically are present. However, this is a more positive pattern than if the **7** and **8** scales are high and the **A** scale is low (below 50 T-score points) because this combination would suggest the possibility of a more chronic adjustment problem and one less likely to change as a result of therapy.

Beginning interpreters sometimes make the mistake of taking each elevated scale and only interpreting it separately. The MMPI interpreter needs to keep in mind that elevated scores tend to modify and change each other. An elevated scale will not necessarily indicate exactly the same characteristic when other scales or combinations of scales also are elevated. We have attempted to represent examples in the previous chapters of some of these scale modifications.

4. The next point in developing an interpretation is to consider the low scales (below 45 T-score points) on the profile and to look at the high scale and low scale interpretations together for additional insights. An example would be that an individual with a low 4 scale (45 or below) and an elevated 0 scale (65 or above) would likely be someone who is not only shy and withdrawn (0 scale) but also someone who is probably sexually inexperienced (4 scale). A female profile with a low 5 scale and high 4 scale would suggest that she is an individual who uses sex as a way of manipulating and controlling men. A low 2 scale with a high 9 scale on a profile would suggest an unusually buoyant, outgoing individual who may not be appropriately responsive to the problems of other people.

5. Having completed the first four points, the more creative aspect of interpreting MMPI can be done; that is, interpreting the inconsistencies. Much of what we have discussed up to this point can be done in a more or less routine manner. This step requires experience with the test and some knowledge of the relationships between scales. One must ask what are the inconsistencies in the test, what does not relate in a logical manner? The interpreter then thinks through possible reasons as to why these relationship may exist. For example, what can be made out of a profile in which the **Do** and **Dy** scales are both above 60? Or the 2 scale and 9 scale both above 70? What can one make of a high **Es** scale and low **K**? A study of these inconsistencies will help the interpreter form a clearer picture of the individual who is being considered.

As an example, I have a college student's profile with a **F** scale of 80 and a **K** scale at 45. The Clinical scales generally are elevated with the 8 scale at 80 and the 4, 6, and 9 scales at 75. So far the test is quite consistent. In looking at the Research scales however I find the **Pr** scale to be at 65 and the **St** scale at 64. This does not fit my expectations. These scores usually are negatively correlated with each other (see Appendix C). In a college population, when the **Pr** scale is low, the **St** usually is elevated and vice versa. The mean **Pr** scale scale score for college students is 40 and the mean **St** scale score for students is 60 (Anderson & Duckworth, 1969). I would like to know why this interesting inconsistency in these profile scores exists. The **Pr** score is consistent with the rest of the test, because it is a sign of general maladjustment and difficulty in relating to others as are the elevated scores on the Clinical scales. The **St** score, on the other hand, seems to correlate more with a healthy outlook on life and with the giving of socially desirable answers. At this point, I may not have a good hypothesis as to how these scores can exist together, but it is a point I can explore with the client.

Occasionally one will have an MMPI profile about which a consistent report can be written, but when talking to the client the report does not match with either the client's overt behavior or with what the client evidently believes about himself/herself. I have found no good explanation for this situation. It is rather rare; but it does occur, and an interpreter should come to expect it occasionally. Some deeper level at which the interpretation is true may exist, but a client should not be forced to fit a particular interpretation if the tester and the client do not view it as applicable.

As examples of how I interpret the MMPI, three brief interpretations will be made of sample profiles.

Profile #1

Profile #1 (Figure 18) is that of an 18-year-old male who was referred to a college counseling center for personal adjustment counseling. The **F-K** index shows that the client is saying that he feels bad, and the possibility exists that he may be exaggerating his symptoms.

The **4-8** would be a fairly frequent two point code in a psychiatric population but is rare in a college population. The **8** scale modifies the **4** scale rather markedly, and the following characteristics could be predicted at a fairly high level of probability for this individual.

    1. He may get into trouble because of bad judgment (**8** scale) as to when to act out against whatever it is he may be fighting (**4** scale). His history probably will show that he has had trouble not only with his family but also with other authority figures such as school personnel and employers.

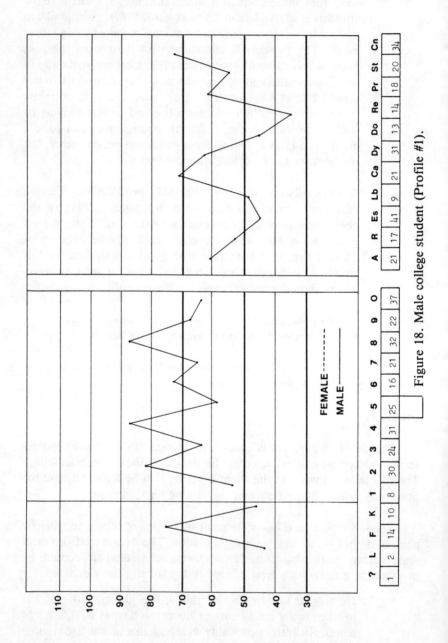

?	L	F	K	1	2	3	4	5	6	7	8	9	O	A	R	Es	Lb	Ca	Dy	Do	Re	Pr	St	Cn
1	2	14	10	8	30	24	31	25	16	21	32	22	37	21	17	41	9	21	31	13	14	18	20	34

FEMALE --------
MALE ————

Figure 18. Male college student (Profile #1).

332

2. He is likely to distrust others and have problems with close relationships.

3. He probably will engage in unpredictable, impulsive behavior.

4. Because of either his dress or behavior, he will strike others as being strange or odd.

The addition of the elevated **2** scale in this pattern brings in the descriptors "depressed, tense, irritable, and hostile." When the **2** scale is this high, it indicates an individual who has various escape methods in stress situations, such as using drugs, alcohol or the actual physical avoidance of situations such as dropping out of school.

The **6** scale adds a definite possibility of violence, and as it is over 70, the possibility of delusional thinking also exists. The individual with a **4-8** pattern tends to be suspicious and the addition of the high **6** scale increases the possibility of increased suspicion and a feeling of being treated unjustly.

These elevations would suggest that the client is coming for therapy because he sees himself as the victim of outside influences or pressures and not because of his awareness of personal defects. This attitude is likely to make him a poor therapy risk.

The Research scales in this case add support to the Clinical scale interpretation but not too much new information. The elevated **Ca, A,** and **Cn** scales support the general maladjustment hypothesis. The **A** scale may be a bit low for an elevated profile like his, but along with the **Cn** scale suggests that he is likely to be able to hold things together so that hospitalization will not be necessary.

The low **Re** scale is supportive of the tendency toward impulsiveness and trouble with authority indicated by the **4-8** combination. On a student's profile it would suggest also the likelihood of academic difficulties.

The elevated **Dy** scale in conjunction with the elevated **4** scale is an interesting inconsistency; that is, he has a need to fight authority (**4** scale) at the same time that he has a need for a dependent relationship (**Dy** scale). This is not such an unusual pattern, but it is an interesting one to

333

consider. The **Dy-Do** pattern shows that he feels unable to take charge of his life at this time (**Do** scale) and wants to lean on someone (**Dy** scale). Given the other indices in this profile however whether or not a therapist would be able to hold him in therapy is questionable in spite of his felt need for dependency.

We have, then, an impulsive, irritable, hostile person with dependency needs. His bad judgment, difficulty with authority, and probable delusional thinking combine to make him a poor therapy risk.

The actual client was quite delusional in that he felt that others were persecuting him. He thought that he was able to hear people talking about him at long distances because of his very good hearing. He had some real doubts about his masculinity. He took pride in the fact that he was very manipulative and liked things that way. He did many things to draw attention to himself. One of his problems was his inability to get along with other people in the dormitory in which he lived. He also admitted he had trouble interacting with women and that he had a bad temper.

Profile #2

Profile #2 (Figure 19) is that of a female college student. The **L, F, K** pattern suggests a long-standing set of problems to which she has become adjusted, at least to the extent that she feels good about herself (**K** scale) but has some bad feelings about her situation (**F** scale).

On the Clinical scales, scale **9** frequently is high for college students. The high score on this profile indicates that the client probably is overactive, and makes little progress for the amount of effort expended. We would expect her to be usually good humored but to become irritable at times and have outbursts of temper. Because this profile is of a college counselee, we also would expect her to be aggressive and/or opinionated.

The height of the **8** scale would, on the face of it, be a pathological sign. A profile with a **9-8** like this is frequent in mental hospital populations. Ordinarily, we would expect a person with this elevation to have delusional thinking, anxiety, and rumination. At this point, however, the strength of the Research scales in modifying the Clinical scales becomes apparent. The signs of general maladjustment and anxiety on the Research scales (scales **A** and **Ca**) are low. The ego strength (**Es** scale), on the other hand, has a mild elevation. This elevation would suggest that she is holding things together rather well. We are going to have to look for another interpretation other than pathology therefore to explain the **9-8** combination in this profile.

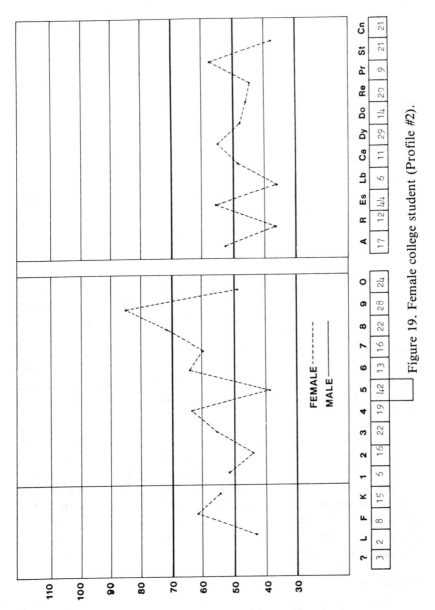

Figure 19. Female college student (Profile #2).

335

The **6** scale is moderately elevated on this profile (T-score = 65) and with the **8** scale elevation would certainly suggest some trouble with her environment. She probably is uncomfortable with people, suspicious of them, and feels cut off and misunderstood. This would lead us to predict she has some difficulties with her sense of identity; that is, she is either dissatisfied with her present identity or she is undergoing a period of identity change. She may be quite anxious about how others are responding to the image that she presents. This interpretation of course is inconsistent with the statement based on the **L, F,** and **K** scales relationship. It seems a better hypothesis about the client, given the total profile, but both interpretations should be considered in an interview with the client.

The low **2** scale in combination with the high **9** scale may indicate a basically extroverted personality which could lead this girl to some corresponding lack of feeling in identifying with other people's problems. When others present problems to her therefore she may not be very sympathetic about what concerns them.

The low **5** scale with the moderate **4** scale suggests some tendency to use sex to manipulate situations.

The Research scales of **A, Es,** and **Ca** have been commented on as being inconsistent with the Clinical profile but as adding a meaningful modification to what would otherwise be a pathological profile. Two other scores on the Research scales deserve some attention. The low **Lb** scale score suggests that the client is easily angered by people and probably is outspoken about her reactions. This is supported, of course, by the interpretation of the high **9** scale. The low **R** scale score would suggest a willingness to discuss her problems, especially those which she has admitted to in filling out the MMPI.

In summary, what we have is a highly energetic, somewhat irritable individual who is having difficulty relating to others and feels misunderstood by them. The counselor should look for the possibility of identity problems and be prepared to help this individual make some changes in self-concept. The client may at times be somewhat unfeeling about others, and the possibility of sex being used as a manipulative device exists. Given the general features of the profile, the prognosis for this case should be rather good.

Profile #3

Profile #3 (Figure 20) also is for a female college student. The Validity scores indicate the classic "cry for help" pattern. The high **F** and low **K** scales border on indicating that she is exaggerating her symptoms, probably to insure that the therapist will see her problems as serious enough to demand attention.

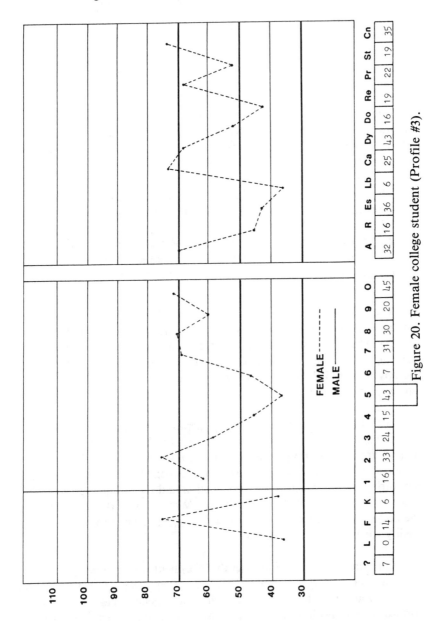

Figure 20. Female college student (Profile #3).

On the Clinical scales the elevated **2** scale shows gloom, sadness, and dissatisfaction with life, but because of the height of the **7** and **8** scales, we need to consider a modification of the **2** scale. The three scores together suggest a tense, anxious, depressed individual who may exhibit confused thinking and much self-doubt. A not unusual score concurrent with this pattern is a low **5** scale which in college women intensifies what we have just said about tenseness, anxiety, and depression and brings in the strong possibility of lack of skills with the opposite sex. Study problems also are indicated for this combination of scales.

The elevated **0** scale adds emphasis to the shyness and introversion symptoms and again supports the possibility of difficulty in relations with the opposite sex. The general maladjustment of the pattern also is supported by the elevations on the **A** and **Ca** scale in the Research scales.

The high **Pr** scale is unusual in a college student; however, as the rest of the profile also is elevated, this scale may be a reflection of some of the difficulties the client is having in adjusting at this time. This scale may reflect a temporary depressed attitude because of her situation; that is, because of her own unhappiness she is feeling that no one is any good, and her prejudice is extended to almost all groups and individuals.

The low **Es** score is certainly not a good therapy indicator; but the **F-K** combination suggests she is hurting. We also know she is voluntarily seeking help, and is young and intelligent. The elevation of the **Cn** scale also suggests that she probably is holding together at least in public. The therapy potential therefore is much better than the low **Es** score would suggest.

A factor which will help in doing therapy with this individual is the elevated **Dy** scale, which shows a strong need to be dependent on someone. If appropriate rapport is established by the therapist, this woman should stay as a client. She will have some tendency toward passivity and permitting the therapist to set the direction and pace. The therapist will need to be aware of this possibility. While using the dependency therapeutically, the therapist should encourage the client to take responsibility for herself and her behavior.

In summary, this test indicates that the client is a depressed, tense individual who is having trouble relating to others. She probably is concerned about relationships with men and has a general negative attitude toward people. Both negative and positive signs are present for her as a therapy risk, although I would suggest that signs for positive prognosis are stronger at this time.

INTERPRETING THE MMPI TO THE CLIENT

Several reasons exist for interpreting an MMPI:

1. a mental health agency may need a diagnostic statement for treatment planning,

2. a rehabilitation agency may need to know a client's potential for a training program,

3. a company may be screening personnel for sensitive positions, or

4. a client may wish to know more about himself/herself.

What is brought into focus by the test interpreter will be different in each of these situations and even the language in which the results are reported is likely to vary.

Most of what has been written about interpreting the MMPI is for its use in the preparation of diagnostic reports in clinical settings. Much of the rest of the previously written material concerns interpretations of the MMPI for screening purposes. Success in a job or in a training program is predictable by interpreting critical scales or specific profile patterns.

Interpretations of the MMPI may be used either as hypotheses for the therapist to test out in therapy or in discussion of the test results with the client.

In interpreting the MMPI to clients, keep certain points in mind:

1. As a therapist interpreting the MMPI, you are trying to create some viable and useful hypotheses about the client and the client's behavior. You are looking for ideas about problem areas and behaviors which may be causing the client difficulties with others and ideas about dynamics which interfere with effective living such as life patterns which may be

restrictive of growth. One of the goals of a therapist is to increase the client's awareness of self and of his/her behavior so that control over the behavior is increased.

2. Because you will be dealing with the client directly, the opportunity to verify the accuracy of your hypotheses is greater. If you are wrong about a particular hypothesis, you should be able to determine the error in discussion with the client. Most of the time therefore interpretations should be given to the client as tentative possibilities and not as finalities. A potential problem occurs in that the rejection by a client of an interpretation may not invalidate the hypothesis. On the other hand, ready acceptance on the part of the client of an interpretation does not always indicate that the hypothesis is valid. For an individual with a high **1-3** scale combination to reject the hypothesis that he/she may have psychological factors in his/her physical problems is to be expected, given the dynamics of the high **1-3** combination. The client's rejection does not invalidate the hypothesis.

3. Frequently, as a test interpreter, you can arrive at some generalities about the client and the client's behavior, but the client must be given an opportunity to provide the specifics. For example, a client with a high **2** scale (T of 70 or above) will have the interpretation made that he/she is depressed. The client should then be ale to be more specific about why he/she feels depressed and in what areas of life this is being felt.

4. When several likely interpretations for an elevated score exist, explain to the client that more than one possibility exists and allow the client to sort out which interpretation is the most accurate. For example, an elevated **2-7** combination indicating depression and anxiety may be the result of current difficulties such as current vocational and/or marital dissatisfactions. On the other hand, it may be the result of a long-standing chronic condition. The client should be able to indicate which of these two interpretations is more accurate or even whether parts of both interpretations are applicable to him/her.

5. Of necessity, you must be well aware of the norms for the client populations. This is particularly true for the Research

scales with college students where the average scores are not those given on the profile. An "average" score of 50 T-score points on scale **A** in a college population, for example, is actually quite elevated, because a score of 40 is the average for this particular group (Anderson & Duckworth, 1969). An **St** scale score of 50, on the other hand is quite low in a college population because scores of 58 and 60 are more the norm.

The need to know special group norms is very important in interpreting profiles for individuals from different racial or cultural backgrounds. The profiles of Northern Europeans tend to be consistent with those found in the United States. However, profiles for people from other countries may look elevated when in fact the individual's adjustment is quite normal for his cultural group (Butcher & Pancheri, 1976).

6. When working with a new population, you should remember that the interpretation of profiles may vary depending upon the group with which you are working. A profile that looks like that of a relatively acute schizophrenic in a mental hospital population may indicate, for example, an identity crisis in a college student population. The difference in potential for treatment is rather great; therefore, the possibilities of what a particular profile means for one's population needs to be checked with much care.

7. Some counselors interpreting an MMPI to a client worry that the client will see the height of some of the scores on the profile and become upset. Keep in mind that the client does not know what scale height means. If you treat an interpretation calmly, the client will most frequently react similarly.

What is important for the client is to have a meaningful interpretation at a level that is appropriate for the client's present needs. Part of the problem of giving an adequate interpretation revolves around the language the counselor may use in discussing the profile. The interpreter should stay away from using such terms as "schizophrenic," "emotionally disturbed," "passive-aggressive," and as much as possible go back to behavioral references. Such phrases as "You often feel cut off from other people," "People really don't seem to understand you or your intentions," "You find yourself brooding a lot," or "There are times when things feel unreal to you," may be less threatening. Because this is behavior the client has reported and is very close to what the client already feels, most clients accept these interpretations quite readily. They then form the basis for discussion of the problems and reassure the client that the tester is an individual who really understands him/her in a way that others do not.

8. Finally, you should not interpret too much material in one session. The client should be given ample time to deal with, elaborate, or give examples of the behavior that you are presenting. The approach to the client should not be one of an expert laying out or dissecting the client's personality, but rather of two people trying to understand what makes one of the two behave in the way in which he/she does.

Hopefully, this chapter showing two different methods of MMPI interpretation using the three types of MMPI scales (Validity, Clinical, and Research) will be helpful in demonstrating the possibilities available in developing a personal style of interpretation.

APPENDICES

APPENDIX A
RESEARCH SCALE ITEM COMPOSITION
Group Booklet Form

The item numbers are from the group form of the test otherwise known as "The Booklet Form."

A Scale (First Factor): 39 Items

True 32 41 67 76 94 138 147 236 259 267 278 301 321 337 343 344 345 356 359 374 382 383 384 389 396 397 411 414 418 431 443 465 499 511 544 555

False 379

R Scale (Second Factor): 40 Items

True None

False 1 6 9 12 39 51 81 112 126 131 140 145 154 156 191 208 219 221 271 272 281 282 327 406 415 429 440 445 447 449 450 451 462 468 472 502 516 529 550 556

Es Scale (Ego Strength): 68 Items

True 2 36 51 95 109 153 174 181 187 192 208 221 231 234 253 270 355 367 380 410 421 430 458 513 515

False 14 22 32 33 34 43 48 58 62 82 94 100 132 140 189 209 217 236 241 244 251 261 341 344 349 359 378 384 389 420 483 488 489 494 510 525 541 544 548 554 555 559 561

Lb Scale (Low Back Pain): 25 Items

    True 67 111 127 238 346

    False 3 45 98 109 148 153 180 190 230 267 321 327 378 394 429 483 502 504 516 536

Ca Scale (Caudality): 36 Items

    True 28 39 76 94 142 147 159 180 182 189 236 239 273 313 338 343 361 389 499 512 544 549 551 560

    False 8 46 57 69 163 188 242 407 412 450 513 523

Dy Scale (Dependency): 57 Items

    True 19 21 24 41 63 67 70 82 86 98 100 138 141 158 165 180 189 201 212 236 239 259 267 304 305 321 337 338 343 357 361 362 375 382 383 390 394 397 398 408 443 487 488 489 509 531 549 554 564

    False 9 79 107 163 170 193 264 369

Do Scale (Dominance): 28 Items

    True 64 229 255 270 368 432 523

    False 32 61 82 86 94 186 223 224 240 249 250 267 268 304 343 356 395 419 483 558 562

Re Scale (Social Responsibility): 32 Items

True 58 111 173 221 294 412 501 552

False 6 28 30 33 56 116 118 157 175 181 223 224 260 304 419 434
437 468 469 471 472 529 553 558

Pr Scale (Prejudice): 32 Items

True 47 84 93 106 117 124 136 139 157 171 186 250 280 304 307 313
319 323 338 349 373 395 406 411 435 437 469 485 543

False 78 176 221

St Scale (Social Status): 34 Items

True 78 118 126 149 199 204 229 237 289 430 441 452 491 513 521

False 136 138 180 213 249 267 280 297 304 314 324 352 365 378 388
427 448 480 488

Cn Scale (Control): 50 Items

True 6 20 30 56 67 105 116 134 145 162 169 181 225 236 238 285
296 319 337 382 411 418 436 446 447 460 529 555

False 58 80 92 96 111 167 174 220 242 249 250 291 313 360 378 439
444 483 488 489 527 548

Mac Scale (MacAndrew Addiction): 49 Items

True 6 27 34 50 56 57 58 61 81 94 116 118 127 128 140 156 186 224

235 243 251 263 283 309 413 419 426 445 446 477 482 483 488 500 507 529 562

False 86 120 130 149 173 179 278 294 320 335 356 378

Rs Scale (Race-Sensitive): 27 Items

True 11 16 59 67 73 84 93 117 124 135 147 157 222 226 229 239 241 264 275 284 298 316 319 343 364

False 81 347

Tr Scale (Test-Retest): 16 Items

8-318	24-333
13-290	32-328
15-314	33-323
16-315	35-331
20-310	37-302
21-308	38-311
22-326	305-366
23-288	317-362

APPENDIX B

RESEARCH SCALE ITEM COMPOSITION
R Form

A Scale (First Factor): 39 Items

> True 32 41 67 76 94 138 147 236 259 267 278 301 305 321 337 343
> 344 345 356 359 368 370 372 376 414 418 431 443 461 462 465
> 482 499 511 518 544 549 555

> False 450

R Scale (Second Factor): 40 Items

> True None

> False 1 6 9 12 39 51 81 112 126 131 140 145 154 156 191 208 219 221
> 271 272 281 282 327 375 377 380 382 383 384 387 394 429 445
> 447 468 472 516 529 550 556

Es Scale (Ego Strength): 68 Items

> True 2 36 51 95 109 153 174 181 187 192 208 221 231 234 253 270
> 355 400 410 421 430 451 458 513 515

> False 14 22 32 33 34 43 48 58 62 82 94 100 132 140 189 209 217 236
> 241 244 251 261 341 344 349 359 420 449 462 482 483 488 489
> 494 510 525 541 544 548 554 555 559 561

Lb Scale (Low Back Pain): 25 Items

    True 67 111 127 238 346

    False 3 45 98 109 148 153 180 190 230 267 321 327 394 429 449 483 504 516 521 536

Ca Scale (Caudality): 36 Items

    True 28 39 76 94 142 147 159 180 182 189 236 239 273 313 338 343 361 398 482 499 512 544 551 560

    False 8 46 57 69 163 188 242 383 407 412 513 523

Dy Scale (Dependency): 57 Items

    True 19 21 24 41 63 67 70 82 86 98 100 138 141 158 165 180 189 201 212 236 239 259 267 304 305 321 337 338 343 357 361 362 370 372 373 393 398 399 408 440 443 461 487 488 489 509 521 531 554

    False 9 79 107 163 170 193 264 411

Do Scale (Dominance): 28 Items

    True 64 229 255 270 400 432 523

    False 32 61 82 86 94 186 223 224 240 249 250 267 268 304 343 356 419 483 547 558 562

Re Scale (Social Responsibility): 32 Items

True 58 111 173 221 294 412 501 552

False 6 28 30 33 56 116 118 157 175 181 223 224 260 304 388 419
434 437 468 471 472 529 553 558

Pr Scale (Prejudice): 32 Items

True 47 84 93 106 117 124 136 139 157 171 186 250 280 304 307 313
319 323 338 349 375 376 388 435 436 437 485 543 547

False 78 178 221

St Scale (Social Status): 34 Items

True 78 118 126 149 199 204 229 237 289 396 430 441 452 491 513

False 136 138 180 213 249 267 280 297 304 314 324 352 365 378 448
449 480 481 488

Cn Scale (Control): 50 Items

True 6 20 30 56 67 105 116 134 145 162 169 181 225 236 238 285
296 319 337 376 379 381 418 447 460 461 529 555

False 58 80 92 111 167 174 220 242 249 250 291 313 360 439 444 449
483 488 489 527 548

Mac Scale (MacAndrew Addiction): 49 Items

True 6 27 34 50 56 57 58 61 81 94 116 118 127 128 140 156 186 224
235 243 251 263 283 309 381 392 413 419 426 445 477 483 488
500 507 529 562

False 86 120 130 149 173 179 278 294 320 335 356 449

Rs Scale (Race-Sensitive): 27 Items

True 11 16 59 67 73 84 93 117 124 135 147 157 222 226 229 239 241
264 275 284 298 316 319 343 364

False 81 347

Tr Scale (Test-Retest): 16 Items

8-318	24-333
13-290	32-328
15-314	33-323
16-315	35-331
20-310	37-302
21-308	38-311
22-326	305-366
23-288	317-362

APPENDIX C

VALIDITY, CLINICAL, AND RESEARCH SCALES

Intercorrelations for Two Normal Populations*

	L	F	K	1	2	3	4	5	6	7	8	9	0
	Validity								Clinical Scales				
L		—.10	.38	—.01	.05	.07	—.20	.11	—.05	—.29	—.27	—.22	—.07
		—.06	.26	.14	.07	.19	—.03	—.05	.04	.00	.06	—.17	—.02
F	—.10		—.25	.36	.31	.06	.40	—.05	.28	.34	.54	.25	.27
	—.06		—.44	.24	.45	.11	.34	.08	.29	.43	.60	.23	.36
K	.38	—.25		—.21	—.15	.13	—.15	.02	—.00	—.62	—.54	—.30	—.45
	.26	—.44		.14	—.25	.27	.20	.12	—.02	—.04	—.02	—.13	—.51
1	—.01	.36	.—21		.51	.29	.24	.19	.21	.44	.43	.13	.25
	.14	.24	.14		.45	.66	.33	.14	.24	.47	.47	.06	.12
2	.05	.31	—.15	.51		.28	.39	.23	.33	.62	.52	—.03	.52
	.07	.45	—.25	.45		.35	.30	.06	.32	.64	.48	—.14	.57
3	.07	.06	.13	.29	.28		.16	.13	.17	.12	.13	.03	—.00
	.19	.11	.27	.66	.35		.44	.15	.37	.42	.39	.06	—.08
4	—.20	.40	—.15	.24	.39	.16		—.05	.43	.47	.56	.42	.13
	—.03	.34	.20	.33	.30	.44		.17	.31	.44	.53	.33	—.08
5	.11	—.05	.02	.19	.23	.13	—.05		.07	.16	.08	—.06	.12
	—.05	.08	.12	.14	.06	.15	.17		.03	.18	.19	.19	—.18
6	—.05	.28	—.00	.21	.33	.17	.43	.07		.39	.44	.20	.13
	.04	.29	—.02	.24	.32	.37	.31	.03		.44	.45	.10	.11
7	—.29	.34	—.62	.44	.62	.12	.47	.16	.39		.83	.32	.61
	.00	.43	—.04	.47	.64	.42	.44	.18	.44		.72	.16	.36
8	—.27	.54	—.54	.43	.52	.13	.56	.08	.44	.83		.44	.48
	—.06	.60	—.02	.47	.48	.39	.53	.19	.45	.72		.33	.21
9	—.22	.25	—.30	.13	—.03	.03	.42	—.06	.20	.32	.44		—.14
	—.17	.23	—.13	.06	—.14	.06	.33	.19	.10	.16	.33		—.31
0	—.07	.27	—.45	.25	.52	—.00	.13	.12	.13	.61	.48	—.14	
	—.02	.36	—.51	.12	.57	—.08	—.08	—.18	.11	.36	.21	—.31	
A	—.30	.39	—.71	.37	.52	.05	.42	.14	.31	.90	.79	.32	.61
	—.15	.58	—.71	.19	.61	.06	.14	.02	.29	.59	.48	.11	.64
R	.32	—.00	.40	.13	.39	.18	—.06	.18	.10	—.07	—.11	—.42	.30
	.30	—.05	.34	.27	.32	.26	.03	.07	.09	.17	.06	—.41	.29
Es	—.10	—.09	.14	—.25	—.24	—.09	—.02	—.39	—.07	—.25	—.20	.03	—.19
	—.07	—.42	.45	—.37	—.51	—.24	—.03	—.01	—.29	—.49	—.39	.03	—.51
Lb	.19	.06	.36	.21	.28	.26	.20	.10	.20	—.01	.00	.05	.14
	.17	—.01	.29	.32	.18	.39	17	—.03	.14	.14	.09	—.04	—.09
Ca	—.25	.39	—.61	.47	.63	.13	.42	.14	.30	.86	.74	.23	.66
	—.13	.53	—.65	.32	.62	.13	.18	.05	.24	.57	.44	.12	.63
Dy	—.06	.16	—.21	.17	.22	.04	.13	.21	.13	.32	.27	.07	.25
	—.16	.49	—.66	.17	.54	.00	.08	.06	.28	.56	.40	.08	.63
Do	—.03	—.10	.15	—.10	—.13	—.02	—.10	—.04	—.06	—.18	—.19	.01	—.19
	—.09	—.38	.44	—.17	—.46	.00	.00	.12	—.15	—.44	—.29	.07	—.57
Re	.39	—.25	.52	—.06	—.01	.11	—.29	.19	—.07	—.37	—.38	—.31	—.12
	.29	—.41	.51	.07	—.11	.18	—.14	.05	—.07	—.12	—.20	—.32	—.15
Pr	—.16	.34	—.67	.24	.26	—.07	.27	—.02	—.00	.59	.59	.31	.47
	—.13	.53	—.69	.09	.35	—.13	.02	—.00	—.00	.26	.30	.19	.46
St	—.05	—.12	.38	—.16	—.23	.06	—.00	—.26	.14	—.38	—.31	.17	—.53
	—.02	—.23	.41	—.14	—.33	.03	.08	.14	—.11	—.29	—.19	.18	—.61
Cn	—.54	.24	—.42	—.14	.20	.01	.38	.08	.21	.45	.43	.44	.13
	—.40	.36	—.46	—.01	.25	—.06	.20	.11	.11	.20	.23	.32	.14

*Bold figures—847 graduate students from Ball State U. and non-student volunteers from the community. No known clinical patients included.

Light figures—50,000 medical outpatients at the Mayo Clinic. No psychiatric patients included (Swenson, Pearson, & Osborne, 1973).

APPENDIX C
VALIDITY, CLINICAL, AND RESEARCH SCALES
Intercorrelations for Two Normal Populations*

New Scales

	A	R	Es	Lb	Ca	Dy	Do	Re	Pr	St	Cn
L	−.30	.32	−.10	.19	−.25	−.06	−.03	.39	−.16	−.05	−.54
	−.15	.30	−.07	.17	−.13	−.16	−.09	.29	−.13	−.02	−.40
F	.39	.00	−.09	.06	.39	.16	−.10	−.25	.34	−.12	.24
	.58	−.05	−.42	−.01	.53	.49	−.38	−.41	.53	−.23	.36
K	−.71	.40	.14	.36	−.61	−.21	.15	.52	−.67	.38	−.42
	−.71	.34	.45	.29	−.65	−.66	.44	.51	−.69	.41	−.46
1	.37	.13	−.25	.21	.47	.17	−.10	−.06	.24	−.16	−.14
	.19	.27	−.37	.32	.32	.17	−.17	.07	.09	−.14	−.01
2	.52	.39	−.24	.28	.63	.22	−.13	−.01	.26	−.23	.20
	.61	.32	−.51	.18	.62	.54	−.46	−.11	.35	−.33	.25
3	.05	.18	−.09	.26	.13	.04	−.02	.11	−.07	.06	.01
	.06	.26	−.24	.39	.13	.00	−.00	.18	−.13	.03	−.06
4	.42	−.06	−.02	.20	.42	.13	−.10	−.29	.27	.00	.38
	.14	.03	−.03	.17	.18	.08	−.00	−.14	.02	.08	.20
5	.14	.18	−.39	.10	.14	.21	−.04	.19	−.02	−.26	.08
	.02	.07	−.01	−.03	.05	.06	.12	.05	.00	.14	.11
6	.31	.10	−.07	.20	.30	.13	−.06	−.07	−.00	.14	.21
	.29	.09	−.29	.14	.24	.28	−.15	−.07	−.00	−.11	.11
7	.90	−.07	−.25	−.01	.86	.32	−.18	−.37	.59	−.38	.45
	.59	.17	−.49	.14	.57	.56	−.44	−.12	.26	−.29	.20
8	.79	−.11	−.20	.00	.74	.27	−.19	−.38	.59	−.31	.43
	.48	.06	−.39	.09	.44	.40	−.29	−.20	.30	−.19	.23
9	.32	−.42	.03	.05	.23	.07	.01	−.31	.31	.17	.44
	.11	−.41	.03	−.04	.12	.08	.07	−.32	.19	.18	.32
0	.61	.30	−.19	−.14	.66	.25	−.19	−.12	.47	−.53	.13
	.64	.29	−.51	−.09	.63	.63	−.57	−.15	.46	−.61	.14
A		−.16	−.32	−.12	.85	.31	−.19	−.39	.64	−.38	.49
		−.10	−.68	−.13	.84	.88	−.60	−.41	.66	−.49	.45
R	−.16		−.09	.33	.00	.00	−.07	.37	−.18	−.15	−.33
	−.10		−.12	.31	−.03	−.08	−.09	.36	−.16	−.21	−.37
Es	−.32	−.09		.00	−.23	−.57	.56	.00	−.15	.20	.09
	−.68	−.12		.03	−.61	−.64	.60	.25	−.53	.54	−.02
Lb	−.12	.33	.00		−.05	−.04	.07	.22	−.17	.29	.08
	−.13	.31	.03		−.10	−.20	.10	.12	−.15	.14	−.04
Ca	.85	.00	−.23	−.05		.30	−.19	−.33	.58	−.40	.41
	.84	−.03	−.61	−.10		.80	−.57	−.38	.61	−.51	.44
Dy	.31	.00	−.57	−.04	.30		−.55	−.09	.20	−.16	.11
	.88	−.08	−.64	−.20	.80		−.63	−.39	.61	−.53	.35
Do	−.19	−.07	.56	.07	−.19	−.55		.08	−.18	.21	−.14
	−.60	−.09	.60	.10	−.57	−.63		.33	−.54	.61	−.02
Re	−.39	.37	.00	.22	−.33	−.09	.08		−.49	.20	−.43
	−.41	.36	.25	.12	−.38	−.39	.33		−.54	.17	−.47
Pr	.64	−.18	−.15	−.17	.58	.20	−.18	−.49		−.30	.27
	.66	−.16	−.53	−.15	.61	.61	−.54	−.54		−.48	.30
St	−.38	−.15	.20	.29	−.40	−.16	.21	.20	−.30		.20
	−.49	−.21	.54	.14	−.51	−.53	.61	.17	−.48		.06
Cn	.49	−.33	.09	.08	.41	.11	−.14	−.43	.27	.20	
	.45	−.37	−.02	−.04	.44	.35	−.02	−.47	.30	.06	

*Bold figures—847 graduate students from Ball State U. and non-student volunteers from the community. No known clinical patients included.

Light figures—50,000 medical outpatients at the Mayo Clinic. No psychiatric patients included (Swenson, Pearson & Osborne, 1973).

354

REFERENCES

REFERENCES

Adams, J. (1971). Defensiveness on the MMPI as a function of the warmth of test introduction. *Journal of Consulting and Clinical Psychology, 36,* 444.

Altman, H., Gynther, M., Warbin, R., & Sletten, I. (1972) A new empirical automated MMPI interpretive program: The **6-8/8-6** code type. **Journal of Clinical Psychology, 28,** 495-498.

Altman, H., Warbin, R., Sletten, I., & Gynther, M. (1973). Replicated empirical correlates of the MMPI **8-9/9-8** code type. *Journal of Personality Assessment, 37,* 369-371.

Anderson, W. (1956). The MMPI: Low **Pa** scores. *Journal of Counseling Psychology, 3,* 226-228.

Anderson, W., & Bauer, B. (1985). Clients with MMPI high **D-Pd:** Therapy implications. *Journal of Clinical Psychology, 41,* 181-188.

Anderson, W., & Duckworth, J. (1969). *New MMPI scales and the college student.* University of Missouri Testing and Counseling Service Report, 23(7).

Anderson, W., & Holcomb, W.R. (1983). Accused murderers: Five MMPI personality types. *Journal of Clinical Psychology, 39,* 761-768.

Anderson, W.P., & Kunce, J.T. (1984). Diagnostic implications of markedly elevated MMPI **Sc** scale scores for nonhospitalized clients. *Journal of Clinical Psychology, 40,* 925-930.

Anderson, W., Kunce, J., & Rich, R. (1979). Sex offenders: Three personality types. *Journal of Clinical Psychology, 35,* 671-676.

Appledorf, M., & Hunley, P. (1975). Application of MMPI alcoholism scales to older alcoholics and problem drinkers. *Journal of Studies on Alcohol, 36,* 645-653.

Arnold, P. (1970). Marriage counselee MMPI profile characteristics with objective signs that discriminate them from married couples in general. Unpublished doctoral dissertation, University of Minnesota.

Astin, A.W. (1959). A factor study of the MMPI Psychopathic Deviate scale. *Journal of Consulting Psychology, 23,* 550-554.

Barger, B., & Hall, E. (1964). Personality patterns and achievement in college. *Educational and Psychological Measurement, 24,* 339-346.

Barron, F. (1953). An ego-strength scale which predicts response to psychotherapy. *Journal of Consulting Psychology, 17,* 327-333.

Barron, F. (1956). Ego strength and the management of aggression. In G.S. Welsh & W.G. Dahlstrom (Eds.) *Basic readings on the MMPI in psychology and medicine.* Minneapolis: University of Minnesota Press.

Barron, F. (1969). *Creative persons and creative process.* New York: Holt, Rinehart, and Wilson.

Bertelson, A.D., Marks, P.A., & May, G.D. (1982). MMPI and race: A controlled study. *Journal of Consulting and Clinical Psychology, 50,* 316-318.

Bieliauskas, L.A., & Shekelle, R. (1983). Stable behaviors associated with high-point **D** MMPI profiles in a non-psychiatric population. *Journal of Clinical Psychology, 39,* 422-426.

Birtchnell, J., & Kennard, J. (1983). What does the MMPI Dependency scale really measure? *Journal of Clinical Psychology, 39,* 532-542.

Black, J.D. (1953). The interpretation of MMPI profiles of college women. Unpublished doctoral dissertation, University of Minnesota.

Blazer, J. (1965a). MMPI interpretation in outline: II. The **L** scale. *Psychology, 2,* 2-7.

Blazer, J. (1965b). MMPI interpretation in outline: III. The **F** scale. *Psychology, 2,* 7-9.

Block, J., & Bailey, D. (May, 1955). Q-sort item analyses of a number of MMPI scales. Officer Education Research Laboratory, Technical Memorandum, OERL-TM-55-7.

Brill, N., Crumpton, E., & Grayson, H. (1971). Personality factors in marijuana use. *Archives of General Psychiatry, 24,* 163-165.

Burke, H.R. (1983). "Markers" for the MacAndrew and the Cavior Heroin Addiction MMPI scales. *Journal of Studies on Alcohol, 44,* 558-563.

Burke, H.R., & Marcus, R. (1977). MacAndrew MMPI alcoholism scale: Alcoholism and drug addictiveness. *Journal of Psychology, 96,* 141-148.

Burkhart, B.R., Gynther, M.D., & Fromuth, M.E. (1980). The relative predictive validity of the subtle vs. obvious items on the Depression scale. *Journal of Clinical Psychology, 36,* 748-751.

Butcher, J. (1965). Manifest aggression: MMPI correlates in normal boys. *Journal of Consulting Psychology, 29,* 446-454.

Butcher, J. (1969). *MMPI: Research developments and clinical applications.* New York: McGraw-Hill.

Butcher, J.N., Braswell, L., & Raney, D. (1983). A cross-cultural comparison of American Indian, Black, and white inpatients on the MMPI and presenting symptoms. *Journal of Consulting and Clinical Psychology, 51,* 587-584.

Butcher, J., & Pancheri, P. (1976). *A handbook of cross-national MMPI research.* Minneapolis: University of Minnesota Press.

Caldwell, A. (1972). Families of MMPI pattern types. Paper presented at the Seventh Annual Symposium on the MMPI, Mexico City, Mexico.

358

Caldwell, A. (1974). Characteristics of MMPI pattern types. Paper presented at the Ninth Annual Symposium on the MMPI, Los Angeles, CA.

Caldwell, A. (1977). Families of MMPI code types. Paper presented at the Twelfth Annual Symposium on the MMPI, Tampa, FL.

Caldwell, A. (1985). MMPI clinical interpretation. Paper presented at the Advanced psychological Studies Institute. Los Angeles, CA.

Canter, A. (1965). A brief note on shortening Barron's ego strength scale. *Journal of Clinical Psychology, 21,* 285-286.

Canter, A., Day, C.W., Imboden, J.B., & Cluff, L.E. (1962). The influence of age and health status on the MMPI scores of a normal population. *Journal of Clinical Psychology, 18,* 71-73.

Carkhuff, R.R., Barnette, L., & McCall, J.N. (1965). *The counselor's handbook: Scale and profile interpretation of the MMPI.* Urbana, IL: R.W. Parkinson and Associates.

Carson, R. (1969). Interpretative manual to the MMPI. In J. Butcher (Ed.), *MMPI: Research developments and clinical applications.* New York: McGraw-Hill, 279-296.

Carson, R. (1972). MMPI profile interpretation. Paper read at the Seventh Annual Symposium on the MMPI. Mexico City, Mexico.

Carson, R. (1985). The MMPI and DSM-III diagnosis. Paper presented at the Advanced Psychological Studies Institute. Los Angeles, CA.

Cernovsky, Z. (1984). Es scale level and correlates of MMPI elevation: Alcohol abuse vs. MMPI scores in treated alcoholics. *Journal of Clinical Psychology, 40,* 1502-1509.

Clopton, J.R., Weiner, R.H., & Davis, H.G. (1980). Use of the MMPI in identification of alcoholic psychiatric patients. *Journal of Consulting and Clinical Psychology, 48,* 416-417.

Colligan, R.C., Osborne, D., Swenson, W.M., & Offord, K.P. (1984). The MMPI: Development of contemporary norms. *Journal of Clinical Psychology, 40,* 100-107.

Conley, J. (1981). An MMPI typology of male alcoholics: Admission, discharge, and outcome comparisons. *Journal of Personality Assessment, 45,* 33-39.

Conley, J., & Kammeier, M.L. (1980). MMPI item responses of alcoholics in treatment: comparisons with normals and psychiatric patients. *Journal of Consulting and Clinical Psychology, 48,* 668-669.

Cooke, M.K., & Kiesler, D.J. (1967). Prediction of college students who later require personal counseling. *Journal of Counseling Psychology, 14,* 346-349.

Costello, R., & Tiffany, D. (1972). Methodological issues and racial (Black-white) comparisons on the MMPI. *Journal of Consulting and Clinical Psychology, 38,* 161-168.

Cottle, W.C. (1953). *The MMPI: A review.* Lawrence, KS: University of Kansas Press.

Craig, R. (1984a). A comparison of MMPI profiles of heroin addicts based on multiple methods of classification. *Journal of Personality Assessment, 48,* 115-129.

Craig, R. (1984b). MMPI substance abuse scales on drug addicts with and without concurrent alcoholism. *Journal of Personality Assessment, 48,* 495-499.

Crumpton, E., Cantor, J.M., & Batiste, C. (1960). A factor analytic study of Barron's ego-strength scale. *Journal of Clinical Psychology, 16,* 283-291.

Cuadra, C.A. (1953). A psychometric investigation of control factors in psychological adjustment. Unpublished doctoral dissertation, University of California.

Dahlstrom, W.G., & Welsh, G.S. (1960). *An MMPI handbook: A guide to use in clinical practice and research.* Minneapolis: University of Minnesota Press.

Dahlstrom, W.G., Welsh, G., & Dahlstrom, L. (1972). *An MMPI Handbook: Volume I, clinical interpretation.* Minneapolis: University of Minnesota Press.

Daniels, E.E., & Hunter, W.A. (1949). MMPI personality patterns for various occupations. *Journal of Applied Psychology, 33,* 559-565.

Davies, J., & Maliphant, R. (1971). Refractory behavior at school in normal adolescent males in relation to psychopathy and early experience. *Journal of Child Psychology and Psychiatry and Allied Disciplines, 12,* 35-41.

Davis, K. (1971). The actuarial development of a female **4-3** MMPI profile. Unpublished doctoral dissertation, St. Louis University.

Davis, K., & Sines, J. (1971). An antisocial behavioral pattern associated with a specific MMPI profile. *Journal of Consulting and Clinical Psychology, 36,* 229-234.

De Groot, G.W., & Adamson, J.D. (1973). Responses of psychiatric inpatients to the MacAndrew alcoholism scale. *Quarterly Journal of Studies on Alcohol, 34,* 1133-1139.

Doob, L. (1960). *Becoming more civilized: A psychological exploration.* New Haven, CT: Yale University Press.

Drake, L.E. (1962). MMPI patterns predictive of achievement. *Journal of Counseling Psychology, 9,* 164-167.

Drake, L.E., & Oetting, E.R. (1957). An MMPI pattern and suppressor variable predictive of academic achievement. *Journal of Counseling Psychology, 4,* 245-247.

Drake, L.E., & Oetting, E.R. (1959). *An MMPI codebook for counselors.* Minneapolis: University of Minnesota Press.

Drasgow, J., & Barnette, W.L. (Jr.) (1957). **F-K** in a motivated group. *Journal of Consulting Psychology, 21,* 399-401.

Duckworth, J. (1983). The **Mac** scale: A report on three studies. Paper presented to the Eighteenth Annual Symposium on the MMPI, Tampa, Florida.

360

Edwards, A., & Abbott, R. (1969). Further evidence regarding the **R** scale of the MMPI as a measure of acquiescence. *Psychological Reports, 24,* 903-906.

Elion, V.H., & Megargee, E.I. (1975). Validity of the MMPI Pd scale among Black males. *Journal of Consulting and Clinical Psychology, 43,* 166-172.

English, R.W. (1971). Correlates of stigma towards physically disabled persons. *Rehabilitation Research and Practice Review, 2,* 1-17.

Evans, R.G. (1984). The test-retest index and high **F** MMPI profiles. *Journal of Clinical Psychology, 40,* 516-518.

Evans, R.G., & Dinning, W.D. (1982). MMPI correlates of the BEM sex role inventory and extended personal attributes questionnaire in a male psychiatric sample. *Journal of Clinical Psychology, 38,* 811-815.

Evans, R.G., & Dinning, W.D. (1983). Response consistency among high **F** scale scorers on the MMPI. *Journal of Clinical Psychology, 39,* 246-248.

Finney, J.C., Smith, D.F., Skeeters, D.E., & Auvenshire, C.D. (1971). MMPI alcoholism scale: Factor structure and content analysis. *Quarterly Journal of Studies on Alcohol, 32,* 1055-1060.

Fowler, R.D., & Athey, E.B. (1971). A cross-validation of Gilberstadt and Duker's **1-2-3-4** profile type. *Journal of Clinical Psychology, 27,* 238-240.

Fowler, R.D., & Coyle, F.A. (1969). Collegiate normative data on MMPI content scales. *Journal of Clinical Psychology, 25,* 62-63.

Fowler, R.D., Teal, S., & Coyle, F.A. (1967). The measurement of alcoholic response to treatment by Barron's ego strength scale. *Journal of Psychology, 67,* 65-68.

Friedrich, W., & Loftsgard, S. (1978). A comparison of the MacAndrew alcoholism scale and the Michigan Alcohol Screening Test in a sample of problem drinkers. *Journal of Studies on Alcohol, 39,* 1940-1944.

Getter, H., & Sunderland, D.M. (1962). The Barron ego strength scale and psychotherapy outcome. *Journal of Consulting Psychology, 26,* 195.

Gilberstadt, H., & Duker, J. (1965). *A handbook for clinical and actuarial MMPI interpretation.* Philadelphia: W.B. Saunders.

Gilliland, A.R., & Colgin, R. (1951). Norms, reliability, and forms of the MMPI. *Journal of Consulting Psychology, 15,* 435-438.

Glosz, J.T., & Grant, I. (1981). Prognostic validity of the MMPI. *Journal of Clinical Psychology, 37,* 147-151.

Gloye, E., & Zimmerman, I. (1967). MMPI item changes by college students under ideal-self response set. *Journal of Projective Techniques and Personality Assessment, 31,* 63-69.

Good, P., & Brantner, J. (1961). *The physician's guide to the MMPI*. Minneapolis: University of Minnesota Press.

Good, P., & Brantner, J. (1974). *A practical guide to the MMPI*. Minneapolis: University of Minnesota Press.

Goodstein, L.D. (1954). Regional differences in MMPI responses among male college students. *Journal of Consulting Psychology, 18,* 437-441.

Gough, H.G. (1948). A new dimension of status: II. Relationship of the St scale to other variables. *American Sociological Review, 13,* 534-537.

Gough, H.G. (1949). A short social status inventory. *Journal of Educational Psychology, 40,* 52-56.

Gough, H.G. (1951). Studies of Social Intolerance: III. Relationship of the Pr scale to other variables. *Journal of Social Psychology, 33,* 257-262.

Gough, H.G. (1952). A personality scale for social responsibility. *Journal of Abnormal and Social Psychology, 47,* 73-80.

Gough, H.G. (1954). Some common misconceptions about neuroticism. *Journal of Consulting Psychology, 18,* 408-413.

Gough, H.G., McClosky, H., & Meehl, P.E. (1951). A personality scale for dominance. *Journal of Abnormal and Social Psychology, 46,* 360-366.

Gough, H.G., McKee, M.G., & Yandell, R.J. (May, 1955). Adjective check list analyses of a number of selected psychometric and assessment variables. Officer Education Research Laboratory, Technical Memorandum, OERL-TM-55-10.

Graham, J. (1977). *The MMPI: A practical guide*. New York: Oxford University Press.

Graham, J.R., & McCord, G. (March, 1982). Correlates of "normal range" MMPI scores for nonclinical subjects. Paper presented at the 17th Annual Symposium on Recent Developments in the Use of the MMPI, Tampa, Florida.

Graham, J., Schroeder, H., & Lilly, R. (1971). Factor analysis of items on the Social Introversion and Masculinity-femininity scales of the MMPI. *Journal of Clinical Psychology, 27,* 367-370.

Gravitz, M. (1967). Frequency and content of test items normally omitted from MMPI scales. *Journal of Consulting Psychology, 31,* 642.

Gravitz, M. (1968). Self-described depression and scores on the MMPI D scale in normal subjects. *Journal of Projective Techniques and Personality Assessment, 32,* 88-91.

Gravitz, M. (1970a). Use of a short form of Barron's ego-strength scale with normal adults. *Journal of Clinical Psychology, 26,* 223.

Gravitz, M. (1970b). Validity implications of normal adult MMPI L scale endorsement. *Journal of Clinical Psychology, 26,* 497-499.

Gravitz, M. (1971). Declination rates on the MMPI validity and clinical scales. *Journal of Clinical Psychology, 27,* 103.

Grayson, H.M., & Olinger, L.B. (1957). Simulation of "normalcy" by psychiatric patients on the MMPI. *Journal of Consulting Psychology, 21,* 73-77.

Greene, R. (1978). An empirically derived MMPI carelessness scale. *Journal of Clinical Psychology, 34,* 407-410.

Greene, R. (1980). *The MMPI: An interpretive manual.* New York: Grune & Stratton.

Grier, W.H., & Cobbs, P.M. (1968). *Black rage.* New York: Basic Books.

Grow, R., McVaugh, W., & Eno, T.D. (1980). Faking and the MMPI. *Journal of Clinical Psychology, 36,* 910-917.

Gulas, I. (1973). MMPI 2-pt. codes for a "normal" college male population: A replication study. *Journal of Psychology, 84,* 319-322.

Guthrie, G.M. (1949). A study of the personality characteristics associated with the disorders encountered by an internist. Unpublished doctoral dissertation, University of Minnesota.

Guthrie, G.M. (1952). Common characteristics associated with frequent MMPI profile types. *Journal of Clinical Psychology, 8,* 141-145.

Gynther, M. (1961). The clinical utility of "invalid" MMPI F scores. *Journal of Consulting Psychology, 25,* 540-542.

Gynther, M. (1972). White norms and Black MMPI's: A prescription for discrimination? *Psychological Bulletin, 78,* 386-402.

Gynther, M. (1974). Actuarial MMPI interpretation. Paper read at the Ninth Annual Symposium on the MMPI. Los Angeles, CA.

Gynther, M., Altman, H., & Sletten, I. (1973). Replicated correlates of MMPI two-point code types: The Missouri actuarial system. *Journal of Clinical Psychology, 29,* 263-289.

Gynther, M., Altman, H., & Warbin, R. (1972). A new empirical automated MMPI interpretive program: The 2-4/4-2 code type. *Journal of Clinical Psychology, 28,* 598-601.

Gynther, M., Altman, H., & Warbin, R. (1973a). Behavioral correlates for the Minnesota Multiphasic Personality Inventory 4-9/9-4 code types: A case of the emperor's new clothes? *Journal of Consulting Psychology, 40,* 259-263.

Gynther, M., Altman, H., & Warbin, R. (1973b). Interpretation of uninterpretable Minnesota Multiphasic Personality Inventory profiles. *Journal of Consulting and Clinical Psychology, 40,* 78-83.

Gynther, M., Altman, H., & Warbin, R. (1973c). A new actuarial-empirical automated MMPI interpretive program: The 4-3/3-4 code type. *Journal of Clinical Psychology, 29,* 229-231.

Gynther, M., Altman, H., & Warbin, R. (1973d). A new empirical automated MMPI interpretive program: The 6-9/9-6 code type. *Journal of Clinical Psychology, 29,* 60-61.

Gynther, M., Altman, H., & Warbin, R. (1973e). A new empirical automated MMPI interpretive program: The 2-7/7-2 code type. *Journal of Clinical Psychology, 29,* 58-59.

Gynther, M., Altman, H., Warbin, R., & Sletten, I. (1972). A new actuarial system for MMPI interpretation: Rationale and methodology. *Journal of Clinical Psychology, 28,* 173-179.

Gynther, M., Altman, H., Warbin, R., & Sletten, I. (1973). A new empirical automated MMPI interpretative program. The 1-2/2-1 code type. *Journal of Clinical Psychology, 29,* 54-57.

Gynther, M., Burkhart, B.R., & Hovanitz, C. (1979). Do face-valid items have more predictive validity than subtle items? The case of the Pd scale. *Journal of Consulting and Clinical Psychology, 47,* 295-300.

Gynther, M., Fowler, R., & Erdberg, P. (1971). False positives galore: The application of standard MMPI criteria to a rural, isolated Negro sample. *Journal of Clinical Psychology, 27,* 234-237.

Gynther, M., & Greene, S. B. (1980). Accuracy may make a difference, but does a difference make for accuracy? A response to Protchard and Rosenblatt. *Journal of Consulting and Clinical Psychology, 48,* 268-272.

Gynther, M., & Shimkunas, A. (1965a). Age, intelligence, and MMPI F scores. *Journal of Consulting Psychology, 29,* 383-388.

Gynther, M., & Shimkunas, A. (1965b). More data on MMPI F†16 scores. *Journal of Clinical Psychology, 21,* 275-279.

Halbower, C.C. (1955). A comparison of actuarial versus clinical prediction to classes discriminated by MMPI. Unpublished doctoral dissertation, University of Minnesota.

Hanvik, L.J. (1951). MMPI profiles in patients with low-back pain. *Journal of Consulting Psychology, 15,* 350-353.

Harmon, L.R., & Weiner, D.N. (1945). The use of the MMPI in vocational adjustment. *Journal of Applied Psychology, 29,* 132-141.

Harmon, M. (1980). The Barron Ego Strength scale: A study of personality correlates among normals. *Journal of Clinical Psychology, 36,* 433-436.

Harris, R.E., & Lingoes, J.C. (1955). Subscales for the MMPI: An aid to profile interpretation. Unpublished manuscript. University of California.

Hathaway, S.R., & McKinley, J.C. (1951). *The Minnesota Multiphasic Personality Inventory Manual.* Revised. New York: The Psychological Corporation.

Hathaway, S.R., & Monachesi, E.D. (1958). MMPI studies of ninth-grade students in Minnesota schools. Unpublished materials.

Hathaway, S.R., Reynolds, P.C., & Monachesi, E.D. (1969). Follow up of the later careers and lives of 1,000 boys who dropped out of high school. *Journal of Consulting and Clinical Psychology, 33,* 370-380.

Haun, K.W. (1965). A note on the prediction of academic performance from personality test scores. *Psychological Reports, 16,* 294.

Heppner, P., & Anderson, W. (1985). The relationship between problem solving, self-appraisal, and psychological adjustment. *Cognitive Therapy & Research, 9,* 415-427.

Hibbs, B.J., Kobas, J.C., & Gonzalez, J. (1979). Effects of ethnicity, sex, and age on MMPI profiles. *Psychological Reports, 45,* 591-597.

Hiner, D., Ogren, D., & Baxter, J. (1969). Ideal-self responding on the MMPI. *Journal of Projective Techniques and Personality Assessment, 33,* 389-396.

Hoffman, H., Loper, R., & Kammeier, M. (1974). Identifying future alcoholics with MMPI alcoholism scales. *Quarterly Journal of Studies on Alcohol, 35,* 490-498.

Hokanson, J.E., & Calden, G. (1960). Negro-white differences on the MMPI. *Journal of Clinical Psychology, 16,* 32-33.

Holcomb, W.R., Adams, N.A., & Ponder, H.M. (1984). Are separate Black and white norms needed?: An IQ-controlled comparison of accused murderers. *Journal of Clinical Psychology, 40,* 189-193.

Holland, T. (1979). Ethnic group differences in MMPI profile pattern and factorial structure among adult offenders. *Journal of Personality Assessment, 43,* 72-77.

Holmes, D. (1967). Male-female differences in MMPI ego-strength: An artifact. *Journal of Consulting Psychology, 31,* 408-410.

Hovanitz, C., & Gynther, M.D. (1980). The prediction of impulsive behavior: Comparative validities of obvious vs. subtle MMPI hypomania (**Ma**) items. *Journal of Clinical Psychology, 36,* 422-427.

Hovanitz, C., Gynther, M.G., & Marks, P. (1983). The prediction of paranoid behavior: Comparative validities of obvious vs. subtle MMPI paranoid (**Pa**) items. *Journal of Clinical Psychology, 39,* 407-411.

Hovey, H.B. (1953). MMPI profiles and personality characteristics. *Journal of Consulting Psychology, 17,* 142-146.

Hovey, H., & Lewis, E. (1967). Semi-automatic interpretation of the MMPI. *Journal of Clinical Psychology, 23,* 123-124.

Huber, N., & Danahy, S. (1975). Use of the MMPI in predicting completion and evaluating changes in a long-term alcoholism treatment program. *Journal of Studies on Alcohol, 36,* 1230-1237.

Jensen, A.R. (1957). Authoritarian attitudes and personality maladjustment. *Journal of Abnormal and Social Psychology, 54,* 303-311.

Jurjevich, R.M. (1966). Short interval test-retest stability of MMPI, CPI, Cornell Index, and Symptom Check List. *Journal of General Psychology, 74,* 201-206.

Kahn, H., & Singer, E. (1949). An investigation of some of the factors related to success or failure of School of Commerce students. *Journal of Educational Psychology, 40,* 107-117.

Kelley, C.K., & King, G.D. (1979a). Behavioral correlates of infrequent two-point MMPI code types at a university mental health center. *Journal of Clinical Psychology, 35,* 576-585.

Kelley, C.K., & King G.D. (1979b). Behavioral correlates of the 2-7-8 MMPI profile type in students at a university mental health center. *Journal of Consulting and Clinical Psychology, 47,* 679-685.

Kelley, C.K., & King, G.D. (1980). Two and three point classification of MMPI profiles in which scales 2, 7, and 8 are the highest elevations. *Journal of Personality Assessment, 44,* 25-33.

Kennedy, W.A. (1962). MMPI profiles of gifted adolescents. *Journal of Clinical Psychology, 18,* 148-149.

King, G.D., & Kelley, C.K. (1977a). Behavioral correlates for spike 4, spike 9, and 4-9/9-4 MMPI profiles in students at a university mental health clinic. *Journal of Clinical Psychology, 33,* 718-724.

King, G.D., & Kelley, C.K. (1977b). MMPI behavioral correlates of spike 5 and two-point code types with scale 5 as one elevation. *Journal of Clinical Psychology, 33,* 180-185.

Klein, S., & Cross, H. (1984). Correlates of the MMPI Lb scale in a college population. *Journal of Clinical Psychology, 40,* 185-188.

Kleinmutz, B. (1960). An extension of the construct validity of the ego-strength scale. *Journal of Consulting Psychology, 24,* 463-464.

Kranitz, L. (1972). Alcoholics, heroin addicts, and nonaddicts: Comparisons on the MacAndrew alcoholism scale of the MMPI. *Quarterly Journal of Studies on Alcohol, 33,* 807-809.

Kunce, J., & Anderson, W. (1976). Normalizing the MMPI. *Journal of Clinical Psychology, 32,* 776-780.

Kunce, J., & Anderson, W. (1984). Perspectives on uses of the MMPI in nonpsychiatric settings. In P. McReynolds & G.J. Chelune (Eds.), *Advances in Psychological Assessment.* San Francisco: Jossey-Bass.

366

Kunce, J., & Callis, R. (1969). Vocational interest and personality. *Vocational Guidance Quarterly, 18,* 34-40.

Kurlychek, R., & Jordan, L. (1980). MMPI profiles and code types of responsible and non-responsible criminal defendants. *Journal of Clinical Psychology, 36,* 590-593.

Lachar, D. (1974). *The MMPI: Clinical Assessment and Automated Interpretation.* Los Angeles, CA: Western Psychological Services.

Lachar, D., Berman, W., Grisell, J.L., & Schoof, K. (1976). The MacAndrew alcoholism scale as a general measure of substance misuse. *Journal of Studies on Alcohol, 37,* 1609-1615.

Lanyon, R. (1967). Simulation of normal and psychopathic patterns. *Journal of Consulting Psychology, 31,* 94-97.

Lanyon, R., Primo, R., Terrell, f., & Weiner, A. (1972). An aversion-desenitization treatment for alcoholism. *Journal of Consulting and Clinical Psychology, 38,* 394-398.

Lewandowski, D., & Graham, J.R. (1972). Empirical correlates of frequently occurring two-point MMPI code types: A replicated study. *Journal of Consulting & Clinical Psychology, 39,* 467-472.

Long, C.J. (1981). The relationship between surgical outcome and MMPI profiles in chronic pain patients. *Journal of Clinical Psychology, 37,* 744-749.

Loper, R. (1976). MMPI in a counseling service setting. Paper presented at the Eleventh Annual Symposium on the MMPI. Minneapolis, MN.

Lough, O., & Green, M. (1950). A comparison of the Minnesota Multiphasic Personality Inventory and the Washburne **S-A** Inventory as measures of personality of college women. *Journal of Social Psychology, 32,* 23-30.

MacAndrew, C. (1965). The differentiation of male alcoholic outpatients from nonalcoholic psychiatric outpatients by means of the MMPI. *Quarterly Journal of Studies on Alcohol, 26,* 238-246.

MacAndrew, C. (1979a). **Mac** scale scores of three samples of men under conditions of conventional versus independent scale administration. *Journal of Studies on Alcohol, 40,* 138-141.

MacAndrew, C. (1979b). On the possibility of the psychometric detection of persons who are prone to the abuse of alcohol and other substances. *Addictive Behavior, 4,* 11-20.

MacAndrew, C. (1981). What the **Mac** scale tells us about men alcoholics: An interpretive review. *Journal of Studies on Alcohol, 42,* 604-625.

MacKinnon, D.W. (1962). The nature and nurture of creative talent. *American Psychologist, 17,* 484-495.

Maloney, M.P., Duvall, S.W., & Friesen, J. (1980). Evaluation of response consistency on the MMPI. *Psychological Reports, 46,* 295-298.

Marks, P., & Haller, D. (1974). Adolescent profiles: A new typology. Paper read at the Ninth Annual Symposium on the MMPI, Los Angeles, CA.

Marks, P., & Seeman, W. (1963). *The actuarial description of abnormal personality.* Baltimore, MD: The Williams and Wilkins.

Marks, P., Seeman, W., & Haller, D. (1974). *The actuarial use of the MMPI with adolescents and adults.* Baltimore, MD: The Williams and Wilkins.

McDonald, R., & Gynther, M. (1963). MMPI differences associated with sex, race and class in two adolescent samples. *Journal of Consulting Psychology, 27,* 112-116.

Meehl, P. (1951). *Research results for counselors.* St. Paul, MN: State Department of Education.

Megargee, E., & Bohn, M. (1979). *Classifying criminal offenders.* Beverly Hills, Ca: Sage Publications.

Mello, N., & Guthrie, G. (1958). MMPI profiles and behavior in counseling. *Journal of Counseling Psychology, 5,* 125-129.

Mitler, C., Wertz, C., & Counts, S. (1961). Racial differences on the MMPI. *Journal of Clinical Psychology, 17,* 159-161.

Morgan, H.H. (1952). A psychometric comparison of achieving and non-achieving college students of high ability. *Journal of Consulting Psychology, 16,* 292-298.

Munley, M.J., & Gilbert, T.E. (1965). The **Pd** scale of the MMPI for college students. *Journal of Clinical Psychology, 21,* 48-51.

Murray, J.B., Munley, M.J., & Gilbert, I.E. (1965). The **Pd** scale of the MMPI for college students. *Journal of Clinical Psychology, 21,* 48-51.

Nacev, V. (1980). Dependency and ego-strength as indicators of patient's attendance in psychotherapy. *Journal of Clinical Psychology, 36,* 691-695.

Navran, L. (1954). A rationally derived MMPI scale to measure dependence. *Journal of Consulting Psychology, 18,* 192.

Nelson, S.E. (1952). The development of an indirect objective measure of social status and its relationship to certain psychiatric syndromes. Unpublished doctoral dissertation, University of Minnesota.

Newmark, C.S., & Hutchins, T.C. (1980). Age and MMPI indices of schizophrenia. *Journal of Clinical Psychology, 36,* 768-769.

Norman, R.D., & Redlo, M. (1952). MMPI personality patterns for various college major groups. *Journal of Applied Psychology, 36,* 404-409.

Nyman, A.J., & LeMay, M.L. (1967). Differentiation of types of college misconduct offenses with MMPI subscales. *Journal of Clinical Psychology, 23,* 99-100.

Oetting, E.R. (1966). Examination anxiety: Prediction, physical response, and relation to scholastic performance. *Journal of Counseling Psychology, 13,* 224-227.

Ollendick, D., Otto, B., & Heider, S. (1983). Marital MMPI characteristics: A test of Arnold's signs. *Journal of Clinical Psychology, 39,* 240-246.

Osborne, R.T., Sander, W.B., & Young, F.M. (1956). MMPI patterns of college disciplinary cases. *Journal of Counseling Psychology, 3,* 52-56.

Page, R., & Bozler, S. (1982). A cross-cultural MMPI comparison of alcoholics. *Psychological Reports, 50,* 639-646.

Palau, N. (1972). Aggression and hostility in Mexican women as measured by the MMPI. Paper presented at the Seventh Annual Symposium on the MMPI, Mexico City, Mexico.

Panton, J.H. (1962). The identity of habitual criminalism with the MMPI. *Journal of Clinical Psychology, 18,* 133-136.

Panton, J.H. (1979). MMPI profile configurations associated with incestuous and non-incestuous child molesting. *Psychological Reports, 45,* 335-338.

Parsons, O.A., Yourshaw, S., & Borstelmann, L. (1968). Self-ideal-self-discrepancies on the MMPI: Consistencies over time and geographic region. *Journal of Counseling Psychology, 15,* 160-166.

Patalano, F. (1980). MMPI two point code type frequencies of drug abusers in a therapeutic community. *Psychological Reports, 46,* 1091-1027.

Perlman, M. (1950). Social class membership and test-taking attitude. Unpublished master's thesis, University of Chicago.

Persons, R., & Marks, P. (1971). The violent **4-3** MMPI personality type. *Journal of Consulting and Clinical Psychology, 36,* 189-196.

Post, R.D., & Lobitz, W.C. (1980). The utility of Mezzick's MMPI regression formula as a diagnostic criterion in depression research. *Journal of Consulting and Clinical Psychology, 48,* 673-674.

Pothast, M.D. (1956). A personality study of two types of murderers. Unpublished doctoral dissertation, Michigan State University.

Pritchard, D., & Rosenblatt, A. (1980). Racial bias in the MMPI: A methodological review. *Journal of Consulting and Clinical Psychology, 48,* 263-267.

Rhodes, R.J. (1969). The MacAndrew alcoholism scale: A replication. *Journal of Clinical Psychology, 25,* 189-191.

Rohan, W. (1972). MMPI changes in hospitalized alcoholics: A second study. *Quarterly Journal of Studies on Alcohol, 33,* 65-76.

Rohan, W., Tatro, R., & Rotman, S. (1969). MMPI changes in alcoholics during hospitalization. *Quarterly Journal of Studies on Alcohol, 30,* 389-400.

Rose, A. (1947). A study of homesickness in college freshman. *Journal of Social Psychology, 26,* 185-202.

Rosen, E. (1956). Self-appraisal and perceived desirablity of MMPI personality traits. *Journal of Counseling Psychology, 5,* 44-51.

Rosen, H., & Rosen, R.A. (1957). Personality variables and role in a union business agent group. *Journal of Applied Psychology, 41,* 131-136.

Schenkenberg, T., Gottfredson, D., & Christensen, P. (1984). Age differences in MMPI scale scores from 1,189 psychiatric patient. *Journal of Clinical Psychology, 40,* 1420-1426.

Schroeder, D.J., & Piercy, D.C. (1979). A comparison of MMPI two-point codes in four alcoholism treatment facilities. *Journal of Clinical Psychology, 35,* 656-663.

Schwartz, M., & Graham, J. (1979). Construct validity of the MacAndrew alcoholism scale. *Journal of Consulting and Clinical Psychology, 47,* 1090-1095.

Schwartz, M., & Green, S.B. (1983). Diagnostic accuracy of actuarial one-point MMPI code systems with college students. *Journal of Clinical Psychology, 39,* 58-66.

Schwartz, M., & Krupp, N. (1971). The MMPI "conversion V" among 50,000 medical patients: A study of incidence, criteria and profile elevation. *Journal of Clinical Psychology, 27,* 89-95.

Schwartz, M., Osborne, D., & Krupp, N. (1972). Moderation effects of age and sex in the association of medical diagrams and 1-3/3-1 MMPI profiles. *Journal of Clinical Psychology, 28,* 502-505.

Sines, L.K., Baucom, D.H., & Gruba, G.H. (1979). A validity scale sign calling for caution in the interpretation of MMPIs among psychiatric inpatients. *Journal of Personality Assessment, 43,* 604-607.

Singer, M. (1970). Comparison of indicators of homosexuality on the MMPI. *Journal of Consulting and Clinical Psychology, 34,* 15-18.

Smart, R., & Jones, D. (1970). Illicit LSD users: Their personality characteristics and psychopathology. *Journal of Abnormal Psychology, 75,* 286-292.

Smith, C.P., & Graham, J.R. (1981). Behavioral correlates for the MMPI standard F scale and for a modified F scale for Black and white psychiatric patients. *Journal of Consulting and Clinical Psychology, 49,* 455-459.

Snyder, C.M., & Graham, J.R. (1984). The utility of subtle and obvious subscales based on scale-specific ratings. *Journal of Clinical Psychology, 40,* 981-985.

Stone, F.B., & Rowley, V.N. (1963). MMPI differences between emotionally disturbed and delinquent adolescent girls. *Journal of Clinical Psychology, 19,* 227-230.

Streiner, P.L., & Miller, H.R. (1981). Prorating incomplete Wiggins and MacAndrew scales. *Journal of Personality Assessment, 45,* 427-429.

Sutker, P.B., Archer, R.P., Brantley, P.J., & Kilpatrick, D. (1979). Alcoholics and opiate addicts: Comparison of personality characteristics. *Journal of Studies on Alcohol, 40*, 635-644.

Sutker, P.B., Brantley, P.J., & Allain, A. (1980). MMPI response patterns and alcohol consumption in DUI offenders. *Journal of Consulting and Clinical Psychology, 48*, 350-355.

Svanum, S., Levitt, E., & McAdoo, W. (1982). Differentiating male and female alcoholics from psychiatric outpatients: The MacAndrew and Rosenberg alcoholism scales. *Journal of Personality Assessment, 46*, 81-84.

Swenson, W. (1961). Structured personality testing in the aged: An MMPI study of the geriatric population. *Journal of Clinical Psychology, 17*, 302-304.

Swenson, W., Pearson, J., & Osborne, O. (1973). *An MMPI source book*. Minneapolis: University of Minnesota Press.

Tamkin, A.S., & Klett, C.J. (1957). Barron's ego strength scale: A replication of an evaluation of its construct validity. *Journal of Consulting Psychology, 21*, 412.

Trimboli, R., & Kilgore, R. (1983). A psychodynamic approach to MMPI interpretation. *Journal of Personality Assessment, 47*, 614-626.

Uecker, A., Boutilier, L., & Richardson, E. (1980). "Indianism" and MMPI scores of men alcoholics. *Journal of Studies on Alcohol, 41*, 357-362.

Volentine, S.Z. (1981). The assessment of masculinity and femininity: Scale 5 of the MMPI compared with the BSRI and the PAQ. *Journal of Clinical Psychology, 37*, 367-374.

Wadden, T.A., & Lucas, R.A. (1980). MMPI as a predictor of weight loss. *Psychological Reports, 46*, 984-986.

Walters, G.D., Greene, R.L., Jeffrey, T.B., Kruzick, D.J., & Haskin, J.J. (1983). Racial variations on the MacAndrew alcoholism scale of the MMPI. *Journal of Consulting and Clinical Psychology, 51*, 947-948.

Walters, G.D., & Solomon, G.S. (1982). Methodological note on deriving behavioral correlates for MMPI profile patterns: Case of the female 4-5-6 configuration. *Psychological Reports, 50*, 1071-1076.

Webb, J., McNamara, K., & Rogers, A. (1981). *Configural interpretation of the MMPI and CPI*. Columbus, OH: Ohio Publishing.

Weiner, D.N. (1948). Subtle and obvious keys for the MMPI. *Journal of Consulting Psychology, 12*, 164-170.

Welsh, G.S. (1956). Factor Dimensions A and R. In G.S. Welsh and W.G. Dahlstrom (Eds.) *Basic readings on the MMPI in psychology and medicine*. Minneapolis: University of Minnesota Press. 264-281.

371

Welsh, G.S. (1965). MMPI profile and factor scales **A** and R. *Journal of Clinical Psychology, 21,* 43-47.

Welsh, G.S., & Dahlstrom, W.G. (Eds.). (1956). *Basic readings on the MMPI in psychology and medicine.* Minneapolis: University of Minnesota Press.

White, W.G. (1974). A psychometric approach for adjusting selected MMPI scale scores obtained by Blacks. Unpublished doctoral dissertation, University of Missouri—Columbia.

Wiggins, J.S., & Rumrill, C. (1959). Social desirability in the MMPI and Welsh's factor scales **A** and **R**. *Journal of Consulting Psychology, 23,* 100-106.

Williams, H.L. (1952). The development of a caudality scale for the MMPI. *Journal of Clinical Psychology, 8,* 293-297.

Wilson, R.L. (1980). Comparative validities of subtle vs. obvious MMPI Hysteria items: Predicting the elusive neurosis. Master's Thesis, Auburn University.

Wiltse, L., & Rocchio, P. (1975). Preoperative psychological tests as predictors of success of chemonucleolysis in the treatment of the low-back syndrome. *The Journal of Bone and Joint Surgery, 57,* 478-483.

Young, R., Gould, E., Gluck, I.D., & Hargraves, W. (1980). Personality inventory correlates of outcome in a follow up study of psychiatric hospitalization. *Psychological Reports, 46,* 903-906.

INDEX

INDEX

SCALE COMBINATION INDEX

ABOUT
THE
AUTHOR

JANE C.
DUCKWORTH

Jane Duckworth has a Ph.D. in psychology from the University of Missouri at Columbia and presently is a professor in the Department of Counseling Psychology and Guidance Services at Ball State University. She has worked with the MMPI in two college counseling centers and a psychiatric clinic and has done MMPI research with the following groups: divorced people, married couples, college students, and sex offenders. A current research interest is the interface between the MMPI and the Rorschach in personality assessment. She teaches the MMPI course in the graduate Counseling Psychology program at Ball State University and conducts workshops on the MMPI in various parts of the United States and foreign countries. She is a diplomat in counseling psychology.

WAYNE
ANDERSON

Wayne Anderson has a Ph.D. in psychology from the University of Missouri-Columbia and is presently Chair of the Joint Training Program in Counseling Psychology at the University of Missouri-Columbia. He has a dual appointment as a Professor of Psychology and a Counseling Psychologist with the Counseling Services. Previously he was with VA psychiatric hospitals for seven years. After coming to Missouri in 1963, he developed the graduate course on the MMPI. He is presently involved as a consultant with the VA and with both the Columbia Police Department and extension law enforcement training. His research interests are the psychology of aggressive offenders (murder and rape) and the effects of counselor self-disclosure upon client behavior. Dr. Anderson has published over 70 articles and book chapters on various aspects of psychology (15 on the MMPI).

386

FEEDBACK

To:
Jane Duckworth, Ph.D.
2004 Euclid
Muncie, Indiana 47304

The parts of *MMPI Interpretation Manual for Counselors and Clinicians,* 1986 edition, that I have found most helpful are (please note pages and reasons if appropriate):

I would find the book more useful if you would elaborate on the following (please note pages and reasons if appropriate):

Other Comments:

Name: _____
Organization: _____
Street: _____
City: _____
State: _____

SUGGESTIONS

To:
Jane Duckworth, Ph.D.
2004 Euclid
Muncie, Indiana 47304

A resource not listed in your *MMPI Interpretation Manual for Counselors and Clinicians,* 1986 edition, that I have found useful is the following:

I am enclosing a copy of an article I found useful. The article was taken from the following source:

Other Comments:

Name: _____
Organization: _____
Street: _____
City: _____
State: _____